Contents

Contents - *continued* Page

OFFICE OF POPULATION CENSUSES AND SURVEYS
GENERAL REGISTER OFFICE FOR SCOTLAND

1991 Census

Definitions
Great Britain

Laid before Parliament pursuant to Section 4(1)
Census Act 1920

London: HMSO

First published 1992

ISBN 0 11 691361 4

Contents - *continued*

Page

Maps

Contents - *continued*

Page

Summary

The statistics to be made available from the 1991 Census are more extensive than those produced for any previous population census of Great Britain. The presentation of definitions and explanatory notes in a single comprehensive volume reduces the amount of such material required to be reproduced in many individual reports.

The structure of this volume is similar to the corresponding publication in 1981 (*1981 Census, Definitions, Great Britain*, HMSO, 1981) so that comparisons in definitions and terms used between the two censuses can more easily be made.

Chapter 1 is a general introduction and describes briefly the authority for the Census, the topics included, how it was taken and how the returns are processed, and confidentiality measures. Chapter 2 deals specifically with the construction of the population bases from the Census questions, while Chapter 3 defines the population groups that make up the composition of these bases. Chapter 4 describes the classification of communal establishments. Chapter 5 covers the classifications of household spaces and types of dwelling, and other definitions used in the tables on housing and availability of cars.

In Chapters 6 and 7 the definitions of the main terms used, respectively, in 100 per cent and 10 per cent processed output, are described for each of the 1991 Census topics, with reference to any differences between 1981 and 1991 in the treatment of particular topics in output.

Chapter 8 describes and defines, with maps, the various standard area levels for which local and topic statistics are made available in published output.

A more comprehensive account of intercensal changes and census procedures will be published in the *1991 Census General Report* in due course.

OPCS/GRO(S)
April 1992

1 Introduction

Legal basis

1.1 The 1991 Census was taken under the authority of the Census Act 1920. The *Census Order* (Statutory Instrument 1990 No. 243)[1], directing that a census be taken in Great Britain on 21 April 1991, was made by Counsellors of State on behalf of HM the Queen in Council on 14 February 1990. This specified the persons with respect to whom the Census returns were to be made, the persons by whom the returns were to be made, and the particulars to be stated in the returns. The *Census Regulations* (Statutory Instruments 1990 No. 307 in England and Wales[2] and 1990 No. 326 in Scotland[3]), setting out the detailed arrangements for the conduct of the Census, were laid before Parliament on 8 March 1990 and came into force on 29 March 1990.

1.2 Censuses were also taken on the same date in Northern Ireland, the Isle of Man, and Guernsey; and on 10 March 1991 in Jersey.

Number of questions

1.3 The 1991 Census form contained 25 basic questions (though additional questions were asked on Welsh language in Wales and on Gaelic language and floor level of accommodation in Scotland). This was four more than in 1981. The new questions were on ethnic group, limiting long-term illness and term-time address of students, and on weekly hours worked. This last question had been included in the 1971 Census but omitted in 1981. The amenities question included a new section on central heating which replaced the section in the 1981 question on outside WCs. Furthermore, a method based on identifying and classifying household spaces in multi-occupied buildings with a separate or shared entrance, provided a count of dwellings that was not available from the 1981 Census.

1.4 There was no separate question on employment status in the 1991 Census but categories for the self-employed were included in the economic position question. Information on managers and supervisors is obtained from the occupation question.

Full and sample processing

1.5 The 1991 Census questions have, like those in the 1981 Census, been divided into those to which the responses are easy to code (most often answered by means of a tick box) and those to which the responses often require write-in answers and are thus more difficult - and consequently more costly - to process. In general, this division determines whether the question is fully processed (a *100 per cent item*) or whether it is processed only for a ten per cent sample of household forms and a ten per cent sample of persons returned on forms for communal establishments (a *10 per cent item*).

1.6 In the 1991 Census the 100 per cent questions were:

sex and date of birth;
marital status;
whereabouts on Census night;
usual address;
term-time address of students;
usual address one year before census;
country of birth;
ethnic group;
long-term illness;
Welsh/Gaelic language;
economic activity in the week before the Census;
type of accommodation and extent of sharing;
number of rooms;
tenure of household;
household amenities;
availability of cars and vans; and lowest floor level of accommodation (Scotland only).

The 10 per cent questions were:

relationship in household;
hours worked;
occupation;
name and business of employer (industry);
workplace;
journey to work; and
higher qualifications.

Order of processing and output

Preliminary Reports

1.7 The first reports to be produced from the 1991 Census were the *Preliminary Reports*[4,5] of counts of population and household spaces for local authority districts in England and Wales and, separately, for districts in Scotland. They were published in July 1991 (and a corrected version for England and Wales published in December 1991). The figures were based on summaries prepared by the temporary field staff (enumerators and census officers) and, as in 1981, will not tally precisely with subsequent reports prepared after computer processing of the completed Census forms.

Local Statistics

1.8 As in previous censuses, returns from the 1991 Census are processed on a county-by-county basis (regions in Scotland), although at any one time work proceeds on several counties in parallel.

1.9 The first returns became available for processing at the Census Offices some six weeks after Census day and work started initially on coding the 100 per cent items. After the data for each county/region is coded, keyed and validated, the Local Base Statistics (LBS) and Small Area Statistics (SAS) are prepared for each area. Summary statistics from the 100 per cent LBS will be published as *County/Region Monitors* to be followed by the full statistics for counties, Scottish regions and local authority districts in the *County/Region Reports* (part 1). Abstracts of the LBS and the SAS in machine-readable form will be available in the same county order down to the ward and enumeration district levels respectively (postcode sector and output area levels in Scotland).

1.10 During the 100 per cent processing, a sample of one in ten households and one in ten persons in communal establishments will be drawn from the validated records. The data in this sample which require more time-consuming coding and processing (see paragraph 1.6) will then be processed and the corresponding LBS and SAS tables prepared. The 10 per cent *County/Region Reports* and abstracts for each area are planned to be available some 4-5 months after the corresponding 100 per cent statistics.

1.11 The planned order of the 100 per cent processing of counties in England and Wales and of Scottish regions is shown in the table below. There may be some slight differences in the order of the 10 per cent processing.

1.12 On completion of the processing of the counties and regions, national versions of the LBS and SAS will be available.

Topic Statistics

1.13 Following the production of the local statistics, more detailed reports on all of the topics covered in the 1991 Census will appear (over the period around late 1992 to around end 1993) presenting statistics at the national and sub-national level. The following list of planned topic reports shows, in the expected publication order, whether the tables are based on 100 per cent or 10 per cent processing.

	Processing level (per cent)
Sex, Age and Marital Status*	100
Historical Tables*	100
Usual Residence*	100
Persons Aged 60 and Over*	100
Housing and Availability of Cars**	100
Communal Establishments*	100
Household Composition*	100
Limiting Long-term Illness*	100
Ethnic Group and Country of Birth*	100/10
Welsh Language in Wales	100/10
Gaelic Language in Scotland	100/10
National Migration - part 1*	100
National Migration - part 2*	10
Regional Migration - part 1	100
Regional Migration - part 2	10
Topics Report for Health Areas*	100
Economic Activity**	10
Workplace and Transport to Work**	10
Household and Family Composition*	10
Qualified Manpower*	10
Children and Young Adults*	100/10

1.14 The reports marked * will be published in single volumes for Great Britain, and those marked ** will be available additionally in volumes for Scotland. The *Regional Migration* reports will consist of separate volumes for each standard region of England and for Wales and Scotland.

County/Region	County/Region	County/Region
Isle of Wight	*continued*	*continued*
Powys	Hampshire	Cheshire
Borders	West Yorkshire	Islands Areas †
Northumberland	Clwyd	Gwynedd
West Glamorgan	North Yorkshire	Lancashire
Cornwall	Devon	Fife
Cumbria	Greater Manchester	Hertfordshire
Suffolk	Buckinghamshire	Warwickshire
Grampian	Avon	Kent
Lincolnshire	Leicestershire	Surrey
Merseyside	Cleveland	Essex
Lothian	Strathclyde	Mid Glamorgan
Cambridgeshire	Dyfed	Central
Oxfordshire	Humberside	Dorset
Inner/Outer London	Gwent	Somerset
West Midlands	Nottinghamshire	Dumfries and Galloway
Berkshire	Tayside	West Sussex
Tyne and Wear	East Sussex	Norfolk
Bedfordshire	Northants	Staffordshire
Gloucestershire	Derbyshire	Hereford and Worcester
Wiltshire	Highland	Durham
South Yorkshire	Shropshire	South Glamorgan

† Orkney, Shetland, and Western Isles will be produced as three separate publications

Enumeration procedures

The field force

1.15 The 1991 Census was organised in the traditional way, with the delivery of the self-completion forms by enumerators to households and to managers in charge of communal establishments, and their subsequent collection. Most forms were delivered during the period 12-19 April and it was planned to collect the completed forms in most areas between 22 and 25 April; for certain inner city areas this collection period was extended to 28 April, to include the weekend after Census day. In practice, however, it was necessary to extend collection in many other areas to include the weekend, and in some inner city areas, into the following week. This was mainly because of difficulties experienced in contacting some households, and omissions on the forms necessitating call-backs by the enumerators.

1.16 The concept of a four-tier field force, used successfully in 1981, was retained for the 1991 Census. This comprised 135 *Census Areas Managers* (known as Supervisors in 1981) responsible for the conduct of the Census in an area containing up to about half a million people. Each Census Area Manager (CAM) recruited up to 25 *Census Officers* (COs) who each took control of a local area containing about 25,000 people (a *Census District*). In total there were about 2,500 COs appointed throughout Great Britain.

1.17 The Census Officers were subsequently responsible, in turn, for the recruitment and training of some 7,800 *Assistant Census Officers* (ACOs) and 117,500 *Enumerators*, the field staff who delivered and collected the forms. The duties of the ACO were substantially increased in comparison with 1981, to take on board quality control responsibilities and the supervision of small teams of enumerators.

Enumeration Districts

1.18 The country was divided into around 130,000 small areas (*Enumeration Districts*) and to each of these areas an enumerator was appointed, though in some cases enumerators were responsible for more than one district. In England and Wales an average enumeration district (ED) comprised about 200 households, containing about 400 persons. In Scotland EDs were, on average, slightly smaller.

1.19 ED boundaries were drawn up by the Census Offices in such a way as to produce reasonable workloads for enumerators to complete their tasks of delivery and collection of the forms in the allocated time. The basis of planning EDs was the expected number of households in the area, but allowances were made for other factors which have an effect on the workload. For example, there is a considerable variation between the work of enumerating a scattered population in a rural area, or in a city centre with mixed residential and commercial premises (where even finding the living accommodation is a task in itself), and the work involved in an area of suburban semi-detached housing. Account was also taken of other factors, such as the percentage of persons expected to be living in communal establishments, the extent of multi-occupied housing, and indications that households would not have English as their first language.

1.20 EDs were defined so that they generally did not cross the boundaries of administrative areas such as counties, local authority districts or wards. In England and Wales, the 1991 boundaries also took into account, as far as possible, the 1981 Census ED boundaries and the requirements of local authorities for statistics for special areas. In Scotland, as in the 1981 Census, EDs were defined as aggregations of unit postcodes and took account of the boundaries of postcode sectors, districts and Islands Areas.

1.21 In England and Wales, the ED is, as in 1981, the basic area unit for standard output, such as the Small Area Statistics (SAS). In Scotland, EDs are not used for output; instead, Output Areas (OAs) are created that nest, as far as possible, within the areas used for SAS in 1981.

Households and communal establishments

1.22 Each enumerator underwent detailed training and was supplied with a Field Manual that described both the procedures for enumerating households and those to be applied in other situations, such as houses not occupied on Census night, non-residential premises (such as shops and factories) and communal establishments (such as hotels and hospitals).

1.23 Establishments which were expected to contain more than 100 people, such as prisons and army barracks, were designated as *Special Enumeration Districts* (SEDs) and were enumerated either directly by the Census Officers or by specially appointed enumerators.

The forms

1.24 Each household was enumerated on a 12-page H form (W form in Wales). The names of persons spending Census night in communal establishments and on HM Ships and other vessels were listed on an L form with each person being enumerated separately on an I form (Iw form in Wales). A person in a household could make an individual return using an I form, if they so wished, but the details of name, relationship in household, and whereabouts on Census night for that person was required to be entered on the appropriate H form. Welsh translations of the forms W, L and Iw were available in Wales. Copies of the forms for England, Scotland, and Wales are given at Appendix 1.

1.25 Enumerators also had the responsibility for recording certain housing information (Panel A on the H form) and making an assessment of the nature of the accommodation if it was not occupied on Census night.

Special arrangements

1.26 It was not possible to enumerate all persons by the conventional methods described above and special arrangements had to be made for certain groups, though the standard forms were used in all cases. For example:

(a) British and foreign registered commercial shipping, non-commercial shipping and pleasure craft in areas normally covered by HM Customs and Excise, were enumerated by Customs Officers appointed as special enumerators.

(b) arrangements were made with the Ministry of Defence for the enumeration of naval vessels;

(c) Trinity House, the Northern Lighthouse Board and the Nature Conservancy Council enumerated lightships and isolated lighthouses, and other very remote locations; and

(d) workers from voluntary organisations, such as the Salvation Army, were appointed, wherever possible, as special enumerators to help count persons sleeping rough.

1.27 Other organisations and government departments assisted in the enumeration by issuing circulars containing guidance or instruction, for example, the Home Office to each Prison Service establishment and the Ministry of Defence to service and military establishments. Help was given on the location of special groups; for example, the Department of the Environment and the Welsh Office supplied information of the location of sites of travelling people.

Confidentiality

Restricted access to data

1.28 A census is taken solely to produce statistics, and steps have been taken to safeguard the anonymity of the individual person or household. Confidentiality is protected by the terms of the 1920 Census Act as amended by the Census (Confidentiality) Act 1991, which provides legal penalties for the unlawful disclosure of census information.

1.29 Though names and addresses were required to be entered on the Census form, these are only used:

(a) to help the form-filler identify each person on the form;

(b) to enable the Census Office to refer to the appropriate person if information on the form was missing;

(c) to indicate whether or not the householder had fulfilled his or her legal obligation to provide the required information;

(d) to enable validation checks and follow-up surveys to be directed to specific individuals;

(e) to enable the linking of a sample of records into the OPCS Longitudinal Study; and

(f) for other statistical purposes, for example, in identifying types of family.

1.30 No information on identified individuals or households from the Census, or from any follow-up surveys or secondary analysis, is revealed to any persons not working for the Registrars General*. On completion of the data processing, the Census forms themselves will be kept securely within the Census Offices and treated as confidential for 100 years, and only in the year 2092 will they be made available for general inspection by the public.

1.31 Precautions are also taken to ensure that statistical tabulations neither directly, nor indirectly by linkage with other sources of data, reveal information about identifiable individuals or households.

Thresholds for the release of Small Area Statistics

1.32 A small proportion of 1991 EDs in England and Wales have very small populations, for example, because of recognition of all Civil Parishes in England as EDs, however small their populations.

1.33 In order to lessen the risk of inadvertent disclosure of information about identifiable individuals or households in small EDs, the *Small Area Statistics* (SAS) will not be released for areas with fewer than 50 usually resident persons *and* 16 resident households (but a count of persons present, residents and households will be provided). Statistics for such suppressed EDs are merged with those of a contiguous ED, provided that the resulting *amalgamated* total numbers of persons and households also exceed the same thresholds. Separate SAS will not be issued for any ED that has 'imported' statistics from a suppressed area in this way but, in output, areas that contain such imported statistics will be identified.

1.34 The contiguous ED to be amalgamated with an ED falling below the thresholds will generally be that with the fewest people, including an ED which may itself fall below the thresholds. But other relevant local circumstances will be taken into consideration; for example, amalgamations will be within statutory areas wherever possible.

1.35 In Scotland, those areas defined for the production of Small Area Statistics (provisional Output Areas), but which do not pass the thresholds, will be amalgamated with a *predetermined* contiguous area in the final stage of creating Output Areas. Thus it will be possible to issue SAS for all *final* Output Areas (see paragraph 8.13).

Arrangements for Special Enumeration Districts

1.36 SEDs were planned where 100 or more people were expected to be present in a communal establishment on Census night, and they are characterised by populations that are often markedly different from those in the surrounding area, particularly having a virtual absence of resident households. Thus, for SEDs a variation of the confidentiality measures for the release of SAS will apply.

---

* However, if a person is prosecuted under the 1920 Census Act for refusing to complete a form properly, the form may be produced as evidence in court.

1.37 Three basic counts:

(a) total persons present;
(b) total residents; and
(c) total resident households

will be issued for *all* SEDs. The SAS tables counting residents only as the base (that is, not households) and the 'residents' part of the SAS tables showing both households and residents will be issued for an SED which has 50 or more residents but which does not exceed the threshold of 16 resident households. All SAS tables will be issued for an SED exceeding the thresholds for both residents and resident households. In Scotland, an SED failing both thresholds is merged with the surrounding OA.

Thresholds for the release of Local Base Statistics

1.38 The full Local Base Statistics (LBS) will be issued in England and Wales as abstracts for wards or sub-divisions of wards with both 1,000 or more residents *and* 320 or more resident households. Otherwise, the statistics for a ward will be amalgamated with those of a contiguous ward, generally following the procedures for EDs. The SAS will, however, be issued for wards which fall below the thresholds for LBS but which are above the minimum thresholds defined in paragraph 1.33 above.

1.39 The same arrangements apply for the release of LBS for postcode sectors and sub-divisions in Scotland, with the exception that the tables relating to ethnic groups will not be released as standard for these area levels.

Modification

1.40 Counts in the SAS and LBS abstracts based on the 100 per cent processing at ward level and below are modified to counter the risk that an individual could be identified through a table and hence information about that individual inadvertently disclosed. All such counts are modified by the addition of +1, 0 or -1 in quasi-random patterns. Exceptions will be the basic counts given in Tables 1, 27 and 71 of the SAS/LBS abstracts and the counts of establishments in Table 3, where modification would impair the usefulness of the tables.

1.41 SAS and LBS based on 10 per cent processing, and counts published in the *County/Region Reports* are not modified.

Computer security

1.42 The computer system used by the Census Offices has built-in safeguards preventing unauthorised access to data, and physical security has been reinforced at the computer installations.

1.43 In the White Paper on the 1991 Census (Cm 430)[6], published in July 1988, the Government announced its intention to carry out an independent review of the Census Offices' computing arrangements, and the British Computer Society (BCS) was awarded the contract following competitive tender. The terms of reference for the 1991 Review were to review the appropriateness and adequacy of the arrangements made by the Census Offices so far as they relate to computing, taking account of the principles set out in the Data Protection Act 1984, the sensitivity of the information held, the risk of a breach of confidentiality, and the cost of precautionary measures.

1.44 The scope of the Review included all activities from the reception of the Census forms in the processing centre, through their processing, to their subsequent removal for permanent storage.

1.45 The report of the Review was published in February 1991 commending the arrangements then being made for processing the Census and a White Paper (*1991 Census of Population: Confidentiality and Computing*, Cm 1447)[7] was presented to Parliament by the Secretaries of State for Health and for Scotland. The report of a Supplementary Review was issued in July 1991 with an OPCS Press Notice[7a].

Edit system

1.46 Answers to questions included in the 100 per cent processing are checked within the computer system for consistency. Answers found to be inconsistent and any missing answers are imputed with an acceptable value by reference to the most recently processed record of a person or household with similar characteristics. Those EDs with more than a prescribed number of errors or missing items are rejected for clerical scrutiny prior to imputation. Consequently, the 100 per cent tables do not, generally, need to include 'not stated' categories.

1.47 The imputation system is not used in editing the 10 per cent sample items because of the difficulty in imputing accurately for the complex variables. For these, editing is performed clerically and, thus, tables based on the sample processing do include 'not stated' categories.

Imputation of data for absent households

1.48 In the 1981 Census, some 700,000 households, containing an estimated million people, were classified as *wholly absent households* (that is, no person was present in the household on Census night) and the residents of such households were excluded from the enumeration at their usual addresses. Many were enumerated at some other address in Great Britain where they happened to be staying on Census night but, because of the way in which the population base was defined for most census output, absent households were omitted from almost all 1981 Census tabulations.

1.49 In an attempt to improve the coverage of the Census in 1991, all households absent on Census night were left a form with a letter asking them to complete the form on their return home and post it to the Census Officer or to Census Headquarters. Not all such absent households completed a form that could be incorporated into the processing. The two reasons that this was so were that:

- the Census Offices could only ask for the completion of the form *on a voluntary basis*, as the household would already have been required to be included on a form if it was elsewhere in Great Britain on Census night; and

- not all absent households returned home early enough after Census day to be able to return their form in time for processing.

1.50 For those absent households for whom a completed form was not received, certain data are imputed using some basic information (such as number of people living at the address and details of the accommodation) collected by the enumerator and also drawing on information from similar absent households which did complete and return census forms.

1.51 Four key variables (the area, number of usual residents, number of rooms and whether the accommodation is self-contained) were recorded for all absent households on a form completed by the enumerator from information supplied either by someone in the household before they went away or by a neighbour or, as a last resort, by estimating the values.

1.52 As the processing system encounters *completed* forms from absent households, the information on housing and household members is stored and referenced by the four key variables. When a non-responding absent household is encountered, details of the 100 per cent items are imputed by copying the most recently stored absent household record which matches the four key variables. This ensures that any geographically clustered variables are imputed as accurately as possible.

1.53 Investigation by OPCS has shown that absent households, as a group, have markedly different characteristics compared with other households; for example, they are smaller on average (most having only one resident) and have residents more likely to be aged between 16-24 or 65 and over than in the population as a whole. The method of imputation adopted takes account of this general difference in household composition. By only imputing details from one absent household to another, distortions in aggregate distributions should be minimised - although the probability of imputing every detail correctly for any single household is very small.

1.54 Cases where the enumerator failed to contact a household throughout the Collection stage were referred to the Census Officer. The overall number of such cases was around 370,000 and special measures were taken with the aim of obtaining a completed return through the post, but between ½ and ¾ of a per cent of households remained for whom a completed form was not received. As there was *prima facie* evidence that someone lived at these addresses, those households for whom a completed form was not received were included in the usually resident database by imputing characteristics of a neighbouring household. Although some of these 'no contacts' may have actually been present on Census night, the imputed data for these households is grouped together with that for absent households in tabulated output (see, for example, Table 1 of the LBS/SAS and *County/Region Report*).

2 Population bases

Population bases in tables

2.1 Census results are generally presented as cross-tabulations of two or more variables, each table counting a particular population (such as *Residents in households, Students and schoolchildren aged 5 and over,* or *Persons aged 60 and over with limiting long-term illness*). It is important to know exactly what is being counted - the *population base* - especially when comparing tables from the 1991 Census with those from 1981 or earlier censuses or from non-census sources.

2.2 As in 1981, the form-filler was instructed to include on the Census form:

(a) "every person who spends Census night (21-22 April) in this household, **including anyone staying temporarily**";

(b) "any other people who are usually members of the household but on Census night are absent on holiday, at school or college, or for any other reason, even if they are being included on another census form elsewhere";

(c) "anyone who arrives here on Monday 22 April who was in Great Britain on the Sunday and who has not been included as present on another census form"; and

(d) "any newly born baby born before 22 April, even if still in hospital".

2.3 The group of people included under (b) are termed *absent residents.*

2.4 Information on *whereabouts* and *usual address,* given for each person included on the Census form, can be used to derive the several population bases used in tabulations.

6	**Whereabouts on night of 21-22 April 1991** Please tick the appropriate box to indicate where the person was on the night of 21-22 April 1991.	At this address, out on night work or travelling to this address ☐ 0 Elsewhere in England, Scotland or Wales ☐ 1 Outside Great Britain ☐ 2
7	**Usual address** If the person usually lives here, please tick 'This address'. If not, tick 'Elsewhere' and write in the person's usual address. For students and children away from home during term time, the home address should be taken as the usual address. For any person who lives away from home for part of the week, the home address should be taken as the usual address. Any person who is not a permanent member of the household should be asked what he or she considers to be his or her usual address.	This address ☐ 1 Elsewhere ☐ If elsewhere, please write the person's usual address and postcode below in BLOCK CAPITALS Post-code

2.5 If, in Question 7, the box 'Elsewhere' had been ticked and an address elsewhere in Great Britain had been given, then the input is the postcode of that address; if an address outside GB had been given, then the input is the country of usual residence (using the same codes as the country of birth classification (see Annex A)). Special procedures are adopted if the answer was missing or entered as "none" or "no fixed address" (see paragraph 3.9).

Construction of bases: counting people

2.6 Combinations of the answers to Questions 6 and 7 form the building bricks for the various population bases as follows:

Whereabouts	Usual Address	Population group
(a) This address	This address	Present residents
(b) This address	Elsewhere in GB	Visitors from within GB
(c) This address	Outside GB	Visitors from outside GB
(d) Elsewhere in GB	This address	Absent residents absent within GB
(e) Outside GB	This address	Absent residents absent outside GB

Categories (d) and (e) are not enumerated in communal establishments. Persons in category (d) should also be in category (b) on the form completed where they are present on Census night.

2.7 *Wholly absent households* (those households where all residents of the household were absent on Census night and no other person was present) were asked to complete, voluntarily, a census form on their return home (see paragraph 1.49). Those which did so are termed *Enumerated wholly absent households*, and households for which no return was received are termed *Imputed wholly absent households.* For convenience, the imputed population of households where no contact was made but where there was *prima facie* evidence that someone lived there, are grouped together with imputed wholly absent households and included under that term in Tables 1 and 18 of the LBS.

2.8 Figure 1 overleaf summarises how the various population bases are constructed from the building blocks identified in paragraphs 2.6 and 2.7.

2.9 The *population present* in an area (referred to, in output, as *Persons present*) is a count of all the persons recorded as spending Census night in the area regardless of whether this was where they usually lived (categories (a)-(c) in paragraph 2.6 above).

2.10 The *usually resident population (topped-up present/absent): 1991 base* (referred to, in output, as *Residents*) is a count of all persons recorded as resident in households in an area, even if they were present elsewhere on Census night, plus residents in communal establishments who were present in the establishment on Census night (categories (a), (d) and (e) in paragraph 2.6). This population is 'topped-up' with persons from enumerated wholly absent households and imputed wholly absent households.

Fig 1 Inter-relationship of population bases

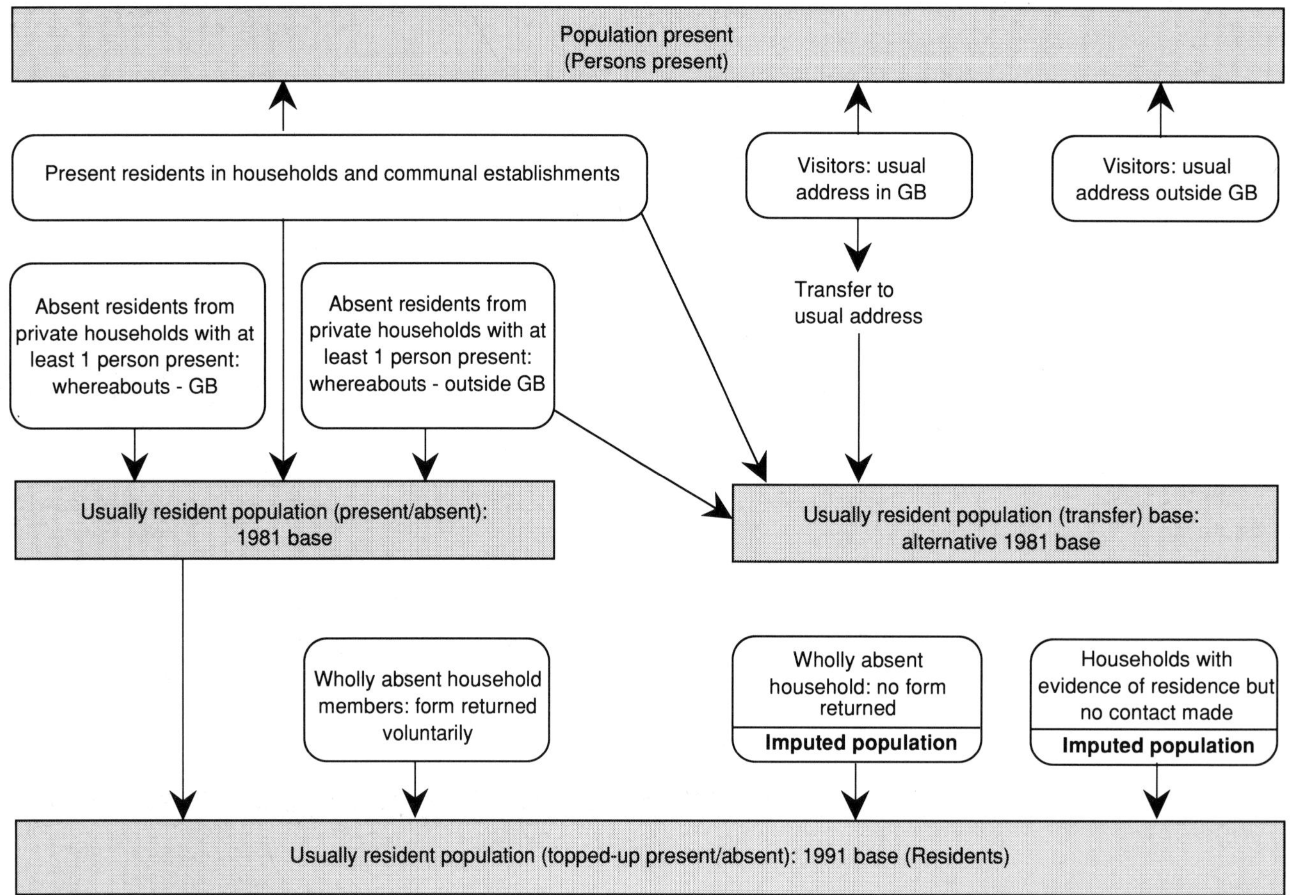

2.11 The *usually resident population (present/absent): 1981 base* did not include any residents in wholly absent households (see paragraph 1.48) and so was an incomplete count of the resident population in the 1981 Census.

2.12 The *usually resident population (transfer): 1981 base* was also compiled in 1981 by counting present residents in an area, plus a 'transfer' count of visitors elsewhere in GB back to the area of residence, plus absent residents in enumerated households who were outside GB on Census night (categories (a), (b) and (e)). In 1981 this population base gave a better count of the resident population than the present/absent base then used, but was of limited use because 'transferred' persons could not be allocated to households and the base could not be counted until all areas had been processed.

2.13 As the full range of census information is given on the H forms for absent residents in households and because the present/absent base can be produced area by area with the processing sequence, this usually resident population is the base that is most commonly used in the Small Area Statistics, Local Base Statistics and *County/Region Reports*, where it is more often referred to as the *resident population* or, more simply, *residents*. Some tables, however, use a different base to allow intercensal comparisons. Additionally, in Table 1 of the LBS/SAS and *County/Region Reports, Visitors* are sub-divided into 'Resident in UK' and 'Resident outside UK' to allow a direct comparison with the equivalent 1981 table.

2.14 For consistency, the same base will generally be carried forward into all the published *Topic Report* volumes, though volumes on specific topics, such as *Workplace and Transport to Work*, will contain slight variations (see Chapter 7).

Term-time address and the Registrars General's annual estimates of population

2.15 The Registrars General's annual estimates of the population usually resident in each district during the 1980s were based on 1981 Census figures compiled by the 'transfer' method (paragraph 2.12), but they adopt a different convention in defining the usual address of the armed forces and some other categories. Thus, a student's usual address is taken, for annual estimates purposes, as the term-time address, but in the 1981 Census this was considered to be the student's home address. Statistics derived from the 1981 Census were therefore not directly comparable with the Registrars General's annual estimates.

2.16 The date of the 1991 Census (21 April) fell in term-time for some educational establishments, but in vacation-time in others. The Census, however, included a new question on *term-time address of students and schoolchildren.*

2.17 Answers to this question (see opposite page) allow the compilation of the term-time population for an area, by omitting resident students with a term-time address outside

8 **Term time address of students and schoolchildren**

If not a student or schoolchild, please tick first box.

For a student or schoolchild who lives here during term time, tick 'This address'.

If he or she does not live here during term time, tick 'Elsewhere' and write in the current or most recent term time address.

Not a student or schoolchild ☐

This address ☐ 1

Elsewhere ☐

If elsewhere, please write the term time address and postcode below in BLOCK CAPITALS

Post-code

the area and including any students resident outside the area but living in the area in term-time. This will provide information for re-calibrating the Registrars General's annual estimates using the 1991 Census as a base.

Construction of bases: counting people in households

2.18 For the 1991 Census the base for the *Housing* and *Household Composition* tables is, as in the 1981 Census, the (usually) resident population in (private) households, referred to, in the tables, as *Residents in households*. In other reports a table that counts *Residents* includes those persons resident in communal establishments (if present there on Census night) as well as those in households.

3 Population and household definitions

Population present

3.1 The number of *persons present* in an area is the count of persons alive at midnight on 21/22 April 1991 who spent that night with a household, in a communal establishment, on board a vessel or elsewhere in the area.

Shipping

3.2 Apart from houseboats (which are enumerated as households), vessels were treated in a similar way to communal establishments (see Chapter 4) with a listing form (L) and individual return form (I) for each person on the ship. Persons on naval vessels in British waters or ports on Census night are included as present in the home base port of the ship. Generally, persons on other vessels are counted as present in the area where the forms were collected.

3.3 For the 1991 Census there were some minor changes made to the enumeration of shipping. Vessels on coastal trips, fishing voyages and voyages between Great Britain and Northern Ireland, Isle of Man and the Channel Isles were not enumerated. However, foreign-registered ships in British ports, excluded in 1981, were enumerated in 1991.

Persons sleeping rough and campers

3.4 The population present also includes persons not enumerated in households, communal establishments or on board vessels. An example is persons who were sleeping rough on Census night. This group should not be confused with the 'homeless', of which it may be part, since homeless persons or families could have spent Census night in a hostel or some other accommodation.

3.5 A further example is persons who spent Census night in a non-permanent structure which was not their usual residence; for example, persons camping or staying in caravans while on holiday.

3.6 Where people were present in non-permanent accommodation with no residents (either present or absent) and with communal catering, they are included in the category for campers. Where caravans or other non-permanent structures with no residents had individual catering, persons present were enumerated on H forms and are included in the household population. This is a change from the 1981 Census when all non-permanent accommodation with no residents was included in the communal establishments category for campers. The number of households affected by this change can be seen, for example, in Table 56 in the LBS and *County/Region Reports.*

3.7 In many tables 'persons sleeping rough' and 'campers' are shown as separate categories within the communal establishments classification, as part of the population not enumerated in households. However, in some tables the two categories are included in a residual group in the classification (for example, in Table 3 of the SAS).

Residents

3.8 For most persons the answer to the question on usual address is straightforward. For some, however, it is not so, particularly when a person lives at more than one address throughout the year. Guidance issued by the Census Office took a number of forms:

To students
Question 7 (see paragraph 2.4) on the H and I forms included the instruction that, for students or (school)children away from home during term-time, their home address should be taken as their usual address.

To enumerators
Guidance to enumerators on whom to treat as usually living at an address for the purposes of completing an H form was provided in the Field Manual. A copy of the relevant extract is shown at Appendix 2.

To patients in communal establishments
Leaflets distributed in communal establishments for the sick and disabled advised patients how to answer the question on usual address. A copy of the leaflet is shown at Appendix 3.

For persons in prisons and community homes
The governors of prisons were advised that, if a prisoner had served six months or more of a sentence in custody (though not necessarily at the same establishment) immediately prior to Census night, the usual address should be taken to be the address of the prison. If less than six months had been served, the usual address before admission should be given. A similar procedure was followed for children in community homes.

3.9 Where there was no answer to the question on usual address, or where the answer was "none" or "no fixed address", the imputation procedure provides a code of either 'this address' or 'elsewhere not stated'.

3.10 *Visitors* are those persons present 'at this address' on Census night whose usual address was not 'this address' (that is, categories (b) and (c) in paragraph 2.6). A *visitor to a specified area* is a person present in that area with a usual address located outside the area.

Households

3.11 A *household* is either:

(a) one person living alone; or

(b) a group of people (who may or may not be related) living, or staying temporarily, at the same address, with common housekeeping.

3.12 As in 1981, enumerators were instructed to treat a group of people as a household if there was any regular arrangement to share at least one meal (including breakfast) a day, or if the occupants shared a common living or sitting room. The occupants of one-room accommodation or of a caravan are treated as a single household.

Head of household

3.13 It should be noted that in 1991 the H form was addressed "to the Head or Joint Head or members of the Household aged 16 or over" (thus allowing for households with no head). Furthermore, the question on relationship in household (see paragraph 7.4) asked for the relationship of the second and subsequent persons to the person entered in the first column on the form. For *statistical* purposes however, in the 100 per cent processed tables the *head of household* is usually taken to be the person entered in the first column. (For the procedures for selecting the head of a household see paragraph 6.49.)

4 Communal establishments: definitions and classifications

Enumeration

4.1 The 1991 Census enumerated all persons present on Census night in a variety of types of *communal establishment* in addition to those living in households. The term covers all establishments in which some form of communal catering is provided. Such establishments were enumerated using the L form on which were listed the names of all persons present on Census night together with individual (I) forms containing the relevant census questions (See Appendix 1 for copies of the L and I forms).

4.2 In 1981 the population in communal establishments (referred to then as the population in non-private households) made up 2½ per cent of the total present population. Included in the communal establishment population are campers with communal catering, and persons sleeping rough.

4.3 In 1991, enumerators were instructed to contact the person in charge of the establishment, for example, the proprietor or manager, who then had the responsibility of listing on an L form all those present in the establishment on Census night and all who arrived on Monday, 22 April and who had not been included as present on a census form elsewhere. The names of any non-resident staff who happened to be on duty on the premises on Census night were not required to be listed.

4.4 The person in charge also had the responsibility of issuing I forms to persons present in the establishment on Census night and of collecting the completed forms, or of completing the forms where necessary in the cases, for example, of any persons who were incapable of completing the forms for themselves.

Special types of establishment

4.5 *Small hotels* and *guest houses* containing ten rooms or more were treated as communal establishments. Those that contained fewer than ten rooms were classified as communal establishments if there were present on Census night any resident staff other than the proprietor and his family *or* five or more guests. Otherwise, they were treated as households. *Inns* and *public houses* with no accommodation were treated as partly residential premises and H forms were issued in the usual way.

4.6 *Nurses' homes* and *students' hostels,* etc, with self-catering facilities were enumerated as communal establishments if there was someone in charge to take responsibility for issuing I forms. Otherwise, each person, or group of persons sharing meals or accommodation, was treated as a separate household.

4.7 *Private residences in the grounds of an establishment,* such as a doctor's house, a caretaker's cottage or a porter's lodge, were treated as households, but *flats or suites of rooms, within the main building* were treated as part of the main establishment, and persons living in such accommodation were enumerated on L and I forms.

4.8 *Service families or civilians, living in married quarters* as part of a military establishment were enumerated as households whether the quarters were located within or outside the boundaries of the establishment.

4.9 *Sheltered housing*, that is, accommodation provided for the elderly, handicapped etc, often fell between a communal establishment and a household, in that a main meal could be taken communally though each person had their own separate accommodation with facilities for cooking their own meals. If at least half the people within the sheltered housing complex *possessed* such facilities, they were all treated as separate households, and, if fewer than half, as members of a communal establishment.

4.10 *Annexes to communal establishments* were treated as part of the main establishment if located in the same ED *or* if meals were taken at the main establishment even though the annexe was in a different ED. The annexe was treated as a separate establishment if located in a different ED *and* meals were provided at the annexe (breakfast counting as a meal) or there were facilities for self-catering; in these circumstances, if there was no one in charge to complete the L form and issue/collect I forms, the annexe was enumerated as though it were accommodation occupied by households, but at coding, such households were transcribed onto L and I forms.

4.11 *Itinerant caravan dwellers,* for example, with circuses or fairs, were treated as households.

Classification of establishments

4.12 The classification of communal establishments shown below comprises 18 major categories used in the standard published output, and 25 sub-categories relating to 'client groups' which will only be identified separately in commissioned tables.

4.13 The first digit of the following classification represents the major group and the second digit the more detailed client group classification. In standard output, such as Table 3 in the LBS and *County/Region Reports* and Table 3 of the *Communal Establishments* volume, only the first digit categories are identified.

MEDICAL AND CARE ESTABLISHMENTS

1 NHS HOSPITALS/HOMES - PSYCHIATRIC

2 NHS HOSPITALS/HOMES - OTHER
- 2.1 Mentally handicapped
- 2.2 Other (including general)

3 NON-NHS HOSPITALS - PSYCHIATRIC

4 NON-NHS HOSPITALS - OTHER
- 4.1 Mentally handicapped
- 4.2 Other

5 LOCAL AUTHORITY HOMES
- 5.1 Mentally ill (including children)
- 5.2 Mentally handicapped (including children)
- 5.3 Elderly
- 5.4 Other

6 HOUSING ASSOCIATION HOMES AND HOSTELS
- 6.1 Mentally ill (including children)
- 6.2 Mentally handicapped (including children)
- 6.3 Elderly
- 6.4 Other

7 NURSING HOMES (non-NHS/LA/HA)
- 7.1 Mentally ill
- 7.2 Mentally handicapped
- 7.3 Elderly mentally infirm
- 7.4 Elderly
- 7.5 Other

8 RESIDENTIAL HOMES (non-NHS/LA/HA)
- 8.1 Mentally ill
- 8.2 Mentally handicapped
- 8.3 Elderly
- 8.4 Other

9 CHILDREN'S HOMES
- 9.1 Local authority
- 9.2 Other

DETENTION, DEFENCE AND EDUCATION ESTABLISHMENTS

10 PRISON SERVICE ESTABLISHMENTS

11 DEFENCE ESTABLISHMENTS

12 EDUCATION ESTABLISHMENTS

OTHER GROUPS

13 HOTELS, BOARDING HOUSES, ETC

14 HOSTELS AND COMMON LODGING HOUSES (non-HA)

15 OTHER MISCELLANEOUS ESTABLISHMENTS
- 15.1 Miscellaneous family establishments
- 15.2 Others

16 PERSONS SLEEPING ROUGH

17 CAMPERS

18 CIVILIAN SHIPS, BOATS AND BARGES

4.14 *Groups 1 and 2* comprise:

- hospitals and nursing homes which are self-governed or managed by a Hospital Management Committee, a Board of Governors or a Hospital Trust, or directly by the Department of Health;
- nurses' homes and hostels managed by a Hospital Management Committee or a Board of Governors, even when the accommodation is separate from the main hospital premises; and
- rehabilitation centres provided within the NHS.

Homes and hostels for district nurses and private nurses' associations are included in *Group 15.2.* Separate accommodation occupied by, for example, a Medical Superintendent and his family, is treated as a household.

4.15 The 1981 term *psychiatric* has been retained for output from the 1991 Census, although this category consists only of hospitals and homes for the mentally ill. Hospitals in *Group 1* include those classified as such by the Department of Health and the three Special Hospitals (Broadmoor, Rampton and Ashworth - formerly Moss Side).

4.16 *Groups 3 and 4* include hospitals not managed under the NHS or by the Department of Health, and nurses' homes and hostels linked to such hospitals, even when separate from the main premises. *Group 3* includes mental/mental care hospitals, hospitals for the mentally ill and mental after-care units. *Group 4.1* comprises hospitals for the mentally handicapped and *Group 4.2* all other non-NHS hospitals.

4.17 *Group 5* comprises homes managed by local authorities but excludes homes run by voluntary, charitable or private organisations (see paragraph 4.20), and hostels managed by religious institutions, private individuals, commercial or voluntary organisations (included in *Group 14).*

4.18 *Group 6* includes:

- almshouses or Abbeyfield Societies registered with the Housing Corporation and Scottish Homes;
- residential homes registered with a local authority and managed by a housing association; and
- other homes and hostels managed by a housing association (except for housing association children's homes, which are included in *Group 9.2*).

4.19 *Group 7* includes nursing homes, convalescent homes and hospices run by voluntary, charitable or private organisations.

4.20 *Group 8* includes residential homes registered with the local authority, or exempt from registration and managed or funded by a voluntary, charitable or private organisation, such as Cheshire Homes. Residential homes managed by the NHS, a local authority or a housing association are classified to *Groups 1, 2, 5,* or *6* as appropriate.

4.21 *Group 9.1* comprises children's homes maintained, controlled or assisted by the local authority, and *Group 9.2* includes children's homes and hostels provided, or maintained, by voluntary organisations, and 'households' with five or more foster children. Residential schools and homes for physically handicapped and disabled children, maintained or assisted by educational authorities, are included in *Group 12* (see paragraph 4.24).

4.22 *Group 10* includes prisons, detention centres and young offender institutions. Excluded are: approved schools, ex-offenders' hostels, and probation and remand homes (included in *Group 5.4*); police stations with a lock-up (included in *Group 15.2*); and Special Hospitals (see paragraph 4.15).

4.23 *Group 11* comprises:

- Army and Air Force camps or establishments, naval shore stations and vessels maintained by service personnel, Fleet Auxiliary vessels and Service hospitals;
- hostels and similar establishments for NAAFI personnel, even if located outside the grounds of the camp; and
- civilians in services establishments including NAAFI staff.

Married quarters for service personnel or civilians are excluded (see paragraph 4.8).

4.24 *Group 12* comprises:

- residential schools, training colleges, theological colleges, and university halls of residence and students' hostels administered by schools, colleges and universities;
- residential schools and homes for physically handicapped and disabled children maintained or assisted by education authorities; and
- religious institutions which are boarding schools or which have living accommodation for teachers.

Training schools provided exclusively for a single employer or for a trade association or government department are classified in *Group 15.2*. Wholly separate accommodation for teachers, caretakers, groundsmen, etc are treated as households.

4.25 *Group 13* includes hotels, boarding houses, apartment houses, inns, public houses with sleeping accommodation, residential clubs, health farms, holiday camps, YHA/YMCA/YWCA hostels, and other similar establishments providing board and accommodation for visitors. Households with 5 or more paying guests and/or resident staff are also included. Establishments described as hotels or inns but with no sleeping accommodation for guests are excluded, along with bed-and-breakfast accommodation for homeless families (included in *Group 15.1*), hotels with less than 10 rooms and less than 5 guests and 5 resident staff (which are treated as households), and youth hostels managed by a Housing Association (included in *Group 6.4*).

4.26 *Group 14* includes hostels not covered in other groups, such as, common lodging houses and reception centres with resident staff, used by people as their main or only residence and run by religious institutions or voluntary organisations (for example, Salvation Army), or by private individuals, commercial organisations or local authorities. All housing association hostels are coded to *Group 6*.

4.27 *Group 15.1* includes bed-and-breakfast accommodation for homeless families, homes for families, hostels and shelters for women, and mother-and-baby homes. Maternity homes are classified elsewhere according to the management type. *Group 15.2* is a heterogeneous group consisting of fire stations, lighthouses and lightships, and hostels, homes, training centres, camps and institutions not classified elsewhere.

4.28 *Group 16* comprises *persons sleeping rough* at sites identified before the Census by voluntary organisations, local authorities and churches, as well as those persons who were counted by ordinary enumerators. In output, figures relate only to those persons sleeping rough in the open air on Census night and do not include persons of no fixed abode who spent Census night in shelters, hostels or squats, etc. *Group 17* includes persons sleeping in a tent or caravan with communal catering, or spending Census night out of doors for recreational purposes (often at a recognised camp site) with a stated permanent address elsewhere (see paragraph 3.6). Travelling people, encampments and circuses are treated as households (see paragraph 4.11).

4.29 *Group 18* includes all civilian boats, barges, ferries and ships with sleeping accommodation, but excludes naval vessels (*Group 11*), and lightships (*Group 15.2*). Houseboats are treated as households.

Changes since 1981

4.30 Compared with the 1981 Census, the number of major categories in the classification of communal establishments identifiable in tables has been expanded from 12 to 18. The changes are:

- NHS hospitals/homes and non-NHS hospitals/homes become separate categories;
- nursing and residential homes covered by the 1984 Registration of Homes Act, and homes and hostels managed by housing associations, are identified as three separate additional groups; in 1981 these were collectively included in the *Hospitals and homes - other* category;
- homes for the old and the disabled, identified as a separate category in 1981 output, are included in Groups 5, 6, 7 or 8 as appropriate; and
- persons sleeping rough *(Group 16)* and campers *(Group 17)* become separate categories.

Residence classification and status

4.31 The status of persons enumerated in communal establishments is obtained from the information given on *position in establishment* on the I form

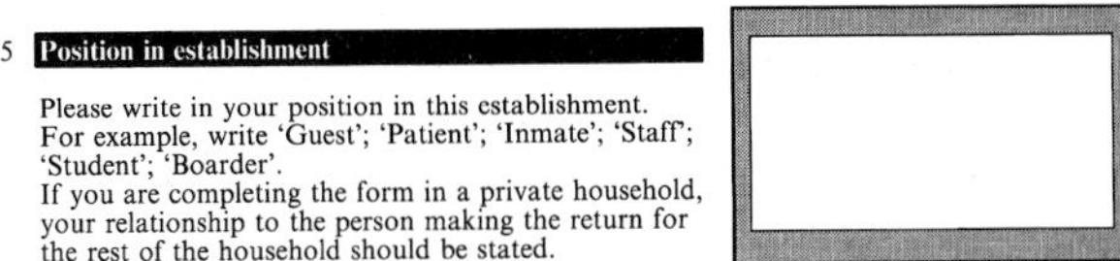
5 Position in establishment

Please write in your position in this establishment.
For example, write 'Guest'; 'Patient'; 'Inmate'; 'Staff'; 'Student'; 'Boarder'.
If you are completing the form in a private household, your relationship to the person making the return for the rest of the household should be stated.

and the response to the *usual address* question (see paragraph 2.4). The full range of categories is:

1 Residents (non-staff)

Visitors/guests
2 Residents in the UK
2a *of which* Visiting staff/relatives of staff
3 Resident outside the UK
3a *of which* Visiting staff/relatives of staff

4 Resident staff
5 Resident relatives of staff

4.32 *Residents* are persons stating 'this address' as their usual address; persons with a stated usual address of 'elsewhere' are classified as *visitors*. Visiting relatives of visiting staff are included in (3a). This classification is used in full in Table 8 in the *Communal Establishments* topic report. More generally, however, an abbreviated version of the classification, giving just three categories, is used in output. In terms of the groups shown above these are:

- Residents (non-staff) (1);
- Visitors (2)+(3); and
- Residents (staff) (4)+(5).

4.33 *Residents (non-staff)* comprises resident guests and inmates; *visitors* comprises guests, inmates, staff and relatives of staff with usual address 'elsewhere'; *residents (staff)* includes resident relatives of managers and staff. *Staff* includes managers of establishments.

4.34 Persons in defence establishments, civilian ships, boats and barges, sleeping rough or camping are all allocated to either category (1) or (2) depending on their answer to the usual address question, irrespective of their response to the question on position in establishment.

5 Housing and availability of cars

The Census questions

5.1 Statistics on housing and cars are derived from:

(a) the information supplied by the enumerator at Panel A of the Census form and the householder's answers to Questions H1-H5 and, additionally in Scotland, Question HL; and

(b) information recorded by the enumerator in his/her record book on the accommodation at each address and on those household spaces sharing a building.

5.2 Output on housing from the Local and Small Area Statistics and *Housing and Availability of Cars* reports for Great Britain and Scotland covers analyses of residential accommodation for households including any unoccupied on Census night. Analyses for people enumerated in communal establishments such as hotels and hospitals are covered in separate tables (see Chapter 4).

5.3 The main source of information on accommodation is taken from Panel A of the Census form and Question H2. Use is also made of the information provided by the building bracket linking household spaces in a converted or shared house, bungalow or flat (Panel A boxes 7 or 8).

Panel A
To be completed by the Enumerator and amended, if necessary, by the person(s) signing this form.

Tick one box to show the type of accommodation which this household occupies.

A caravan or other mobile or temporary structure		☐	1
A whole house or bungalow that is	detached	☐	2
	semi-detached	☐	3
	terraced (include end of terrace)	☐	4
The whole of a purpose built flat or maisonette	in a commercial building (for example in an office building or hotel or over a shop)	☐	5
	in a block of flats or tenement	☐	6
Part of a converted or shared house, bungalow or flat	separate entrance into the building	☐	7
	shared entrance into the building	☐	8

5.4 Enumerators were given guidance on identifying caravans and other mobile or temporary (*non-permanent*) structures. While towable caravans, mobile homes, converted railway carriages, and houseboats were treated as non-permanent, other structures, such as huts and holiday chalets were not always so easy to classify. Enumerators were thus instructed to consider as a *permanent building* any structure which satisfied at least one of the following criteria:

- that the walls are of brick, stone and mortar, concrete, breeze block, or similar material;
- that the roof is of ceramic tiles, slate, thatch, shingle, or concrete; and
- that the length of the shortest wall is at least 15 feet.

Otherwise, enumerators were instructed to tick box 1 of Panel A if the accommodation was occupied on Census night or, where unoccupied, if it was the usual residence of a household.

5.5 All occupants in a non-permanent structure were treated as a single household; separate caravans in, for example, sites for travelling people or circuses were enumerated as separate households.

Dwellings

5.6 *Dwellings* are defined as 'structurally separate accommodation'. For *permanent accommodation*, this is determined on the basis of the information from Panel A (boxes 2-8) and Question H2, which applies to Panel A codes 7 (unshared entrance) and 8 (shared entrance) in accommodation occupying part of a converted or shared house, bungalow or flat. *Non-permanent accommodation*, such as caravans, houseboats and other temporary structures (see paragraph 5.4), were identified from box 1 of Panel A.

H2 Accommodation
If box 7 or box 8 in Panel A is ticked, tick one box below to show the type of accommodation which your household occupies.

A one roomed flatlet with private bath or shower, WC and kitchen facilities.	☐	1
One room or bedsit, not self-contained (to move from your room to bathroom, WC or kitchen facilities you have to use a hall, landing or stairway open to other household(s)).	☐	2
A self-contained flat or accommodation with 2 or more rooms, having bath or shower, WC and kitchen facilities all behind its own private door.	☐	3
2 or more rooms, not self-contained (to move between rooms or to bathroom, WC or kitchen facilities you have to use a hall, landing or stairway open to other household(s)).	☐	4

5.7 Boxes 2-6 on Panel A are classified as *Unshared dwellings - purpose built.*

5.8 Accommodation which forms part of a converted building or shares part of a building is allocated either box 7 or box 8 at Panel A and, in these cases, Question H2 further identifies the type of such accommodation. These dwelling categories are defined as:

Unshared dwellings - converted, comprising self-contained accommodation in part of a converted or shared house, bungalow or flat with either separate or shared access to the building;

Unshared dwellings - not self-contained, comprising accommodation which is not self-contained but which has a separate entrance into the building; and

Shared dwellings - not self-contained, comprising accommodation which is not self-contained and which has a shared entrance into the building.

5.9 In terms of the responses to Panel A and Question H2, these dwelling types may be summarised as:

	Panel A	H2
Unshared dwellings - purpose built	2-6	-
Unshared dwellings - converted	7 or 8	1 or 3
Unshared dwellings - not self-contained	7	2 or 4
Shared dwellings - not self-contained	8	2 or 4

5.10 Accommodation sharing an entrance into the building (Panel A, box 8) that is not self-contained (H2, box 2 or 4) group to form a single *shared dwelling*. However, where there is one such household in the shared house, bungalow or flat, the accommodation does not form, or belong to the dwelling but is classified as an *unattached household space* (see paragraph 5.18 below).

Dwelling type

5.11 Information on dwellings is available for all household spaces, whether occupied or not (see *Occupancy type* - paragraph 5.81 below) since Panel A is completed by the enumerator whether or not there are any persons present on Census night.

5.12 Accommodation in permanent buildings may be classified in some tables by *dwelling type*. For example, in Tables 20-22 in the *Housing and Availability of Cars* reports, the following dwelling type classification is used:

- Unshared dwellings
  - Purpose built
  - Converted
  - Not self-contained
- Shared dwellings
  - 2 household spaces
  - 3 household spaces
  - 4 household spaces
  - 5 or more household spaces

Household space type

5.13 The *household space* is generally defined as the accommodation available for a household. The basic household space classification, used in the LBS/SAS and in the *Housing and Availability of Cars* report, is based on the information obtained from Panel A, Question H2 and Question H4 on amenities (see paragraphs 5.3 and 5.54).

5.14 The following full classification of household spaces used in the 100 per cent census processing is structured in relation to the categories of dwellings and unattached household spaces described above.

FULL CLASSIFICATION OF HOUSEHOLD SPACE TYPES

	HOUSEHOLD SPACES IN PERMANENT ACCOMMODATION
	Unshared dwelling - purpose built
1	Detached
2	Semi-detached
3	Terraced
4	Purpose built flat in residential building
5	Purpose built flat in commercial building
	Unshared dwelling - converted
6	Converted flat - separate entrance into building
7	Converted flat - shared entrance into building
8	Converted flatlet - separate entrance into building
9	Converted flatlet - shared entrance into building
	Unshared dwelling - not self-contained
10	Not self-contained flat
11	Not self-contained 'rooms'
12	Bedsit
13	Not self-contained unoccupied
	Shared dwelling - not self-contained
14	Not self-contained flat
15	Not self-contained 'rooms'
16	Bedsit
17	Not self-contained unoccupied
	Unattached household space - not self-contained
18	Not self-contained flat
19	Not self-contained 'rooms'
20	Bedsit
21	Not self-contained unoccupied
22	NON-PERMANENT ACCOMMODATION

5.15 *Unshared converted accommodation* is a household space with its room(s) including a bath or shower, WC and kitchen facilities behind its own private door. Such accommodation is identified either by Question H2 box 1 (*converted flatlet*) or box 3 (*converted flat*).

5.16 *Unshared not self-contained accommodation* is identified by Panel A box 7, Question H2 box 2 (*bedsit*) or box 4. This latter group is further sub-divided into two household space types - those with exclusive use of bath/shower and inside WC (*flat*) and those without exclusive use of bath/shower and inside WC (*'rooms'*).

5.17 *Shared dwellings* comprise two or more household spaces sharing an entrance into the building (Panel A, box 8) that are not self-contained (Question H2, boxes 2 or 4).

5.18 *Unattached spaces* are household spaces also sharing an entrance into the building but where they are the *only* one not self-contained.

5.19 Where not self-contained accommodation is unoccupied on Census night and no information on amenities is available to the enumerator, the accommodation is classified as *not self-contained unoccupied.*

5.20 Generally, in output, such as Table 1 in the *Housing and Availability of Cars* report, the full household space type classification is reduced to 16 categories by combining *shared dwellings - not self-contained* with *unattached household spaces - not self-contained.*

5.21 The 16-category basic output classification of household spaces, together with the definition of the categories in terms of Panel A, H2 and H4, is shown below.

5.22 In the LBS where household space type is cross-analysed with *occupancy type* (for example, Table 56) or is used with the *Households with residents* base rather than *Household spaces* base (for example, Table 58), the unoccupied household spaces (categories 13 and 17/21) are not shown.

16-CATEGORY OUTPUT CLASSIFICATION OF HOUSEHOLD SPACE TYPES

Household space type	Panel A code	Accommodation code (H2)	Bath/shower and inside WC (H4)
Accommodation in permanent buildings			
Unshared dwellings - purpose built			
1 Detached	2	-	-
2 Semi-detached	3	-	-
3 Terraced	4	-	-
4 Purpose built flat in residential building	6	-	-
5 Purpose built flat in commercial building	5	-	-
Unshared dwelling - converted			
6, 7 Converted flat	7 or 8	3	-
8, 9 Converted flatlet	7 or 8	1	-
Unshared dwelling - not self-contained			
10 Flat	7	4	Exclusive use of both
11 'Rooms'	7	4	Not exclusive use of both
12 Bedsit	7	2	-
13 Unoccupied	7	4	Not known
Other household spaces - not self-contained			
14, 18 Flat	8	4	Exclusive use of both
15, 19 'Rooms'	8	4	Not exclusive use of both
16, 20 Bedsit	8	2	-
17, 21 Unoccupied	8	4	Not known
Non-permanent accommodation (22)	1	-	-

5.23 In the SAS versions of the LBS tables the classification of household space types is generally further reduced by combining the categories into half a dozen or so broad groups. For example, in SAS Tables 57-59 the following six-category grouping is adopted:

	Unshared dwelling - purpose built
1-3	Detached, semi or terraced
4,5	Purpose built flat
	Unshared dwelling
6-9	Converted
10-13	Not self-contained
14-21	Other household spaces - not self-contained
22	Non-permanent accommodation

Comparison with 1981 - dwellings and household space type

5.24 A count of dwellings was not included in the 1981 Census but estimates of the number of dwellings were made from the data supplied on household spaces. This was reported in Appendix 3 of the *1981 Census Definitions* volume[8] which referred readers to the article 'Dwelling stock estimates from the 1981 Census of Population' in *Statistical News no. 49*[9]. Because of a basic change in the definition of self-contained accommodation in 1991, it is not possible to compare accurately 1991 and 1981 statistics on self-contained and not self-contained accommodation.

5.25 In the 1981 Census in England and Wales, self-contained accommodation required a household space sharing an entrance from outside the building with one or more other household(s) to have its rooms (not including a bathroom or WC) enclosed behind its own front door inside the building. For 1991, the definition was changed to require the rooms *and* kitchen facilities, bath or shower, and inside WC, to be contained behind the 'private' door. In Scotland, the most closely corresponding question in 1981 was the one on 'shared access' to the household's accommodation (Question 19).

5.26 In 1981, purpose built flats (categories 4 and 5 of the 1991 household space type classification) were counted as a single group 'in a purpose built block of flats or maisonettes'. The separate 1991 categories of *detached, semi-detached* and *terraced* were only identified in Scotland in 1981. In England and Wales in 1981 these were included with accommodation in converted or shared houses, bungalows or flats as a single group 'household spaces in permanent buildings with separate entrance from outside the building'.

Rooms

5.27 The number of rooms in the household's accommodation was obtained from Question H1.

5.28 Caravans and other non-permanent accommodation recorded as having 6 or more rooms either have the number of rooms re-set to 5 or fewer, or are re-classified to another household space type, by the imputation procedure.

H1 Rooms

Please count the number of rooms your household has for its **own** use.

Do not count: small kitchens, under 2 metres (6 feet 6 inches) wide
bathrooms
toilets

Do count: living rooms
bedrooms
kitchens at least 2 metres (6 feet 6 inches) wide
all other rooms in your accommodation

The total number of rooms is ☐

5.29 The question asked for the inclusion of the same categories of rooms that were included in the 1981 Census in England and Wales, though rooms used solely for business purposes were then excluded. The question in Scotland in 1981 was slightly different in an attempt to identify rooms used as ancillary kitchens. In 1991 the question was the same throughout Great Britain.

5.30 In output, statistics on rooms are given either as the total number of rooms cross-analysed by other housing or non-housing variables, such as dwelling type, occupancy type, or number of students in household, or, in more detailed tables, as the number of households with 1, 2, 3, 4, 5, 6 and 7 or more rooms cross-analysed by other census variables. Tables on rooms are included in the Local Base Statistics and Small Area Statistics as well as in the *Housing and Availability of Cars* report.

Household size

5.31 1991 Census tables relating to housing and households generally refer to the resident population. *Household size*, the number of residents in a household, is derived from the answer to Question 7 (see paragraph 2.10).

5.32 In the *Housing and Availability of Cars* report and in other tables, one of three distributions of household size is commonly used, namely:

1, 2, 3, 4, 5, 6 and 7 or more persons;
1, 2, 3, 4 and 5 or more persons; or
1, 2 and 3 or more persons.

Density of occupation

5.33 Two measures of under-occupancy or overcrowding have been used in the 1991 Census (*persons per room* and *occupancy norm*), following the pattern adopted in 1981. In Scotland, since the definition of a 'room' has changed since 1981 (see paragraph 5.29), comparison of both these measures between censuses must be made with caution.

Number of persons per room

5.34 One measurement of under-occupancy and overcrowding is given by the number of *persons per room*, that is, the ratio of the number of residents in a household, obtained from Question 7 (see paragraph 2.4) to the number of rooms in the accommodation of that household, provided by the response to Question H1.

5.35 In processing, 9 categories are identified:

1 under 0.5
2 0.5
3 over 0.5 but under 0.75
4 0.75
5 over 0.75 but under 1.0
6 1.0
7 over 1.0 but under 1.5
8 1.5
9 over 1.5

5.36 In output, various distributions of households by persons per room are produced. The standard, four category, distribution is:

1,2 Up to 0.5 persons per room
3-6 Over 0.5 and up to 1.0 person per room
7,8 Over 1.0 and up to 1.5 persons per room
9 Over 1.5 persons per room

These grouped categories appear, for example, in Table 23 of the LBS and *County/Region Reports*.

5.37 In other tables, such as Table 3 in the *Housing and Availability of Cars* volume, a three-fold distribution is presented:

1-6 Up to 1.0 person per room
7, 8 Over 1.0 and up to 1.5 persons per room
9 Over 1.5 persons per room

5.38 In the SAS, some tables are presented as abbreviated versions of the LBS tables. Thus, in Table 23 a truncated version of the distribution in paragraph 5.36 above appears:

1,2 Up to 0.5 persons per room
7,8 Over 1.0 and up to 1.5 persons per room
9 Over 1.5 persons per room

allowing the user to derive the missing group (categories 3-6) by differencing.

5.39 Tables in some topic volumes other than *Housing and Availability of Cars* may only present *persons per room* as summary statistics, identifying perhaps just two groups, or as a single indicator. For example, Table 2 in the *Household Composition (100 per cent)* report gives figures of households with residents living at:

1,2 Up to 0.5 persons per room
9 Over 1.5 persons per room

while Table G in the *County/Region Monitors* shows the single percentage of households living at a density of more than 1.0 person per room (categories 7-9).

Occupancy norm (Scotland only)

5.40 The second measure of under-occupancy and overcrowding equates the rooms available with an assessment of the rooms required by the people resident in the household. This measure is labelled the *occupancy norm* and is adopted in some housing and household composition tables for Scotland only (see, for example, Table 5(S) in the *Household Composition (100 per cent)* report or Tables 26-28 in the *Housing and Availability of Cars* volume for Scotland).

5.41 It is an approximate measure developed in the 1981 Census along the lines of the 'bedroom standard' used in survey work. Bedrooms are not counted separately in the Census, and it has been argued that the specific use to which a room is put is often determined by the household occupying the accommodation. The total number of rooms required by a household is calculated as outlined below, and this figure is compared with the number of rooms available.

5.42 The room requirement is calculated as follows:

(a) a one-person household is assumed to require only one room; and

(b) where there are two or more residents it is assumed that they require a minimum of one common room plus one bedroom for:

- each married couple (taken as 2 persons in a household, of the opposite sex, both married);
- any other person aged 21 or over;
- each pair aged 10-20 of the same sex;
- each pair formed from a remaining child aged 10-20 with a child aged under 10 of the same sex;
- each pair of children aged under 10 remaining; and
- each child unable to form a pair.

5.43 This room requirement is compared with the number of rooms available and the resulting difference forms the basis of a 4-category classification. In output the full *occupancy norm* categories are:

	Permanent accommodation	
1	+1 or more	(greater than the norm)
2	0	(the norm)
3	-1	(one room less than the norm)
4	-2 or less	(two or more rooms less than the norm)
5	Non-permanent accommodation	

Tenure of accommodation: household spaces

5.44 The tenure of the household's accommodation was obtained from the answer to Question H3 (see opposite page). The question in Scotland had an additional category - *renting from Scottish Homes*.

England and Wales

H3 Tenure

Please tick the box which best describes how you and your household occupy your accommodation.

If buying by stages from a Council, Housing Association or New Town (under shared ownership, co-ownership or equity sharing scheme), answer as an owner-occupier at box 1.

If your accommodation is occupied by lease originally granted for, or extended to, more than 21 years, answer as an owner-occupier. For shorter leases, answer 'By renting'.

A private landlord may be a person or a company or another organisation not mentioned at 3, 4, 5 or 6 above.

As an owner-occupier:

- -buying the property through mortgage or loan ☐ 1
- -owning the property outright (no loan) ☐ 2

By renting, rent free or by lease:

- -with a job, farm, shop or other business ☐ 3
- -from a local authority (Council) ☐ 4
- -from a New Town Development Corporation (or Commission) or from a Housing Action Trust ☐ 5
- -from a housing association or charitable trust ☐ 6
- -from a private landlord, furnished ☐ 7
- -from a private landlord, unfurnished ☐ 8

In some other way:

- -please give details below ☐

Scotland

H3 Tenure

Please tick the box which best describes how you and your household occupy your accommodation.

If buying by stages from a Council, Housing Association, New Town or Scottish Homes (under shared ownership, co-ownership or equity sharing scheme), answer as an owner-occupier at box 1.

If your accommodation is occupied by lease originally granted for, or extended to, more than 20 years, answer as an owner-occupier. For shorter leases, answer 'By renting'.

A private landlord may be a person or a company or another organisation not mentioned at 3, 4, 5, 0 or 6 above.

As an owner-occupier:

- -buying the property through mortgage or loan ☐ 1
- -owning the property outright (no loan) ☐ 2

By renting, rent free or by lease:

- -with a job, farm, shop or other business ☐ 3
- -from a local authority (Council) ☐ 4
- -from a New Town Development Corporation ☐ 5
- -from Scottish Homes ☐ 0
- -from a housing association or charitable trust ☐ 6
- -from a private landlord, furnished ☐ 7
- -from a private landlord, unfurnished ☐ 8

In some other way:

- -please give details below ☐

5.45 At the processing stage, if more than one box was ticked a priority order of 1, 2, 4, 6, 5, 3, 7, 8 is assigned. A set of coding instructions was devised, in consultation with the Department of Environment, for coding answers written in under the *In some other way* category. For example, answers such as "relative's property" or "squatting" are assigned to an appropriate renting category.

5.46 Tables showing the full and abbreviated tenure categories appear in both the Local Base Statistics and Small Area Statistics as well as in the main *Housing and Availability of Cars* report. Analyses of other household variables by tenure of accommodation are also included in other topic volumes. The full list of tenures in output is:

	Owner occupied
1	Owned outright
2	Buying
	Rented privately
3	Furnished
4	Unfurnished
5	Rented with job or business
6	Rented from a housing association
7	Rented from a local authority or New Town
8	Rented from Scottish Homes

5.47 This classification appears, for example, in Table 6 of the *Housing and Availability of Cars* report and in Table 20 of the LBS/SAS, but may be abbreviated in a number of ways to suit the needs of different topics; for example, in Table 6 in the *Children and Young Adults* report the two owner occupied categories (1 and 2) are combined.

Comparison with 1981

5.48 The division of owner-occupiers into *buying through mortgage or loan* and *owning outright* represents a slight difference from the categories adopted in England and Wales in 1981 when owner-occupation was classified as either freehold or leasehold, irrespective of whether the property was being purchased by mortgage or owned outright.

5.49 In England and Wales the renting categories are the same as in 1981 except that the category *renting from a New Town Development Corporation or from a Housing Action Trust* is separately identified on the 1991 Census form to reflect the increase in this sector of the housing market. In standard output in England and Wales (but not in Scotland), however, numbers in this group are combined with those in the *renting from a local authority* category as in 1981.

5.50 In Scotland there is an additional category identified in Question H3 - *renting from Scottish Homes*. In output, when tenure categories are required to be combined, for example, when statistics at the Great Britain level are shown, numbers in this group will be merged with those for *renting from a local authority or New Town*. In SAS, the *Scottish Homes* category is merged with that for *New Towns*, since, for most small areas, these do not occur together.

Tenure of accommodation: dwellings

5.51 The tenure of a dwelling is chosen with reference to the tenure(s) of the constituent household space(s). For a dwelling of one household space, the tenure of the dwelling will be the same as that of the household space. For a multi-household space dwelling, the tenure is chosen according to a priority order:

1 Owner occupied - owned outright
2 Owner occupied - buying
3 Rented from a housing association
4 Rented from Scottish Homes
5 Rented from a New Town
6 Rented from a local authority
7 Rented privately - unfurnished
8 Rented privately - furnished
9 Rented with a job or business

5.52 In output, category 4 is only used in Scotland; categories 5 and 6 are always combined in England and Wales (see, for example, Table 64 of the LBS and *County/Region Reports*).

5.53 The highest ranked tenure among the household spaces becomes the tenure for the dwelling. For example, a dwelling consisting of one 'owner occupied - buying' household space and one 'rented privately - furnished' household space will be classified as an *owner occupied - buying* dwelling.

Amenities

H4 Amenities

Does your household — that is, you and any people who usually live here with you — **have the use of:**

a A bath or shower?

- **Yes** — for use only by this household ☐ 1
- **Yes** — for use also by another household ☐ 2
- **No** — no bath or shower available ☐ 3

b A flush toilet (WC) with entrance inside the building?

- **Yes** — for use only by this household ☐ 0
- **Yes** — for use also by another household ☐ 1
- **No** — flush toilet with outside entrance only ☐ 2
- **No** — no flush toilet indoors or outdoors ☐ 3

c Central heating in living rooms and bedrooms (including night storage heaters, warm air or under-floor heating), whether actually used or not?

- **Yes** — all living rooms and bedrooms centrally heated ☐ 1
- **Yes** — some (not all) living rooms and bedrooms centrally heated ☐ 2
- **No** — no living rooms or bedrooms centrally heated ☐ 3

5.54 Question H4 on the 1991 Census form asked if the household had exclusive/shared/no use of a bath or shower and a flush toilet (WC) with entrance inside the building, and whether there was central heating in all/some/no living rooms and bedrooms. The same question was asked both in England and Wales and in Scotland.

5.55 Part (a) and boxes 0 and 1 of part (b) of Question H4 were asked in 1981 but the question on central heating was new to the Census in 1991; it replaced the separate question on outside WCs, which was incorporated as boxes 2 and 3 in part (b). In output, the answers for boxes 2 and 3 in part (b) are combined, resulting in 3 categories for use of WC.

5.56 In output, the number of separate amenities categories varies from table to table depending on the detail of other variables being cross-analysed and the area level. The full classification extends to 27 (3 x 3 x 3) categories and hierarchically covers bath/shower, inside WC and central heating:

Exclusive use of bath/shower
Exclusive use of inside WC
1 With central heating - all rooms
2 - some rooms
3 No central heating

Shared use of inside WC
4 With central heating - all rooms
5 - some rooms
6 No central heating

No inside WC
7 With central heating - all rooms
8 - some rooms
9 No central heating

Shared use of bath/shower
Exclusive use of inside WC
10 With central heating - all rooms
11 - some rooms
12 No central heating

Shared use of inside WC
13 With central heating - all rooms
14 - some rooms
15 No central heating

No inside WC
16 With central heating - all rooms
17 - some rooms
18 No central heating

No bath/shower
Exclusive use of inside WC
19 With central heating - all rooms
20 - some rooms
21 No central heating

Shared use of inside WC
22 With central heating - all rooms
23 - some rooms
24 No central heating

No inside WC
25 With central heating - all rooms
26 - some rooms
27 No central heating

This full classification is used, for example in Table 20 in the LBS and *County/Region Reports.*

5.57 More commonly, the full classification is reduced to 18 groups by combining the two *With central heating* categories:

Exclusive use of bath/shower
Exclusive use of inside WC
1,2 With central heating
3 No central heating

Shared use of inside WC
4,5 With central heating
6 No central heating

No inside WC
7,8 With central heating
9 No central heating

Shared use of bath/shower
Exclusive use of inside WC
10,11 With central heating
12 No central heating

Shared use of inside WC
13,14 With central heating
15 No central heating

No inside WC
16,17 With central heating
18 No central heating

No bath/shower
Exclusive use of inside WC
19,20 With central heating
21 No central heating

Shared use of inside WC
22,23 With central heating
24 No central heating

No inside WC
25,26 With central heating
27 No central heating

An example of this classification may be found in Table 7 of the *Housing and Availability of Cars* volume.

5.58 A reduction to a 12-fold classification is achieved by combining the *Shared use* and *No use* categories of each amenity as illustrated in Table 58 of the *County/Region Reports*:

Exclusive use of bath/shower and inside WC
1 With central heating - all rooms
2 - no rooms
3 No central heating

Exclusive use of bath/shower, shared or no inside WC
4,7 With central heating - all rooms
5,8 - no rooms
6,9 No central heating

Exclusive use of inside WC, shared use or no bath/shower
10,19 With central heating - all rooms
11,20 - no rooms
12,21 No central heating

Shared use or no bath/shower and inside WC
13,16,22,25 With central heating - all rooms
14,17,23,26 - no rooms
15,18,24,27 No central heating

5.59 A further reduction to just 8 groups may be achieved by combining both the operations in paragraphs 5.57 and 5.58.

5.60 In some tables the distribution of amenities categories may be further abbreviated to produce just a very few summary groups by excluding central heating and combining bath/shower and inside WC in various ways:

(a) by grouping the *Shared use* and *No use* categories for bath/shower and inside WC (giving 4 groups):

Exclusive use of bath/shower
1 Exclusive use of inside WC
2 Shared use or no inside WC

Shared use or no bath/shower
3 Exclusive use of inside WC
4 Shared use or no inside WC

(b) by separately identifying the *Exclusive use* and *No use* categories of bath/shower and inside WC, and combining all other categories (giving 3 groups):

1 Exclusive use of bath/shower and inside WC

2 Shared use of bath/shower or inside WC and no use of the other amenity

3 No bath/shower and/or inside WC

(c) by combining *Exclusive use* of both amenities and combining *Shared use* and *Lacking* one or both (giving 2 groups):

1 Exclusive use of bath/shower and inside WC
2 Shared use or no bath/shower and inside WC.

Occupancy type: households

5.61 The full list of categories of *occupancy type* in the order that they appear in output, such as Table 4 in the *Housing and Availability of Cars* volume, is as follows:

	Households with residents
1	Enumerated with person(s) present
	Absent households
2	Enumerated
3	Imputed
	Vacant accommodation
4	New, never occupied
5	Under improvement
6	Other
	Accommodation not used as main residence
	No persons present
7	Second residences
8	Holiday accommodation
9	Student accommodation
	Persons enumerated but no residents
10	Owner-occupied
11	Not owner-occupied

5.62 There is no single question on the Census form from which information on *occupancy type* is derived. The enumerator classified residential accommodation by whether it was occupied or vacant (see paragraph 1.25) and attempted to distinguish between the 'unoccupied' categories 4-9.

Occupied accommodation

5.63 Household spaces that were *occupied* on Census night, regardless of whether or not there were persons present on Census night, comprise five of the categories listed in paragraph 5.61 above, that is, 1-3, 10, and 11.

5.64 Accommodation in categories 1, 10, and 11 was enumerated in the usual way and census forms returned in respect of all persons present in the accommodation on Census night (and persons usually resident but absent from category 1 households on Census night). Households in permanent buildings which consist entirely of *visitors*, (included in categories 10 and 11, and shown separately in, for example, LBS and *County/Region Report* Table 56) give an approximate measure of those second homes (*owner-occupied*) and holiday homes (*not owner-occupied*) that were occupied on Census night.

5.65 Accommodation occupied by a wholly absent household is defined as "accommodation from which *all* the occupants who usually live there were away on Census night (for example, on holiday) and in which no other person was present". Such households were identified by the enumerator at the Delivery stage from information obtained either from a member of the household contacted before Census day or from a neighbour or other reliable source. In the absence of any such information enumerators made their own assessment as to whether the household was absent on Census night.

5.66 At the Collection stage, the enumerators were asked to confirm that the household had, in fact, been absent on Census night and, if so, they recorded some basic information about the household (see paragraph 1.51) and left a leaflet and return envelope inviting the householder to complete and return (voluntarily) the census form on their return home. Households completing their census forms in this way were classified as *enumerated absent households* (category 2 in paragraph 5.61). Households originally thought to be absent at the Delivery stage but which, at Collection, were found to have been present on Census night, were enumerated and recorded in the normal way.

5.67 Wholly absent households for which no census forms were returned, and households not personally contacted and from whom no forms were received (see paragraph 1.54), were classified as *imputed absent households* (category 3 in paragraph 5.61). (Details of the imputation of 1991 Census data for such households is given at paragraphs 1.50-1.52.)

Vacant accommodation

5.68 Enumerators were instructed to treat any residential accommodation as *vacant* where:

- the property was new and ready for occupation but not yet occupied (category 4 in paragraph 5.61);
- the accommodation was in the course of conversion or improvement (renovation or decoration) and was not yet occupied (category 5); and
- the property was clearly without furniture, or information was obtained that the property was not occupied, for example, because new tenants were awaited or that the occupier was deceased (category 6).

5.69 The *vacant (under improvement)* category covers a wide range of types of improvement, from major structural alteration to inside decoration. It would not have been practicable to obtain a finer distinction of types because reliable information on the improvement may not have been obvious or easy to obtain. Previous evidence has indicated some mis-classification between categories 5 and 6 but this division of previously occupied accommodation nevertheless provides reasonable measures of distinction.

5.70 Enumerators were instructed to treat any vacant premises previously used as a small hotel or boarding house as a private residence, because of the tendency for such premises to move in and out of the private housing market.

Derelict buildings

5.71 Derelict buildings were not recorded unless occupied on Census night, in which case they were treated in a similar way to any other accommodation occupied by households.

5.72 Enumerators were instructed to treat a building as derelict if the roof was partly missing, if floors or staircases were missing, or if the doors were missing and there was no sign that the building was being converted or renovated. Properties which had their doors and windows boarded or bricked up were not necessarily considered as derelict as this may have only been a precaution against vandalism or squatters during a temporary vacancy. Neighbours were often able to provide information, but in the absence of any reliable source enumerators made their own assessment.

5.73 If enumerators had any reason to believe that persons were sleeping rough in a derelict building, they reported this to their Assistant Census Officer and alternative arrangements were made to enumerate the building. For output purposes, persons sleeping rough are included in the population in communal establishments, that is, not in households (see paragraph 4.28).

5.74 Enumerators were instructed, as in 1981, to treat cases where there were difficulties in distinguishing between vacant and derelict as *vacant (other).*

5.75 In interpreting the statistics on occupancy type it is important to remember that the Census gives a snap-shot of the housing stock at a point in time. Thus, vacant accommodation was classified as at 21 April 1991. Known future plans, for example, to demolish the building, should not have been taken into account. Furthermore, not all accommodation classified as *vacant (other)* was necessarily in the housing market at the time of the Census, since some could have been purchased but awaiting occupation by the new tenants (see paragraph 5.68).

Accommodation not used as a main residence

5.76 *Second residences* were defined as company flats, holiday houses, weekend cottages, etc in permanent buildings which were *known* to be the second residences of people who had a more permanent address elsewhere and which were unoccupied on Census night. This classification was applied even if the premises were occasionally let to others.

5.77 Accommodation in permanent buildings which were let to different occupiers for holidays, for example, self-catering holiday flats, were defined as *holiday accommodation* if they were unoccupied on Census night.

5.78 *Student accommodation* was defined as private accommodation (for example, in a house or flat) which was unoccupied on Census night but *entirely* occupied during term-time by one or more students.

Categories identified in output

5.79 The full 11-fold classification (paragraph 5.61) is used in the *Housing and Availability of Cars* volume (see, for example Table 4), but in other sources abbreviations of the full classification are often adopted; for example, in Table 61 of the LBS the absent household categories (2 and 3) are combined giving a 10-fold classification, whereas in the SAS version of this table a further reduction is achieved by combining 4, 5 and 6 into a single *vacant accommodation* category and identifying only two other categories where accommodation was not used as a main residence: *no persons present* (categories 7, 8 and 9) and *persons enumerated but no residents* (categories 10 and 11).

Comparison with 1981

5.80 In 1981, student accommodation in private residences was classified as *second residences*, otherwise the categories in 1991 are the same as those adopted ten years earlier, but an additional *absent household* category is available in 1991 through the imputation procedure (see paragraphs 1.48-1.54). Categories 10 and 11 (*persons enumerated but no residents*) include non-permanent accommodation with persons present but no residents. In 1981 people enumerated in such accommodation were included as *campers* in the communal establishments population (see paragraph 3.7).

Occupancy type: dwellings

5.81 The occupancy type of a dwelling is chosen with reference to the occupancy type(s) of the constituent household space(s). For a dwelling comprising one household space, the occupancy type will be the same as that of the household space. For a multi-household space dwelling the occupancy type is chosen according to a priority order:

1 With residents - persons present
2 With residents - absent household (no persons present)
3 Vacant - under improvement
4 Vacant - other
5 Persons enumerated but no residents - owner occupied
6 Second residences
7 Persons enumerated but no residents - not owner occupied
8 Holiday accommodation
9 Student accommodation
10 Vacant - new, never occupied

5.82 The highest ranked occupancy type among the household spaces becomes the occupancy type for the dwelling. For example, a dwelling consisting of one 'second residence' household space and one household space 'with residents - persons present' will be classified as a dwelling *with residents - persons present.*

5.83 In output, the full 10-fold occupancy type classification of dwellings is given in Table 20 of the *Housing and Availability of Cars* volume, whereas elsewhere, abbreviated versions of the classification are adopted; for example, in Table 64 of the LBS and *County/Region Reports* a 5-fold classification is shown which combines categories 1, 2 and 3 (from paragraph 5.61) as one group, 4, 5 and 6 as another and 7, 8 and 9 as a third, with the categories 10 and 11 separately identified.

Floor level of household's accommodation (Scotland only)

5.84 In Scotland only, as in the 1981 Census, an additional question was asked on *floor level of accommodation.*

HL Floor level of household's living accommodation

Which is the lowest floor on which any of your household's living accommodation is situated?

Tick box **B** or **G** or write number of floor

Basement ☐ **B**

Ground floor ☐ **G**

Floor number ☐

The 1991 Census question differed from the question asked in 1981 which identified accommodation:

- all on ground floor or on ground and other floors;
- all in basement; and
- all on first or higher floors (stating floor of entry to accommodation).

5.85 In the *Housing and Availability of Cars* volume for Scotland and Local Base Statistics tables the full classification of floor level is:

1 Basement
2 Ground
3 1st or 2nd
4 3rd or 4th
5 5th or 6th
6 7th-9th
7 10th and over

5.86 There was no question in the 1991 Census, as there was in 1981, on shared access or means of access to the household's accommodation.

Cars and vans

5.87 The same question that was asked in 1981 was included on the 1991 Census form.

H5 Cars and vans

Please tick the appropriate box to indicate the number of cars and vans normally available for use by you or members of your household (other than visitors).

Include any car or van provided by employers if normally available for use by you or members of your household, but **exclude** vans used only for carrying goods.

None ☐ 0

One ☐ 1

Two ☐ 2

Three or more ☐ 3

5.88 The same categories are recognised in the full output classification (such as in Table 16 in the *Housing and Availability of Cars* volume and Table 6 in the *Workplace and Transport to Work* volume). Elsewhere, abbreviated categories or summary statistics are given; for example, in Table 83 of the LBS and SAS the classification is reduced to three categories:

- No car
- 1 car
- 2 or more cars

while in LBS/SAS Table 46 and elsewhere, a single *households with no car* variable is given.

6 Population topics (100 per cent)

Age and sex

6.1 This information comes from Questions 2 and 3 of the Census form.

Sex	Male ☐ 1
	Female ☐ 2
Date of birth	
Day ☐ Month ☐ Year ☐	

6.2 *Age* is derived from the date of birth and is the number of *completed* years of age at Census date (21 April 1991), unless specified otherwise in a table. *Pensionable age* is the minimum age at which a person may receive a national insurance retirement pension; that is, 60 for women and 65 for men.

6.3 A national single year of age distribution for all residents is given for ages up to 99 then 100 and over in Table 1 of the *Sex, Age and Marital Status* volume, and local figures of residents in households for ages up to 89 and then 90 and over in Table 38 of the *County/Region Reports (part 1)* and Local Base Statistics (LBS). Elsewhere aggregations of age groups are used as either summary groupings or to focus on particular age bands of the population. For example, some of the aggregations used in the LBS are shown below.

6.4 In LBS Table 67 different age groupings are identified in the Welsh language and Gaelic versions to reflect the specialist uses for this table.

Marital status

6.5 Information on *marital status* comes from Question 4.

4 Marital status	
On the 21st April what is the person's marital status?	Single (never married) ☐ 1
If separated but not divorced, please tick 'Married (first marriage)'	Married (first marriage) ☐ 2
or 'Re-married' as appropriate.	Re-married ☐ 3
Please tick one box.	Divorced (decree absolute) ☐ 4
	Widowed ☐ 5

The question in England and Wales is unchanged from that asked in 1981; in Scotland box 4 is labelled just 'Divorced'. In 1981 the question in Scotland did not distinguish between first and subsequent marriages.

6.6 *Single* persons are those who have never married (bachelors and spinsters). *Married (first marriage)* persons are those whose first marriage had not ended by divorce or death of a spouse. *Re-married* persons are those who have married again after their first or subsequent marriage(s) ended in divorce or death of a spouse and who were still married at the time of the Census. The *total married* population comprises those persons classified as married (first marriage) plus those classified as re-married. *Widowed* and *divorced* persons are those whose most recent marriage ended, respectively, through the death of a spouse or divorce.

Some age aggregations used in the Local Base Statistics

Table 15	Table 11	Table 12	Table 8	Table 52
1-4	0-4	0-4		
5-9	5-9			
10-14	10-14	5-15		0-17
15	15			
16	16-17	16-17	16	
17			17	
			18	
18-19	18-19		19	
20-24	20-24	18-29	20	
25-28			21-24	18-44
29	25-29		25-29	
30-34	30-34		30-34	
35-39	35-39	30-44	35-39	
40-44	40-44		40-44	
45-49	45-49	45-54	45-49	
50-54	50-54		50-54	45-pensionable
55-59	55-59	55-59	55-59	age
60-64	60-64	60-64	60-64	
65-69	65-69		65-69	
70-74	70-74	65-74	70-74	
75-84	75-79		75+	pensionable
	80-84			age +
85+	85-89	85+		
	90+			

Persons who were separated but not divorced from their spouse are classified as either *married (first marriage)* or *re-married.*

6.7 The same categories that appear in the question are also identified in the full output classification (for example, in Table 1 of the *Sex, Age and Marital Status* volume). In other tables, such as in the *County/Region Reports* and LBS/SAS, abbreviated categories are given; for example:

LBS Table 2	SAS Table 2	LBS Table 8
Males		
Single	Single, widowed and divorced	Total males
Married	Married	
Widowed		
Divorced		
Females		
Single	Single, widowed and divorced	Single, widowed and divorced
Married	Married	Married
Widowed		
Divorced		

Migration

6.8 The identification of a migrant is based on answers to the questions on usual address (see paragraph 2.4) and address one year before the Census (Question 9).

9 Usual address one year ago

If the person's usual address one year ago (on the 21st April 1990) was the same as his or her current usual address (given in answer to question 7), please tick 'Same'. If not, tick 'Different' and write in the usual address one year ago.

If everyone on the form has moved from the same address, please write the address in full for the first person and indicate with an arrow that this applies to the other people on the form.

For a child born since the 21st April 1990, tick the 'Child under one' box.

Same as question 7 ☐ 1
Different ☐
Child under one ☐ 3

If different, please write the person's address and postcode on the 21st April 1990 below in BLOCK CAPITALS

Post-code

The question is unchanged from the 1981 Census.

6.9 A *migrant within one year preceding the Census* (often referred to simply as a *migrant*) is a person with a different usual address one year ago to that at the time of the Census. The usual address at the Census provides the *area of destination* and the usual address one year ago the *area of origin* in tables of migration flows.

6.10 A *migrant household* is a household whose head is a migrant.

6.11 A *wholly moving household* is a household all of whose resident members aged one year and over were migrants with the same postcode of usual residence one year before the Census. Children aged under one are included as members of wholly moving households.

6.12 The *resident* population used in tables in the *Migration* volumes is defined according to the topped-up present/absent base (see paragraph 2.10). A *migrant resident* in an area is a resident in the area who was resident at a different address one year before the Census.

6.13 Certain categories of change of usual address during the reference period are excluded from the statistics for various reasons:

(a) children aged under one at Census date, though they are included in tabulations as members of wholly moving households (see paragraph 6.11 above);

(b) persons who died before Census date (not enumerated);

(c) migrants usually resident in communal establishments but absent on Census night (see the definition of the present/absent base at paragraph 2.10); and

(d) persons who emigrated overseas (not enumerated); the Census does, however, provide information on persons with a previous address overseas.

6.14 In the case where a person had moved more than once during the year preceding the Census date, only the net result of those moves is recorded.

Coding a migrant's address by area

6.15 The *usual address* at the Census is coded to the enumeration district (ED) in England and Wales and to the postcode unit in Scotland. Although the postcode of enumeration is captured in England and Wales, it will not be used for standard output.

6.16 The question on *usual address one year ago* is coded to postcode unit for addresses in Great Britain, or to an overseas country (see Annex A for a full list of countries coded - the same as those recognised in the country of birth code list). Non-responses to Question 9 are assigned either a non-migrant code or a migrant (origin not stated) code by the edit/imputation system.

6.17 When the response to Question 9 does not contain a postcode and the address is not complete enough for a full postcode to be assigned, then it is coded as *migrant (origin not stated).* The 1991 Census will have no provision for partial postcodes on the lines adopted in Scotland in 1981.

6.18 When coded to postcode unit, areas of origin in England and Wales are translated into wards and to the higher area levels used in tables via the Central Postcode Directory that links postcodes to wards. In England and Wales, the use of postcodes to define areas of previous residence results in some asymmetry, that is, wards are exact aggregates of EDs (for data on usual address) but only approximate aggregations of postcodes (for data on previous address). Consequently, a person who moved *within* an area may be counted as having moved from *outside* the area (and *vice versa*) for a very small number of cases. In Scotland, both areas of origin and areas of destination are translated into postcode sectors.

Type of move

6.19 Statistics on migrants are available for a wide range of standard census variables, but migration data is also often analysed on a *type of move* (TYMO) basis. Definitions of these are:

- a *migrant within a defined area*, for example a migrant within a local authority district, is one whose former usual address (area of origin) and usual address at Census (area of destination) are within the same defined area;

- a *migrant to a defined area* is a migrant whose usual address at Census was inside the defined area but whose former usual address was outside that area;

- a *migrant from overseas to a defined area* is a migrant whose address at Census was inside the defined area but whose former usual address was outside Great Britain (this definition carries no implication with regard to birthplace or ethnic group of the migrant);

- a *migrant from a defined area* is a migrant whose former usual address was inside the defined area but whose usual address at Census was outside the area but within Great Britain;

- *migrants resident in a defined area* is the sum of migrants within the area and migrants into the area, including those migrants resident in the area with origin not stated; and

- *migrants from/to contiguous areas* are defined as the sum of all migrants from/to areas which have a shared boundary with the defined area (see paragraphs 8.17-8.18 for definition of contiguous areas).

6.20 A migration table will comprise several of these TYMOs depending on the area level being analysed. A typical TYMO classification as used, for example, in Table 4 of the *National Migration (100 per cent)* report is as follows:

1 Migrants resident in [area]
2 Migrants moving within [area]
3 Migrants moving within standard regions of [area]/Scotland
4 Migrants moving within counties/Scottish Regions of [area]
5 Migrants moving within districts of [area]
6 Migrants moving into [area] from rest of GB
7 Migrants moving into [area] from Northern Ireland
8 Migrants moving into [area] from outside UK
9 Migrants moving into [area] from origin not stated
10 Migrants moving from [area] to rest of GB

In 1981 output, categories 8 and 9 were not separately identified.

6.21 In the LBS (which describes only migration flows within and into each local area) there are variations to these TYMOs, with some additional categories. Thus Table 15, for example, has the following column headings:

- Total residents with different address one year before the Census
- Moved within wards/postcode sectors
- Moved between wards/postcode sectors but within district
- Moved between districts but within county/Scottish Region
- Moved between counties/Scottish Regions but within standard region/Scotland
- Moved between regions or between Scotland and England and Wales
- Moved from outside GB

plus

- Moved between neighbouring districts
- Moved between neighbouring counties/Scottish Regions

Distance of move

6.22 An alternative measure in analysing migration flows is to consider the distance of move as, for example, in Table 10 of the *National Migration (100 per cent)* report. The range of distances analysed are:

0- 4 kilometres
5- 9 kilometres
10-19 kilometres (1 km = 0.62 miles)
20-49 kilometres
50-79 kilometres
80 or more kilometres

6.23 Distance is the measurement of the straight line between the postcode of the addresses of origin and destination. For areas in England and Wales the calculation uses the National Grid reference of the first address in the postcode contained in the Central Postcode Directory; the reference is usually given to the nearest 100 metres. In Scotland the references are to the nearest 10 metres and are the centroids of the populated part of the postcode.

6.24 In tables analysing distance of move, moves of migrants from areas of origin outside Great Britain or not stated are excluded.

Migration reports

6.25 Tables on migration are published in volumes at both the national and regional level, each in two parts. The *National Migration (100 per cent)* volume comprises tables cross-analysing migrants by a range of those variables processed at the 100 per cent level, such as economic position, ethnic group and amenities. The set of *Regional Migration (100 per cent)* volumes presents broadly corresponding tables for smaller areas. Part 2 of each report includes tables showing variables processed only at the 10 per cent level (see paragraph 7.100).

6.26 In *Special Migration Statistics,* summary tables are given for customer-specified areas down to the local authority district level for most counts, and to the ward level (in England and Wales) and postcode sector level (in Scotland) for less detailed counts.

Country of birth

6.27 Question 10 asked:

10 Country of birth

Please tick the appropriate box.

If the 'Elsewhere' box is ticked, please write in the present name of the country in which the birthplace is now situated.

England ☐ 1
Scotland ☐ 2
Wales ☐ 3
Northern Ireland ☐ 4
Irish Republic ☐ 5
Elsewhere ☐

If elsewhere, please write in the present name of the country

The question was unchanged from the 1981 Census.

6.28 Although only five pre-coded categories are given, that is, England, Scotland, Wales, Northern Ireland, and Irish Republic, all answers are coded to the countries as listed in Annex A.

6.29 *Great Britain* comprises England, Wales and Scotland; the *United Kingdom* comprises Great Britain and Northern Ireland; the *British Isles* comprises the United Kingdom, the Irish Republic, the Channel Islands and the Isle of Man. The *Irish Republic* is taken to include responses written in under the 'Elsewhere' box as simply 'Ireland', except in tables where *Ireland - part not stated* is shown as a separate category.

6.30 The full country of birth classification is given in Table 1 of the *Ethnic Group and Country of Birth* volume, but in other output tabulations abbreviated versions only of the full classification may be given; for example, a reduction to 90 categories is available from Table 7 of the *County/Region Reports* and LBS while a 24-category classification is provided in Table 2 of the *Ethnic Group and Country of Birth* report; SAS Table 7 presents a further reduction to 19 categories. In summary-type tables even further reductions, or selected groupings, may be adopted; for example in the language indicator table (Table 52) in the *County/Region Reports* and LBS, only two country of birth groupings - (i) New Commonwealth and (ii) Outside of UK, Ireland, Old Commonwealth and USA are presented (see paragraph 6.58).

Country of birth of head of household

6.31 In the absence of a question on ethnic group in the 1981 Census, several household composition analyses were given by country of birth of head of household as a proxy measure. In order to maintain comparability with the previous census, similar cross-analyses are presented for 1991 (see paragraph 6.49 for definition of *head of household*).

6.32 In most tables the number of country of birth categories, when relating to head of household, are further reduced; for example, in Table 3 of the *Ethnic Group and Country of Birth* volume, a 14-category classification is given.

Ethnic group

6.33 Question 11 asked:

11 Ethnic group

Please tick the appropriate box.

If the person is descended from more than one ethnic or racial group, please tick the group to which the person considers he/she belongs, or tick the 'Any other ethnic group' box and describe the person's ancestry in the space provided.

White ☐ 0
Black-Caribbean ☐ 1
Black-African ☐ 2
Black-Other ☐
please describe

Indian ☐ 3
Pakistani ☐ 4
Bangladeshi ☐ 5
Chinese ☐ 6
Any other ethnic group ☐
please describe

The question was new to the Census in Great Britain in 1991.

Coding ethnic group

6.34 Answers to this question are assigned one of 35 codes, given in Annex B. This full classification incorporates each of the 7 pre-coded categories from the question, plus another 28 derived from any multi-ticking of boxes and the written descriptions given in the 'Black-Other' and 'Other ethnic group' boxes.

6.35 Written descriptions which are the same (or generally have the same meaning) as one of the pre-coded categories are assigned the relevant code in the range 0-6. Generally, where the 'Black-Other' box has been ticked, a code in the range 7-17 is allocated, and where the 'Any other ethnic group' box has been ticked a code is allocated in the range 18-34.

Output classifications

6.36 For the purposes of most statistical output on ethnic group, the full classification (35 codes) will be condensed into 10 categories. This *output classification*, together with the constituent codes, is as follows:

Ethnic group output classification

White		0 26-29 33
Black-Caribbean		1 8 20
Black-African		2 10 22
Black-Other		7 14 15 17
Indian		3
Pakistani		4
Bangladeshi		5
Chinese		6
Other groups	- Asian	11-13 23-25
	- Other	9 16 18 19 21 30-32 34

6.37 The full classification is given in one table only (Table A in the *Ethnic Group and Country of Birth* volume). To show the effect of grouping the 35 codes, this table also shows the above 10-fold output classification (*after allocation*), together with the following summary classification (*before allocation* to the output categories):

Ethnic group summary classification	
White	0
Black-Caribbean	1
Black-African	2
Black-Other	7-17
Indian	3
Pakistani	4
Bangladeshi	5
Chinese	6
Other groups	18-34

This provides an indication of the numbers of people who responded to the Census question with write-in answers.

6.38 In most other tables showing ethnic group, the 10-fold output classification is given, though in several SAS tables, which can relate to small areas such as EDs in England and Wales, and Output Areas in Scotland, a reduction to 4 groups is adopted:

White	0
Black	1 2 7-17
Indian, Pakistani and Bangladeshi	3-5
Chinese and other groups	6 18-34

6.39 An additional category, *born in Ireland,* derived from the country of birth question, is given in most tabulations by ethnic group for which there is no equivalent country of birth cross-tabulation. Counts in this category will also be included in the appropriate ethnic group categories.

Limiting long-term illness

6.40 Another question new to the Census related to *limiting long-term illness.*

12 Long-term illness

Does the person have any long-term illness, health problem or handicap which limits his/her daily activities or the work he/she can do?

Include problems which are due to old age.

Yes, has a health problem which limits activities ☐ 1

Has no such health problem ☐ 2

6.41 In tables, statistics are presented simply as numbers in population groups with long-term illness, often compared with the total population in those groups (for example, Tables 1-4 in the *Limiting Long-term Illness* volume), or as analyses of housing or households containing persons with a long-term illness (for example, LBS Table 49).

Household composition

6.42 The 1991 Census adopts two approaches to the analysis of the composition of households, both referring to either households with residents or residents in households as the base population; that is, the base is restricted to persons whose usual address at Question 7 (see paragraph 2.4) was entered as 'this address'.

6.43 The first approach uses only the answers to the questions on age, sex and marital status (see paragraphs 6.1 and 6.4) and the question on long-term illness (see paragraph 6.40) for each person in the household. All four variables are included in the full processing.

6.44 The second approach also uses the answers to the question on relationship in household, the answers for which were only processed for a sample of one in ten household forms. A description of the relationship question and of the output produced for this 10 per cent topic is given in Chapter 7 (paragraphs 7.3-7.21).

Household composition type

6.45 In general, the main classification of *household composition* used in the 100 per cent tables is self-explanatory. The full classification is:

1 No adults, all dependent children

One adult (male)
2 Aged 65 or over with no dependent children
3 Aged under 65 with no dependent children
4 With 1 dependent child
5 With 2 or more dependent children

One adult (female)
6 Aged 60 or over with no dependent children
7 Aged under 60 with no dependent children
8 With 1 dependent child
9 With 2 or more dependent children

Two adults (1 male, 1 female)
10 One or both of pensionable age with no dependent children
11 Both under pensionable age with no dependent children
12 With 1 dependent child
13 With 2 dependent children
14 With 3 or more dependent children

Two adults (same sex)
15 One or both of pensionable age with no dependent children
16 Both under pensionable age with no dependent children
17 With 1 or more dependent children

Three or more adults (male(s) and female(s))
18 With no dependent children
19 With 1 or 2 dependent children
20 With 3 or more dependent children

Three or more adults (same sex)
21 With no dependent children
22 With 1 or more dependent children

6.46 This full classification is used, for example, in Tables 1-10 of the *Household Composition (100 per cent)* volume. In some other tabulations, however, the full classification is collapsed by varying degrees. Thus, for example, in Table 59 of the *County/Region Reports* and the LBS/SAS, the 22 categories are reduced to 11:

2,6	One adult of pensionable age with no dependent children
3,7	One adult under pensionable age with no dependent children
4,5,8,9	One adult, any age with 1 or more dependent children
10,11	Two adults (1 male and 1 female) with no dependent children
12-14	Two adults (1 male and 1 female) with one or more dependent children
15,16	Two adults (same sex) with no dependent children
17	Two adults (same sex) with 1 or more dependent children
18	Three or more adults (male(s) and female(s)) with no dependent children
19,20	Three or more adults (male(s) and female(s)) with 1 or more dependent children
21	Three or more adults (same sex) with no dependent children
22	Three or more adults (same sex) with 1 or more dependent children

6.47 Category 1 is likely to contain only a very small number of households (comprising households of, for example, one or more 18-year old never married students in full-time education). In abbreviated versions of the classification these are included in the Total households but are not shown separately.

6.48 Other tables may focus on particular types of households or will present household composition types in different ways. For example, Table 47 in the *County/Region Reports* and LBS/SAS looks at households with pensioners, separately identifying persons aged 75-84 and 85 and over living alone, while Table 1 of the *Household Composition (100 per cent)* volume presents a cross-analysis of the adult classification by the number of dependent children up to 4 or more.

Definition of terms used in the household composition classification

6.49 The following terms are used in relation to persons included in the 100 per cent processing of household composition:

(a) The *head of household* is regarded as the person entered in the first column of the form, provided that person was: (i) aged 16 years or over; and (ii) usually resident at the address of enumeration.

If one of these conditions was not met, the first person aged 16 or over to be entered on the form and recorded as usually resident at the address of enumeration was coded as the head. In the last resort the oldest resident aged under 16 was taken as the head.

No head was identified in households consisting entirely of visitors. This is the same definition that was adopted in the 1981 Census.

(b) *Dependent children* are defined as: persons aged 0-15 in a household; or persons aged 16-18, never married, in full-time education and economically inactive. The additional qualification 'and economically inactive' has been added to the 1981 Census definition (which also included persons aged 19-24 who were also never married and classified as a student from the question on economic activity).

(c) An *adult* is any person who is not a dependent child.

Household dependant type

6.50 For output from the 1991 Census, an additional, *household dependant type,* classification of households has been introduced and is defined in terms of *dependants* and *non-dependants* in the household.

6.51 In this classification of household types a *dependant* is either a dependent child or a person who both has a limiting long-term illness *and* whose economic position is either 'permanently sick' or 'retired'. A *non-dependant* is any person who is not a dependant.

6.52 In output, the full classification comprises 21 categories:

1	Households with no dependants
	Households with 1 dependant, aged:
2	0- 4
3	5-15
4	16-18
5	19 up to pensionable age
6	Pensionable age and over
	Households with at least 2 dependants
	Age of youngest dependant 0-4 and age of oldest:
7	0- 4
8	5-15
9	16-18
10	19 up to pensionable age
11	Pensionable age and over
	Age of youngest dependant 5-15 and age of oldest:
12	5-15
13	16-18
14	19 up to pensionable age
15	Pensionable age and over
	Age of youngest dependant 16-18 and age of oldest:
16	16-18
17	19 up to pensionable age
18	Pensionable age and over
	Age of youngest dependant 19 up to pensionable age and age of oldest:
19	19 up to pensionable age
20	Pensionable age and over
21	Age of youngest dependant pensionable age and over

6.53 This full classification is used, for example, in Table 28 of the *County/Region Reports* and in the LBS. In other tables, abbreviated versions of the classification may appear. For example: in Table 14 of the *Household Composition (100 per cent)* volume a 15-fold version is adopted, combining categories 2/3, 7/8/12, 9/13, 10/14 and 11/15; and in the SAS version of Table 28 a further reduction to 10 groups is achieved by additionally combining categories 4/5, 9/10/13/14, 16/17/19 and 18/20.

Welsh and Gaelic languages

6.54 In Wales and Scotland respectively the following questions were asked of persons aged 3 and over:

W **Welsh language**

Does the person speak, read or write Welsh?

Please tick the appropriate box(es)

Speaks Welsh ☐ 1
Reads Welsh ☐ 2
Writes Welsh ☐ 4
Does not speak, read or write Welsh ☐ 0

G **Scottish Gaelic**

Can the person speak, read or write Scottish Gaelic?

Please tick the appropriate box(es)

Can speak Gaelic ☐ 1
Can read Gaelic ☐ 2
Can write Gaelic ☐ 4
Does not know Gaelic ☐ 0

6.55 The question in Scotland was unchanged from 1981; the Welsh version varied only slightly from the question in 1981, which had a yes/no filter for 'speaks Welsh'.

6.56 In output, such as Table 67 in the *County/Region Reports* and LBS/SAS, the following are identified:

persons who:

- speak Welsh/Gaelic
- read Welsh/Gaelic
- write Welsh/Gaelic
- speak and read Welsh/Gaelic
- speak, read and write Welsh/Gaelic
- either speak, read or write (that is, have some knowledge of) Welsh/Gaelic.

Language indicator

6.57 In consultation, many users expressed a requirement for the Census to include a question on language other than English usually spoken in the home (or 'mother tongue'). Such a question was not included in the Census, but Table 52 in the *County/Region Reports* and LBS/SAS attempts to provide a general, and approximate, indication, at the local area level, of the possible extent of a language other than English being the first language spoken.

6.58 The table cross-analyses residents in the broad age groups 0-17, 18-44, 45 up to pensionable age, and pensionable age and over, by whether born in (i) the New Commonwealth or (ii) Outside the British Isles, Old Commonwealth and USA (including persons born in the New Commonwealth).

Economic activity

6.59 The general topic of *economic activity* covers a wide range of census characteristics including both those obtained directly from questions on the Census form, such as *economic position, employment status* and *occupation*, and others which are derived by combining answers to these questions, for example, *social class* and *socio-economic group*, which are derived from occupation and employment status.

6.60 The question giving information on economic position and employment status (Question 13) was asked of all persons aged 16 or over at the time of the Census and is fully processed. Subsequent questions were addressed only to those persons who were either in paid employment in the week before Census day or who had had a paid job within the previous ten years. These questions are only processed for a ten per cent sample of households and persons in communal establishments (see paragraphs 7.23, 7.29, 7.42 and 7.70 in Chapter 7).

Economic position and employment status

6.61 These 100 per cent processed items are taken directly from the answers to Question 13:

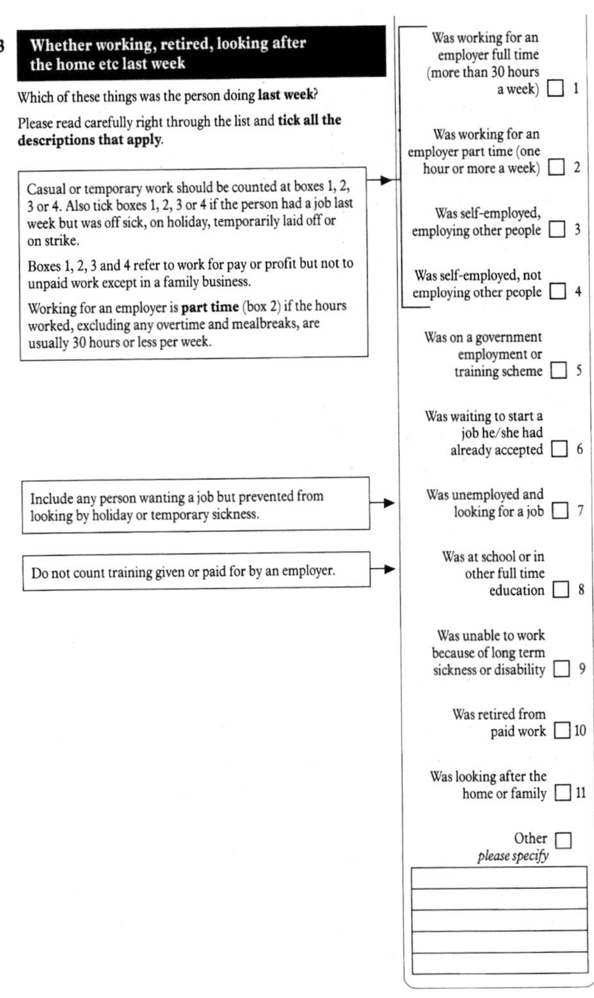

13 **Whether working, retired, looking after the home etc last week**

Which of these things was the person doing **last week**?

Please read carefully right through the list and **tick all the descriptions that apply.**

Casual or temporary work should be counted at boxes 1, 2, 3 or 4. Also tick boxes 1, 2, 3 or 4 if the person had a job last week but was off sick, on holiday, temporarily laid off or on strike.

Boxes 1, 2, 3 and 4 refer to work for pay or profit but not to unpaid work except in a family business.

Working for an employer is **part time** (box 2) if the hours worked, excluding any overtime and mealbreaks, are usually 30 hours or less per week.

Include any person wanting a job but prevented from looking by holiday or temporary sickness.

Do not count training given or paid for by an employer.

Was working for an employer full time (more than 30 hours a week) ☐ 1
Was working for an employer part time (one hour or more a week) ☐ 2
Was self-employed, employing other people ☐ 3
Was self-employed, not employing other people ☐ 4
Was on a government employment or training scheme ☐ 5
Was waiting to start a job he/she had already accepted ☐ 6
Was unemployed and looking for a job ☐ 7
Was at school or in other full time education ☐ 8
Was unable to work because of long term sickness or disability ☐ 9
Was retired from paid work ☐ 10
Was looking after the home or family ☐ 11
Other ☐ *please specify*

Written answers at the 'other-please specify' box are re-coded where possible to one of the eleven numbered categories. For example, entries such as 'au pair' are coded as either 1 or 2 (depending on the number of hours worked); 'job creation scheme' is coded 5; 'handicapped' is coded 9.

6.62 In cases of multiple ticking, up to three codes are entered on the computer file. The three lowest numbered boxes ticked are given priority except for boxes 5 and 8 which take precedence over all other boxes. Thus, for example, ticks in boxes 1, 5 and 11 are coded as 5 (*primary code*), 1 (*secondary code*) and 11 (*tertiary code*), while ticks in, say, boxes 1, 4, 8 and 11 are coded, respectively, as 8, 1 and 4.

6.63 In statistical output such as tables in the *County/Region Reports*, the LBS/SAS and the *Economic Activity* volume, only the primary code is identified, except in the case of students, where the secondary code (if any) is used to distinguish economically active from economically inactive students (see paragraph 6.66 below).

6.64 The full details of the coding instructions are not included in this volume but a copy may be obtained from Census Customers Services at the address given on page 147.

6.65 The full 12-fold *economic position/employment status* classification, as used, for example, in Table 1 of the *Economic Activity* volume, is:

	Economically active
	Persons in employment
	Employees
1	Full-time
2	Part-time
	Self-employed
3	With employees
4	Without employees
5	On a government scheme
	Unemployed
6	Waiting to start a job
7	Seeking work
8	Students (included above)
	Economically inactive
9	Students
10	Permanently sick
11	Retired
12	Other inactive

In many tables, however, categories 6 and 7 are combined to form a single *unemployed* category (see, for example, Table 8 in the *County/Region Reports* and LBS/SAS).

6.66 Category 9, *students - economically inactive*, comprises persons who are allocated a primary code of 8, and no other boxes 1-4 were ticked. However, persons who ticked any box 1-4 in addition to box 8 are separately identified as *students - economically active* as well as being included in the appropriate economically active category. (A tick in box 5 takes priority over all other boxes, and persons ticking this box are thus coded as being *on a Government scheme*.)

6.67 Category 12, *other inactive*, comprises persons *looking after the home or family*, or for whom the last box was ticked and who are not re-allocated to another category, including persons of independent means.

Differences from the 1981 question on economic activity

6.68 Question 13 on the 1991 Census form attempts to obtain the same information that was asked for in two separate questions in 1981. Question 10 on the 1981 form had just two *persons in employment* boxes, which distinguished only between persons with a full-time and a part-time job. The information on *employment status* (that is, whether a person was working for an employer or was self-employed with/without employees) was obtained from a separate question (Question 13).

6.69 The introduction of economically active students in categories 1-4 is also a change from 1981, introduced to follow International Labour Organisation definitions adopted in the early 1980s.

6.70 Additionally, the 1991 question allows for persons on government employment and training schemes - introduced widely only since 1981 - to be identified. The 1981 question on employment status included a box for 'apprentice or articled trainee'.

10 per cent employment status

6.71 A fuller breakdown of employment status, based on the 10 per cent sample processing, is described in Chapter 7 (paragraphs 7.65-7.67).

Lifestages

6.72 Also new to 1991 Census output is a summary household composition/economic activity classification designed to attempt to identify households at different stages in their development. For example, Table 53 in the *County/Region Reports* and LBS/SAS presents figures for persons and household heads:

	Aged 16-24
1	With no children aged 0-15 in household
2	With children aged 0-15 in household
	Aged 25-34
3	With no children aged 0-15 in household
4	With children aged 0-4 in household
5	With youngest child in household aged 5-10
6	With youngest child in household aged 11-15
	Aged 35-54
7	With no children aged 0-15 in household
8	With children aged 0-4 in household
9	With youngest child in household aged 5-10
10	With youngest child in household aged 11-15
	Aged 55 up to pensionable age
11	Working or retired
12	Unemployed
13	Pensionable age-74
14	Aged 75 and over

analysed by whether or not living in a *'couple' household* (defined for this purpose as a household containing two persons aged 16 and over of the opposite sex with no other persons aged 16 and over, with or without children aged 0-15).

7 10 per cent topics

Introduction

7.1 As explained at paragraph 1.10, the responses to the 1991 Census questions that were harder to code, mainly those with write-in answers, were processed only for a 10 per cent sample of households and persons in communal establishments. The 10 per cent questions were:

relationship in household;
hours worked;
occupation;
industry;
workplace;
journey to work; and
higher qualifications.

7.2 Journey to work, though relatively easy to code, is included with the 10 per cent topics because the output is most often used in conjunction with workplace, which is a hard-to-code topic.

Household and family composition

7.3 Paragraphs 6.42-6.44 explained that the 1991 Census adopts two approaches to the analysis of the composition of households. The first (described in paragraphs 6.45-6.53) uses only the answers to the questions on age, sex, marital status and long-term illness, which are processed for 100 per cent of household returns.

7.4 The second approach uses, additionally, the answer to the question on *relationship in household* (Question 5).

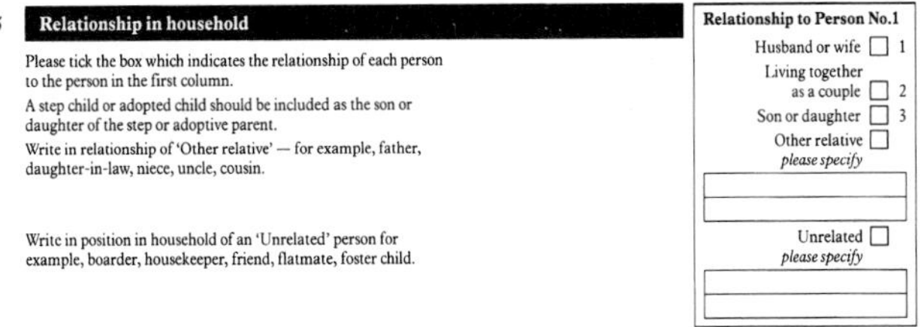

5 **Relationship in household**

Please tick the box which indicates the relationship of each person to the person in the first column.

A step child or adopted child should be included as the son or daughter of the step or adoptive parent.

Write in relationship of 'Other relative' — for example, father, daughter-in-law, niece, uncle, cousin.

Write in position in household of an 'Unrelated' person for example, boarder, housekeeper, friend, flatmate, foster child.

Relationship to Person No.1

Husband or wife ☐ 1
Living together as a couple ☐ 2
Son or daughter ☐ 3
Other relative ☐ *please specify*

Unrelated ☐ *please specify*

The aim of this approach is to classify households, taking account of the inter-relationships between household members. To do this each member's relationship to head of household is coded to a 17-category classification. This is, in turn, used to group individuals into families, and households are classified according to the numbers and type of families they contain.

7.5 The head of household, or a joint head, or other member of the household, is entered as person 1 on the Census household form, and relationship to that person is answered for all other persons on the form.

7.6 The question (which is not asked for person 1) is very similar to the one asked throughout Great Britain in 1981 but, additionally, attempts to identify *cohabiting* by means of a stated category on the form rather than by the coding of write-in answers.

7.7 Written answers at the un-numbered boxes for *other relative* and *unrelated* are coded so that all persons in households are allocated one of the following codes:

0	Head of household	9	Brother/sister
1	Spouse	10	Brother/sister-in-law
2	Cohabitant	11	Grandchild
3	Son/daughter	12	Nephew/niece
4	Child of cohabitant	13	Other related
5	Son/daughter-in-law	14	Boarder, lodger, etc
6	Cohabitant of son/daughter	15	Joint head
7	Parent	16	Other unrelated
8	Parent-in-law		

The accuracy of this allocation will depend on how specific the information given at Question 5 is.

7.8 Step and adopted relationships, when specified as such on the form, are not distinguished from blood relationships. Thus 'adopted son' or 'step-son' is coded 3, but 'foster son' is treated as *unrelated.*

7.9 The list of relationship codes differs from that followed in 1981 only in that *cohabitant* (code 2) replaces the former *de facto spouse* (derived from write-in answers) and that additional codes are introduced for *child of cohabitant* (code 4) and *cohabitant of son/daughter* (code 6) in an attempt to identify 'hidden' families within households. The *other unrelated* category (code 16) now includes domestic servants, who were separately coded - though not identified in tables - in 1981.

7.10 Category 10 (brother/sister-in-law) is intended to comprise the spouses of siblings and the siblings of spouses but *not,* for example, the wife of the brother of the wife of the head (who should be recorded as category 13 - 'other related').

Family unit type

7.11 A computer algorithm is used to allocate individuals within households to one of the 60 detailed family unit types shown at Annex C. The algorithm also defines the number of family units within a household, the relationship of each unit to the head of the household, and the generation within the family unit to which the individual belongs.

7.12 In any family unit within a household where there are two generations, the younger generation must be single (never married) and have no obvious partner or offspring. When a person in a younger generation has, or can be shown to have had, a relationship to a person other than their parent(s), that person is not placed in the same family unit as his or her parent(s). Thus, in two-generation family units, married and divorced children are not put in the same family unit as their parent(s), but single, non-cohabiting children, even those who used to have a cohabiting partner, are put in the same family unit, since their former relationship cannot be deduced from information given on the Census form.

7.13 For the purposes of statistical output the detailed family unit types identified by the algorithm are grouped into one of the following standard types:

(a) *married couple family*: a married couple with or without their never married child(ren) - including a childless married couple;

(b) *cohabiting couple family*: two persons of the opposite sex living together as a couple with or without their never married child(ren) - including a childless cohabiting couple;

(c) *lone parent family*: a father or mother together with his or her never married child(ren); or

(d) *no family person*: an individual member of a household not assigned with other members to a family; for example, a household containing a brother and sister only would be classified as *no family, 2 or more persons* (category 2 in paragraph 7.15 below).

7.14 Grandparent(s) with grandchild(ren), if there are no apparent parents of the grandchild(ren) resident in the household, are classified as type (a), (b) or (c) as appropriate. Households consisting entirely of persons aged under 16 are not grouped into families.

Classification of household and family composition type

7.15 In 10 per cent output the standard classification of households with residents by household and family composition is:

Households with no family
1 1 person
2 2 or more persons

Households with 1 family
Married couple family with no children
3 Without others
4 With others
Married couple family with child(ren)
Without others
5 With dependent children
6 With non-dependent children only
With others
7 With dependent children
8 With non-dependent children only
Cohabiting couple family with no children
9 Without others
10 With others
Cohabiting couple family with child(ren)
Without others
11 With dependent children
12 With non-dependent children only
With others
13 With dependent children
14 With non-dependent children only
Lone parent family
Without others
15 With dependent children
16 With non-dependent children only
With others
17 With dependent children
18 With non-dependent children only

Households with 2 or more families
19 With no children
20 With dependent children
21 With non-dependent children only

7.16 This classification is given, for example, in Tables 1 and 3 in the *Household and Family Composition (10 per cent)* volume.

7.17 More detailed breakdowns of households with two or more residents not in families, and of households with two or more families are also given in tables in the *Household and Family Composition (10 per cent)* volume.

Definition of other terms used in the 10 per cent household and family composition classification

7.18 The following terms are used in relation to persons included in the 10 per cent processing of household and family composition:

(a) *Head of household* takes the same definition as adopted in the 100 per cent processing (see paragraph 6.49(a)).

(b) In this classification of household types there is no age limit to the term *child*. For example, a parent (or parents) living with a never married son aged 40, would be classified as a family consisting of a lone parent (or married or cohabiting couple) with children.

(c) A *dependent child* is a person in the second generation of a family and with the same characteristics as defined in paragraph 6.49(b).

(d) A *non-dependent child* is any person in the second generation of a family who is not a dependent child.

(e) The *head of family* is generally taken to be the head of household if the family contains the head of household, otherwise:

- in a couple family, the head of family is the first member of the couple on the form;
- in a lone parent family, the head of family is the lone parent; or
- in some tables a no family person (type (d) in paragraph 7.13) is treated as a head of family.

(f) *Family size* is the number of residents in a family as defined above. No person can belong to more than one family.

Differences between the 1981 and 1991 classifications

7.19 The main difference between Question 5 on the 1991 Census form and the relationship question asked in 1981 is, as stated in paragraph 7.6, the inclusion of the category *living together as a couple* (box 2).

7.20 In 1981, responses that either indicated cohabitation, such as 'common-law spouse', or which were incompatible with the answer to the marital status question, were coded as *de facto spouse*. But, although some information on *de facto* unions was available from the 1981 Census, such unions were not included with married couples in the classification of married family types. As a consequence, cohabiting couple families (categories 9-14 in the 1991 classification) were not separately identified in 1981. Such households would have appeared as households with no family, or as lone parent families with others, or as 2-family households - depending on the presence of any children of the cohabitants.

7.21 However, in 1981 output, separate categories for families with *all dependent children* and with *both dependent and non-dependent children* were included in the 10 per cent household classification. In 1991 these two groups are combined into a single *with dependent children* category for each standard family type.

Hours worked per week

7.22 Although a question on *hours worked* was included in the 1971 Census, this item was dropped from the 1981 Census form and replaced with additional full-time/part-time job boxes in the 100 per cent question on economic activity.

7.23 In order to obtain more information on the changing working patterns in certain occupations and industries, particularly among women and on part-time working, a question on hours *usually* worked in a person's *main* job was re-introduced in the 1991 Census (Question 14) as well as retaining, for comparison purposes, the full-time/part-time categories in the economic activity question.

14 Hours worked per week

How many hours per week does or did the person usually work in his or her main job?
Do not count overtime or meal breaks.

Number of hours worked per week

7.24 The maximum number of hours worked to be recorded is 99, and any responses in excess of 99 hours are coded as 99. Fractions of an hour are rounded to the nearest even number.

7.25 In output, the standard groupings of hours worked is as follows:

3 and under	31-35
4- 7	36-40
8-15	41-50
16-21	51-60
22-23	61 and over
24-30	not stated

7.26 The full categories are given, for example, in Table 75 of the *County/Region Reports* and LBS and in Table 7 of the *Economic Activity* volume, whereas in other tables, such as the SAS version of Table 75, abbreviated groupings only are provided:

15 and under	31-40
16-21	41 and over
22-23	not stated
24-30	

7.27 For comparison with 100 per cent figures on full-time and part-time workers, total counts of persons working *31 or more hours* and *30 hours or less* are often provided in 10 per cent tables (such as Table 72 in the *County/Region Reports*). In all tables showing hours worked in the *Economic Activity* volume (and elsewhere) a split in the distribution is always made at 31 hours to equate with the *full-time* and *part-time* employment status categories (see paragraph 6.65).

Occupation

7.28 The *occupation* of a person defines the kind of work performed; this generally determines the assignment to an *occupation group*. The nature of the factory, business or service in which the person is employed has no bearing on the classification of the occupation, except to the extent that such information may clarify the nature of the duties. Thus, for example, a 'crane driver' may be employed in a shipyard, in an engineering works or on a construction site, but this makes no difference as to how the occupation is coded, and all crane drivers are classified to the same occupation group. Whereas, in the case, for example, of a 'jeweller', account *is* taken of the nature of the business, so that such a person engaged in manufacture or repair is coded to a different occupation from one employed in wholesaling or retailing.

7.29 Occupation codes are allocated from the write-in answers to Question 15, which was asked of all persons who had had a paid job either in the week before the Census or within the previous ten years.

15 Occupation

Please give the full title of the person's present or last job and describe the main things he/she does or did in the job.
At a, give the full title by which the job is known, for example: 'packing machinist'; 'poultry processor'; 'jig and tool fitter'; 'supervisor of typists'; 'accounts clerk'; rather than general titles like 'machinist'; 'process worker'; 'supervisor' or 'clerk'. Give rank or grade if the person has one.

a Full job title

At b, write down the main things the person actually does or did in the job. If possible ask him/her to say what these things are and write them down.
Armed Forces — enter 'commissioned officer' or 'other rank' as appropriate at **a**, and leave **b** blank.
Civil Servants — give grade at **a** and discipline or specialism, for example: 'electrical engineer'; 'accountant'; 'chemist'; 'administrator' at **b**.

b Main things done in job

7.30 During the late 1980s, OPCS collaborated with the Employment Department Group and the Institute for Employment Research at Warwick University to produce a new *Standard Occupational Classification* (SOC)[10] for use as a single standard classification in the Census and other official statistics, replacing both the OPCS *1980 Classification of Occupations* (CO80)[11], which was used in the 1981 Census, and the *Classification of Occupations and Directory of Occupational Titles* (CODOT)[12], which was used widely in the employment service field.

Aims for the new classification

7.31 The main concept of the new SOC was to classify *jobs* (considered as a set of employment tasks) as opposed to classifying *persons*. Thus the classification is based entirely on information about the type of work done, as indicated by the job title and description, and, unlike CO80, takes no account of ancillary information on employment status (such as whether the person is self-employed) which is not always available from non-census sources.

7.32 A further aim of SOC was to maintain a reasonable degree of comparability with the existing classifications in use, particularly CO80, though the new classification does reflect important differences within the current range of occupations and employment; in particular it draws distinctions between types and levels of work in certain fast-growing industries, such as those involved in Information Technology, and also between types of work which account for high proportions of female employment, such as nursing and teaching. Conversely, an effort was made to remove those distinctions in previous classifications which had become obsolete and to reduce the high proportion of jobs in CO80 which were allocated to residual 'not elsewhere classified' (nec) categories.

7.33 The format of the classification, like CODOT, is hierarchical, offering different levels of aggregation suitable for various analytical purposes. Thus, SOC comprises:

9	Major Groups, sub-divided into
22	Sub-major Groups, sub-divided into
77	Minor Groups, sub-divided into
371	Unit Groups created from the
3,800	CODOT occupational titles.

Continuity with the 1980 Classification of Occupations

7.34 Figure 2 illustrates how the hierarchical structure of SOC is built up from the 3,800 CODOT job titles and how the new classification corresponds to CO80.

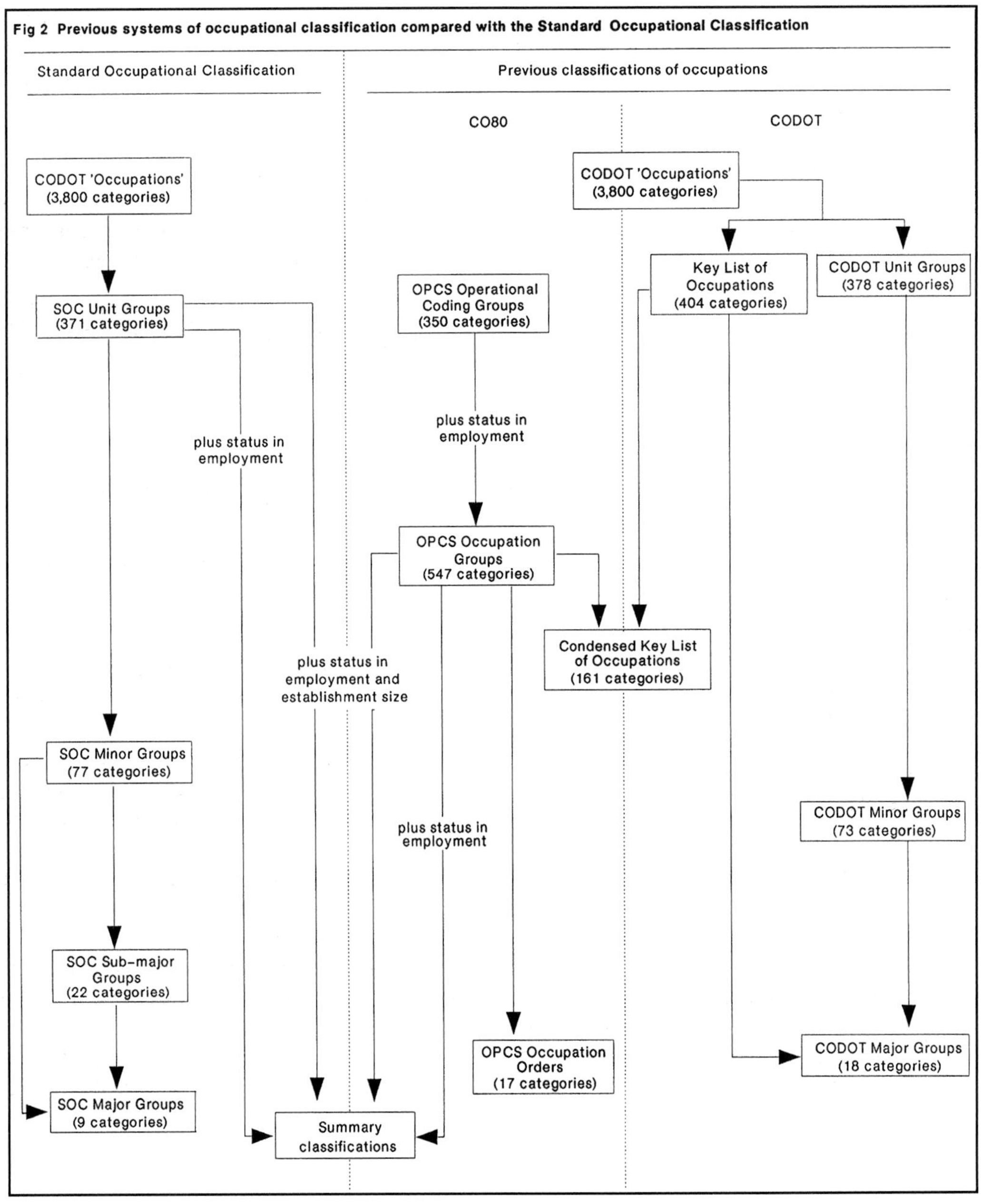
Fig 2 Previous systems of occupational classification compared with the Standard Occupational Classification

7.35 Most of the work in developing SOC went into the definition of the Unit Groups, with which coders and other practical users are mainly concerned. The aim was to adapt the structure of the 350 Occupational Coding Groups (OCGs) used in the CO80 to meet the SOC criteria.

7.36 Over half (56.3 per cent) of the OCGs match with the SOC Unit Groups on a one-to-one basis, and a further 4.9 per cent can be exactly reconstructed by aggregating two or more SOC Unit Groups. Of the others which cannot be exactly matched, a significant number differ only slightly from the SOC Unit Groups thus providing a reasonably good overall fit. Much of the remaining discontinuity affects the residual 'nec' groups in CO80.

1991 Census output

7.37 In most output, 1991 Census statistics on occupation are presented either for *Major, Sub-major* and *Minor Groups*, or *Unit Groups* of the SOC. There are 9/22 *Major/Sub-major Groups*:

1 Managers and Administrators
- 1a Corporate managers and administrators
- 1b Managers/proprietors in agriculture and service

2 Professional Occupations
- 2a Science and engineering professionals
- 2b Health professionals
- 2c Teaching professionals
- 2d Other professional occupations

3 Associate Professional and Technical Occupations
- 3a Service and engineering associate professionals
- 3b Health associate professionals
- 3c Other associate professional occupations

4 Clerical and Secretarial Occupations
- 4a Clerical occupations
- 4b Secretarial occupations

5 Craft and Related Occupations
- 5a Skilled construction trades
- 5b Skilled engineering trades
- 5c Other skilled trades

6 Personal and Protective Service Occupations
- 6a Protective service occupations
- 6b Personal service occupations

7 Sales Occupations
- 7a Buyers, brokers and sales representatives
- 7b Other sales occupations

8 Plant and Machine Operatives
- 8a Industrial plant and machine operators, assemblers
- 8b Drivers and mobile machine operators

9 Other Occupations
- 9a Other occupations in agriculture, forestry and fishing
- 9b Other elementary occupations

7.38 Some tables, such as Table 4 in the *Economic Activity* volume, present, additionally, the 77 Minor Groups and 371 Unit Groups. A summary of the Major, Sub-major and Minor Groups is given in Annex D.

7.39 As an indication of the degree of comparability of output between the 1980 classification and SOC, the information presented in Table 4 of the *Economic Activity* volume for SOC Unit Codes is also given in terms of occupation groups, orders and units from the CO80 (Table A in the same volume). Also Table 98 from the *County/Region Reports* and LBS presents a summary table of 1980 occupation orders for comparison at the local area level.

7.40 A full description of the SOC is published by HMSO in three volumes[10], and users who wish to become more familiar with the details of the classification should consult these volumes (see *References* on page 56 for publication details).

Industry

7.41 The *industry* in which a person is engaged is determined by the business or activity in which his or her occupation is followed. A single business may employ people of various occupations to provide a particular service or to make a particular product. While the occupational classification takes account of the nature of the work performed, the *industrial classification* has regard only to the nature of the service or product to which the labour contributes. For example, a carpenter is classified industrially to *building* if employed by a building firm, but to *brewing* if employed by a brewery.

7.42 The allocation of an industry code is based on the write-in answers to Question 16, which was asked of all persons who had a paid job either in the week before the Census or within the previous ten years.

16 **Name and business of employer (if self-employed give the name and nature of the person's business)**

At a, please give the name of the employer. Give the trading name if one is used. Do not use abbreviations.

At b, describe clearly what the employer (or the person if self-employed) makes or does (or did).

Armed Forces — write 'Armed Forces' at **a** and leave **b** blank. For a member of the Armed Forces of a country other than the UK — add the name of the country.

Civil Servants — give name of Department at **a** and write 'Government Department' at **b**.

Local Government Officers — give name of employing authority at **a** and department in which employed at **b**.

a Name of employer

b Description of employer's business

7.43 Industry codes are assigned, as far as possible, by reference to lists from the Department of Employment which give names and addresses of employers by industry code. Where the employer's name is not listed, a code is allocated based on information given in the description of the employer's (or self-employed person's) business.

7.44 A description of the codes which form the basis of the Standard Industrial Classification (SIC) was published as *Standard Industrial Classification Revised 1980* by HMSO[13] (see *References* for publication details). Users who wish to become familiar with SIC should consult this volume.

7.45 There has been no subsequent revision to the classification which comprises the full range of industries grouped into 10 *Divisions* each denoted by a single digit. The Divisions (with the abbreviated descriptions used in output) are as follows:

0 Agriculture, Forestry and Fishing
1 Energy and Water Supply Industries (Energy and water)
2 Extraction of Minerals and Ores, other than Fuels; Manufacture of Metals, Mineral Products and Chemicals (Mining)
3 Metal Goods, Engineering and Vehicle Industries (Manufacturing, metal, etc)
4 Other Manufacturing Industries (Other manufacturing)
5 Construction
6 Distribution, Hotels and Catering (Distribution and catering)
7 Transport and Communication (Transport)
8 Banking, Finance, Insurance, Business Services and Leasing (Banking and finance etc)
9 Other Services

7.46 The Divisions are divided into 60 *Classes*, each denoted by the addition of a second digit, and divided further into 222 *Groups* and 334 *Activities* by the addition of third and fourth digits. For example:

Division 4 Other manufacturing industries

Class	Group	Activity	
48			Processing of rubber and plastics
	481		Rubber products
		4811	Rubber tyres and inner tubes
		4812	Other rubber products

7.47 Census industry coding is based on the *Activity* heading level with some exceptions where it is not possible to distinguish separate activities/sub-divisions of activities. However, elsewhere further distinctions are made, for example, in activities covering educational establishments in order to identify separately those that are 'maintained' from those 'non-maintained' and the type of establishment (see Industry Activities 9310 and 9320 at Annex E, page 78).

7.48 The classification of some activities presents conceptual problems, for example, head offices which are sited in different locations from the place where the main activities are carried out, or repair work carried out by the manufacturers or distributors of the goods concerned. Methods of dealing with such problems are set out in the introduction to the *Standard Industrial Classification Revised 1980*.

7.49 In most output, such as Tables 10-12 in the *Economic Activity* volume, statistics are presented for Industry Divisions and Classes, although one table in this volume (Table 9) does go down to the Activity level. Elsewhere, such as in the *County/Region Reports* and other topic volumes, statistics at the Division level only are generally presented.

7.50 A summary of the Industry Classes, Groups and Activities is given at Annex E.

Social class based on occupation

7.51 Since the 1911 Census it has been customary, for certain analytical purposes, to arrange the large number of groups in the classification of occupations into a smaller number of summary categories called *Social Classes*. In the 1991 Census, persons with a paid job are assigned to one of the following social classes by reference to their occupation in the week preceding the Census or, where there was no paid job, on the basis of the most recent paid job held within the previous ten years.

I	Professional, etc occupations
II	Managerial and technical occupations
III(N)	Skilled occupations: non-manual
III(M)	Skilled occupations: manual
IV	Partly skilled occupations
V	Unskilled occupations

7.52 Members of the armed forces and those with inadequately described occupations are not allocated a social class and are, generally, separately identified in tables showing social class distributions, for example, Tables 90 and 91 in the *County/Region Reports* and LBS, and in Table 17 of the *Economic Activity* volume. Persons on a government employment or training scheme are similarly not allocated a social class, and are generally omitted from 10 per cent analyses (see paragraph 7.68).

7.53 Late in 1989 OPCS conducted a consultation exercise to ascertain whether there was any user requirement to revise the terminology of the then existing classification in order to answer a long-standing criticism that the name implied that the classification embraced many social characteristics, whereas it is, in fact, based solely on occupation.

7.54 Some of the interested parties consulted supported the proposal to change the name of the classification from *Social Class* to *Occupational Skill Group*, though many preferred a simpler name, such as *Occupational category*. But there was, however, serious opposition to any change; in particular, it was pointed out that, although the classification is indeed based on occupation, it is *related* to other factors, and is applied to all members of a household or family, including those without occupations.

7.55 In the light of the views expressed, OPCS decided to retain the name 'social class' but to expand it to *Social Class based on occupation* in order to make its basis more explicit.

7.56 The proposal to change the name of Social Class II from *Intermediate Occupations* to *Managerial and Technical Occupations* was welcomed and this has been implemented.

7.57 Notwithstanding these minor changes to the nomenclature of the classification, the occupation groups included in each of the social class categories are, as in 1981, selected in such a way as to bring together, as far as possible, people with similar levels of occupational skill. In general, for the 1991 Census, each SOC Unit Group is assigned as a whole to one or other social class and no account is taken of differences between individuals in the same group, such as differences of education or levels of remuneration. However, for persons having the *employment status* of 'foreman' or 'manager' the following additional rules apply:

(a) each occupation is given a basic social class;

(b) persons of 'foreman' status whose basic social class is IV or V are allocated to Social Class III; and

(c) persons of 'manager' status are allocated to Social Class II with certain exceptions.

Continuity between 1981 and 1991 Censuses

7.58 Volume 3 of the *Standard Occupational Classification*[10] presents an analysis of allocated social class based on CO80 tabulated against social class as re-allocated on the basis of SOC, for a sample of 1981 Census occupations.

7.59 The most salient net effects on the distribution of the sample are:

- a decrease from 18.0 per cent to 16.8 per cent in the proportion of cases assigned to Social Class IV; and

- an increase from 6.2 per cent to 7.6 per cent in the proportion of cases assigned to Social Class V.

7.60 In none of the other social classes was there a difference in the proportion of cases allocated which was greater than + 0.3 per cent.

Socio-economic group

7.61 Classification by *socio-economic group* (SEG) was introduced in the 1951 Census and extensively amended in 1961. This non-hierarchical classification aims to bring together people with jobs of similar social and economic status. The allocation of occupied persons to an SEG is determined by considering their *employment status* and *occupation*. The 20-fold classification, with brief descriptions, is as follows:

1 Employers and managers in central and local government, industry, commerce, etc - large establishments
  1.1 Employers
  1.2 Managers
2 Employers and managers in industry, commerce, etc - small establishments
  2.1 Employers
  2.2 Managers
3 Professional workers: self-employed
4 Professional workers: employees
5 Intermediate non-manual workers
  5.1 Ancillary workers and artists
  5.2 Foremen and supervisors
6 Junior non-manual workers
7 Personal service workers
8 Foremen and supervisors: manual
9 Skilled manual workers
10 Semi-skilled manual workers
11 Unskilled manual workers
12 Own account workers (other than professional)
13 Farmers: employers and managers
14 Farmers: own account
15 Agricultural workers
16 Members of armed forces
17 Inadequately described and not stated occupations

7.62 It is not practicable to obtain from a census the degree of responsibility exercised by employers and managers. An indirect, and necessarily rather crude, distinction between greater and lesser responsibility is therefore provided by classifying employers and managers by the size of the establishment in which they work: SEGs 1.1 and 1.2 comprise, respectively, employers and managers in enterprises employing 25 or more persons, while SEGs 2.1 and 2.2 comprise those in enterprises employing fewer than 25 persons. Civil servants, local authority officials and ships' officers are conventionally regarded as working in large establishments.

7.63 A more detailed description of SEGs is given in Annex F, and a full account of the construction of SEGs, in terms of the SOC Unit Groups, is given in Volume 3 of the *Standard Occupational Classification*[10].

7.64 In output, the full SEG classification is generally given (see, for example, Table 92 of the *County/Region Reports* and LBS and in Table 17 in the *Economic Activity* volume). However, in some tables, abbreviated versions of the full classification are adopted: for example, in Table 86 of the LBS groups 1.1 and 1.2 are combined, and 2.1 and 2.2 combined, to form single categories; and in Table 82 further reductions are achieved by combining the following groups:

1,2	Employers and managers
3,4	Professional workers
5	Intermediate non-manual workers
6	Junior non-manual workers
8,9,12	Manual workers (foremen, supervisors, skilled and own account)
7,10	Personal service and semi-skilled manual workers
11	Unskilled manual workers
13,14,15	Farmers and agricultural workers
16,17	Members of armed forces and inadequately described occupations.

Employment status

7.65 For most output, *employment status* is taken from the responses from Question 13, which is processed for 100 per cent of returns (see paragraphs 6.61 and 6.65). In some tables, however, employment status is presented broken down by census characteristics which are processed only for the 10 per cent sample.

7.66 Thus in Table 3 of the *Economic Activity* volume, *employees* are sub-divided into those who are:

- working 31 or more hours per week
- working 16-30 hours per week
- working 15 hours or fewer per week

and also into:

- Managers
  - Large establishments
  - Small establishments
- Foremen
  - Non-manual
  - Manual
- Professional employees
- Other employees

while the *self-employed* are similarly sub-divided by hours worked and also into:

- With employees
  - Large establishments
  - Small establishments
- Without employees.

7.67 Abbreviated versions of these 10 per cent analyses of employment status also appear in the *County/Region Reports* and LBS/SAS (see Tables 79 and 81 for example).

Persons on a Government scheme

7.68 Persons on a Government employment or training scheme are classified as *economically active - in employment* (see paragraph 6.65). Information about the particular scheme was not collected in the Census, however, so tables which analyse occupation, industry, hours worked, social class based on occupation and SEG do not include persons working on such a scheme.

Persons not in employment

7.69 Persons who were not in employment in the week before Census day were asked details of their most recent paid job, if one had been held within the previous ten years. If no paid job had been held in this period, such persons are not included in tables analysing occupation, industry, hours worked, social class and SEG.

Workplace and transport to work

7.70 The questions on *workplace* and *transport to work* (Questions 17 and 18) are similar to those asked in the 1981 Census. However, Question 17 had an additional instruction to members of the armed forces not to enter their address of place of work, and, in Scotland, a note on offshore installations was added. Furthermore, in Question 18 the 1981 means of transport to work category 'car or van - pool, sharing driving' was dropped.

Population base

7.71 The 1991 Census tables on *Workplace and Transport to Work* will be published in volumes for Great Britain and, separately, for Scotland. The population base used for these tables differs slightly from the *resident population,* in that *economically active* persons with a workplace in Great Britain but who are resident outside Great Britain are also included. The resident population base used elsewhere only includes persons resident in Great Britain at the time of the Census (see paragraph 2.10).

17 Address of place of work

Please give the full address of the person's place of work.

For a person employed on a site for a long period, give the address of the site.

For a person not working regularly at one place who reports daily to a depot or other fixed address, give that address.

For a person not reporting daily to a fixed address, tick box 1.

For a person working mainly at home, tick box 2.

Armed Forces — leave blank.

Please write full address and postcode of workplace below in BLOCK CAPITALS

Post-code

No fixed place ☐ 1
Mainly at home ☐ 2

18 Daily journey to work

Please tick the appropriate box to show how the longest part, by distance, of the person's daily journey to work is normally made.

For a person using different means of transport on different days, show the means most often used.

Car or van includes three-wheeled cars and motor caravans.

British Rail train ☐ 1
Underground, tube, metro ☐ 2
Bus, minibus or coach (public or private) ☐ 3
Motor cycle, scooter, moped ☐ 4
Driving a car or van ☐ 5
Passenger in car or van ☐ 6
Pedal cycle ☐ 7
On foot ☐ 8
Other ☐ 9
please specify

Works mainly at home ☐ 0

Usual address

7.72 For some people their *usual address* (see paragraph 2.4) may differ from the address from which they go to work; a note to the usual address question states that 'the home address should be taken as the usual address for any person who lives away from home for part of the week'. Consequently, any cross-tabulation of usual address and address of workplace can produce some unlikely combinations, particularly when the means of transport to work is added as an additional cross-variable.

Address of workplace

7.73 Apart from those cases where the workplace is given as an address outside Great Britain, 'no fixed place', 'mainly at home' or is not stated, the address is postcoded for computer processing. Workplaces are therefore recorded in terms of postcode units and are allocated to local authority wards, districts or counties (postcode sectors and Regions in Scotland) using the OPCS Central Postcode Directory (CPD). Only full postcode units for workplace will be processed and these will be obtained, as far as possible, even for incomplete workplace addresses, by searching lists of workplace establishments obtained from the 1989 Census of Employment and other sources, such as a list of schools from the Department of Education and Science.

7.74 Cases where a full postcode is not obtained are treated as 'not stated'. Members of the armed forces will not be coded to area of workplace but where possible are separately identified in output as 'armed forces' to distinguish them within the *not stated* category (in 1981 they were assigned to their area of workplace where possible).

7.75 Persons working on offshore installations (oil and gas) within the UK sector on Census night were not enumerated in the 1991 Census, but persons who work on them may have been counted at an address in Great Britain, either as present on Census night or as an absent resident member of a household. Where such persons have been enumerated, their area of workplace is coded *offshore installations* and treated as *outside Great Britain*. In 1981, these cases were generally treated as if their area of workplace was the same as their area of residence.

7.76 Persons with 'no fixed workplace' or 'workplace not stated' are, wherever possible, coded as such, though in output they are sometimes included as working in their area of usual residence.

Workplace type

7.77 There are three main categories of workplace type used in output. These relate to the person's residence and workplace in terms of the area of analysis. The categories are:

- (i) resident and working in the area;
- (ii) working in area, resident outside; and
- (iii) resident in area, working outside.

Categories (i) + (ii) give the total population *working* in the area, while (i) + (iii) give the total employed population *resident* in the area.

7.78 In main output, such as Table 1 of the *Workplace and Transport to Work* volume, a more detailed, 12-fold breakdown of the above categories is presented. The full *workplace* categories are:

	Resident in area
1	In employment
2	Unemployed
3	Working in area
	Resident and working in area
4	Total
5	Workplace at home
6	No fixed workplace
	Workplace not stated
7	Armed forces
8	Other
	Working in area, resident outside
9	Total
10	Resident outside GB
	Resident in area, working outside
11	Total
12	Workplace outside GB

Categories 4, 9 and 12 equate, respectively with the main categories (i), (ii) and (iii) in paragraph 7.77 above.

7.79 In the 1991 Census, categories 5-8 are counted as working in their area of residence, whereas in 1981 Census tables these categories were not identified separately (although members of the armed forces were counted in their area of workplace when this was stated). Persons *resident outside GB* (category 10) were, in 1981, counted as resident in the area of enumeration, but for 1991 this practice has been changed and this group is identified as *resident outside area* and shown separately as such wherever possible.

7.80 In *Special Workplace Statistics* three sets of tables (Set A - area of residence, Set B - area of workplace, and Set C - matrix of journeys from residence to workplace) are given for customer-specified areas built up from EDs in England and Wales and Output Areas in Scotland.

Transport to work

7.81 The journey to work question (see paragraph 7.70) asked about the longest part, by distance, of the person's normal daily journey to work. The categories 1-9 listed in the question are the same as those in 1981 except that the former category 'car pool/sharing driving' is no longer separated from 'driving a car or van' (category 5) or 'passenger in car or van' (category 6).

7.82 Where more than one box was ticked the lowest number was coded; for example, if box 1 and box 6 were ticked, then the code for 'British Rail, train' was allocated.

7.83 During the coding of workplace and journey to work a check is made to ensure that no inconsistencies occur. Thus if *workplace* has been given as 'mainly at home' then the corresponding code for 'works mainly at home' is assigned if box 0 in the journey to work question has not been ticked, regardless of any of the other boxes 1-9 being ticked.

7.84 The categories 1-8, plus an 'other' or 'not stated' category, are used in output, for example, in Table 8 of the *Workplace and Transport to Work* volume and in Table 82 of the *County/Region Reports* and LBS/SAS. The 'other' or 'not stated' category comprises those persons who failed to answer the question, or who selected box 9 but cannot be assigned another code, or who selected box 0 but gave an address of workplace other than 'mainly at home'.

Distance to work

7.85 Table 7 in the *Workplace and Transport to Work* volume analyses means of transport to work by *distance to work*. This distance is a measure, in kilometres, of a straight line between the postcode of residence and postcode of workplace. For England and Wales, the calculation is performed using the National Grid reference of the first address in the postcode, contained in the CPD; the reference is usually given to the nearest 100 metres. In Scotland, the references are to the nearest 10 metres and are referenced from the centroid of the populated part of the postcode.

7.86 The accuracy of the distance calculated will be affected by the accuracy of the postcodes of residence and workplace and of the grid references on the CPD. Additionally, anomalies in addresses of residences (for example, persons having a temporary residence near their place of work but with a usual residence elsewhere) may result in an incorrect distance to work.

7.87 The *distance to work* categories, in output, are:

	Workplace stated
1	Less than 2 km
2	2- 4 km
3	5- 9 km
4	10-19 km
5	20-29 km
6	30-39 km
7	40 km and over
8	Workplace at home
9	No fixed workplace
10	Workplace not stated
11	Workplace outside GB

Qualified manpower

7.88 Question 19 on the Census form requested, for all persons aged 18 and over, details of degrees and professional and vocational qualifications obtained.

19 Degrees, professional and vocational qualifications

Has the person obtained any qualifications after reaching the age of 18 such as:
-degrees, diplomas, HNC, HND,
-nursing qualifications,
-teaching qualifications (see * below),
-graduate or corporate membership of professional institutions,
-other professional, educational or vocational qualifications?

Do not count qualifications normally obtained at school such as GCE, CSE, GCSE, SCE and school certificates.

If box 2 is ticked, write in all qualifications even if they are not relevant to the person's present job or if the person is not working.

Please list the qualifications in the order in which they were obtained.

If more than three, please enter in a spare column and link with an arrow.

*For a person with **school teaching qualifications**, give the full title of the qualification, such as 'Certificate of Education' and the subject(s) which the person is qualified to teach. The subject 'education' should then only be shown if the course had no other subject specialisation.

NO — no such qualifications ☐ 1
YES — give details ☐ 2

1 Title
Subject(s)
Year
Institution

2 Title
Subject(s)
Year
Institution

3 Title
Subject(s)
Year
Institution

The question was in the same form as the one included in the 1981 Census.

Coding of qualifications

7.89 Each qualification is allocated a 6-digit code: the first 3 digits indicating the type and level of the qualification, for example, degree, diploma, certificate, etc; and the second 3 indicating the subject, or combination of subjects, in which the qualification was obtained.

7.90 The awarding institution and year of the award are not coded, but this additional information is used to improve the accuracy of the 6-digit coding.

7.91 Each recorded qualification is checked against indexes of acceptable and unacceptable qualifications, which are updated with the help of the Department of Education and Science and the Scottish Office Education Department. The indexes also contain the codes to be applied to the acceptable qualifications. The coded qualifications are subjected to a computer edit by checking against a combination of acceptable qualifications and subjects. Edit failures are re-coded as necessary.

7.92 Cases requiring special treatment include:

(a) *Conjoint degrees and professional qualifications*, such as MB (Bachelor of Medicine), BCh (Bachelor of Surgery) and MRCS (Member of the Royal College of Surgeons of England), which are treated as single qualifications.

(b) *Degrees in combined subjects*: such degrees differ from (a) above. The subject classification contains specific codes to be allocated to degrees in which more than one major subject is stated.

(c) *Teaching qualifications.* Initial teaching qualifications, including non-graduate teaching certificates, certificates in education, post-graduate certificates in education (PGCE) and Bachelor of Education degrees (where obtained in 1967 or later) are subject coded 1.2.1 (see Annex G for the full list of subject codes). Subsequent teaching qualifications are coded 1.2.2 if a special education component (for example, teaching of music) is mentioned, and 1.1 if there was no mention of a specialist subject.

Where a BEd was obtained within two years of a non-graduate certificate of education, the two are treated as a single qualification and coded to the BEd.

(d) *Masters' degrees and Bachelorates.* In general MAs are coded to level a, except those obtained at Cambridge, Oxford and the Scottish universities of Aberdeen, Dundee, Edinburgh, Glasgow and St Andrews, where they are coded to level b (see paragraph 7.94). Bachelorates are generally coded to level b but, conversely, some are coded to level a; for example:

- in Civil Law or Science at Oxford
- in Divinity at Birmingham
- in Letters or Philosophy at all universities
- in Planning at Manchester.

Population base

7.93 The 1991 Census tables on *qualified manpower* cover the resident population aged 18 and over. The 1981 population base also included persons resident outside Great Britain but with a workplace in Great Britain. This latter group added just 1,240 persons in the 10 per cent sample in 1981 and has been omitted from the 1991 base.

Educational level

7.94 For the purposes of output, qualifications are grouped into three *educational levels*:

Level a - higher degrees of UK standard;

Level b - first degrees and all other qualifications of UK first degree standard; and

Level c - qualifications that are: (i) generally obtained at 18 and over; (ii) above GCE 'A' level standard; and (iii) below UK first degree standard.

7.95 Level c includes most nursing and many teaching qualifications, although degrees in education (including PGCE) will be classified as level b.

7.96 A *qualified* person is one who holds at least one qualification at level a, b or c. Persons holding more than one qualification are generally analysed by the highest qualification; if two or more qualifications of the same (highest) level are held, the one most recently obtained is used.

7.97 Tabulations of level of qualification are published in the *Qualified Manpower* volume and in Tables 84 and 85 of the *County/Region Reports* and LBS and Table 84 of the SAS.

Subject group

7.98 The major subject(s) of each qualification that a person holds is coded using a standard subject classification, consisting of 10 *subject groups* and 108 *primary subjects*. The full classification is given at Annex G.

7.99 As stated in paragraph 7.96 above, unless otherwise stated in tables, the most recently obtained qualification at the highest level is used to determine the educational level and subject for each qualified person. In Tables 14a-14e of the *Qualified Manpower* volume, the most recently obtained qualification at the highest level in a *particular* subject area is used. Thus in some cases, for example, where two qualifications in two different subjects are held, a person can be counted in more than one of the tables.

Migration (10 per cent tables)

7.100 Although migration is a 100 per cent topic (that is, the questions on usual address (see paragraph 2.4) and address one year before the Census (see paragraph 6.8) are fully processed), tables on this topic show migrants analysed both by other 100 per cent variables (see paragraph 6.25) and, separately, by 10 per cent variables.

7.101 In both the *National* and *Regional Migration* reports the 10 per cent variables cover occupation, industry and socio-economic group. However, all definitions pertaining to the *migrants* are common to both levels of processing (see paragraphs 6.8-6.26).

Interpretation of the 10 per cent sample statistics

7.102 The 10 per cent sample is a stratified sample covering one in ten enumerated households and one person in ten enumerated in communal establishments (see paragraph 1.5). Evaluation of the 1981 Census 10 per cent sample[14], when the same sampling strategy was used, has shown that a reliable estimate of the enumerated population is achieved by simply multiplying the sample counts by 10. A similar analysis will be carried out for the 1991 Census sample and reported in the *Census Monitor* series.

7.103 For the first time in a British Census, the 1991 Census includes statistics for households with residents where nobody was present on Census night. These *wholly absent households* were left a census form for voluntary completion on their return home (see paragraphs 1.48-1.49). All forms completed and returned to the Census Offices have been processed and, where selected, are included in the 10 per cent sample. In some cases no form was received from an absent household because, for example, the household returned home too late to be included in the census processing. In these cases the items which are processed for 100 per cent level have been imputed (see paragraphs 1.50-1.54).

7.104 Because there is no reliable method of imputing the more complex items processed for the 10 per cent sample (for example, occupation, industry, higher qualifications and family composition), imputed absent households are *excluded* from the 10 per cent sample. This means that grossing-up sample counts by the simple factor of 10 will not give figures comparable with the published figures for the total population (although, as stated in paragraph 7.102, the grossed-up figures will be a reliable estimate of the *enumerated* population, that is, the total population minus members of imputed wholly absent households).

7.105 In each 10 per cent topic report, tables show counts of residents in imputed wholly absent households for all of the geographic areas covered in the particular volume. The tables cover all of the 100 per cent processed items included in the volume and enable users to compare grossed-up counts from 10 per cent sample tables with 100 per cent processed tables. For example, Table 1 in the *Qualified Manpower* volume shows the 10 per cent sample resident population of England age 18 and over. A reliable estimate of the total population aged 18 and over is thus given by:

sample count x 10 = estimate of enumerated population....(1)

(1) + residents in imputed households
= estimate of total population.............(2)

7.106 The residents in imputed wholly absent households are, in effect, an addition to the 'not stated' categories of the 10 per cent processed items.

8 Standard areas for statistical output

Topic Statistics

8.1 Tables in the Great Britain volumes on individual Census topics are generally published at one of five levels of geographic area. In each report, the table contents indicates the areas for which each table is presented and the order in which those areas appear within the table. These levels are:

Great Britain tables:	Great Britain
National level tables:	Great Britain England and Wales England Wales Scotland
Regional level tables:	Great Britain England and Wales England Standard regions [8] Metropolitan counties [7] Inner/Outer London Regional remainders [5] Wales Scotland
County level tables:	same as Regional level tables
plus	Non-met counties of England and Wales [55] Regions and Islands Areas of Scotland [12]
District level tables:	same as Regional level tables
plus	London boroughs [33] Non-met counties of England and Wales [55] Districts of England and Wales [403] Regions and Islands Areas of Scotland [12] Districts of Scotland [53]

8.2 Where tables are produced in Scotland only volumes (see paragraph 1.14) the area levels to be published (though not always for each table) are:

Scotland
Regions and Islands Areas
Districts
Civil Parishes (for *Gaelic language* volume only)

Metropolitan areas

8.3 In output, the 1991 Census adopts the same definition of *metropolitan counties* as in 1981. These are:

North region	Tyne and Wear
Yorkshire and Humberside region	South Yorkshire West Yorkshire
South East region	Greater London
West Midlands region	West Midlands
North West region	Merseyside

These counties are identified in Map 1 (page 50) as the shaded areas.

8.4 At the regional and district level, tables for the South East Region will also be presented for the *Outer Metropolitan Area* and the *Outer South East.* The *Outer Metropolitan Area* is defined in terms of the following districts surrounding Greater London:

Bedfordshire (part)	Luton South Bedfordshire
Berkshire (part)	Bracknell Reading Slough Windsor and Maidenhead Wokingham
Buckinghamshire (part)	Chiltern South Bucks Wycombe
Essex (part)	Basildon Brentwood Castle Point Chelmsford Epping Forest Harlow Rochford Southend-on-Sea Thurrock
Hampshire (part)	Hart Rushmoor
Hertfordshire	All districts
Kent (part)	Dartford Gillingham Gravesham Maidstone Rochester upon Medway Sevenoaks Tonbridge and Malling Tunbridge Wells
Surrey	All districts
West Sussex (part)	Crawley Horsham Mid Sussex

This area is identified on Map 1 by the dotted line and hatched shading. The *Outer South Area* comprises all other remaining districts in the South East region.

Other area levels

8.5 In the *Topics Report for Health Areas*, a selection of the 100 per cent topics tables is presented for the following health administration area levels in Great Britain:

Regional health authority level:	Great Britain
	England
	Regional Health Authorities [14]
	Wales
	Scotland

8.6 The constituent components of each main area level identified in topic report tables are shown on Maps 1-5 (pages 50-55).

8.7 In the *National Migration* and *Regional Migration* reports, 13 additional areas, termed *other main urban centres*, are identified as areas of residence at Census and of origin, in tables at the regional level of output. These areas include:

North region	Cleveland county
Yorkshire and Humberside region	Kingston upon Hull
East Midlands region	Leicester Nottingham
East Anglia region	Norwich
South East region	Portsmouth-Southampton corridor, comprising: Eastleigh Fareham Gosport Havant Portsmouth Southampton
South West region	Bristol Plymouth
Wales	Cardiff
Scotland	City of Aberdeen City of Dundee City of Edinburgh City of Glasgow

8.8 In *Workplace and Transport to Work* tables several areas of special interest for the analysis of travel to work are identified. These are:

City centres of - London (City and West End)
Birmingham
Edinburgh
Glasgow
Leeds
Liverpool
Manchester/Salford
Newcastle-upon-Tyne
Sheffield

plus Heathrow and Gatwick Airports and London Docklands

Local and Small Area Statistics

County/Region Reports

8.9 The Local Base Statistics tables in both the 100 per cent and 10 per cent volumes of the *County/Region Reports* are presented for each county and district in England and Wales, and for each Region, Islands Area and district in Scotland. Maps showing the constituent areas of each county and Scottish Region are included in the respective reports.

8.10 The *Health Regions Summary Report* will present the Local Base Statistics tables at the Regional Health Authority area level.

Abstracts of LBS and SAS

8.11 Machine-readable versions of the Local Base Statistics (LBS) and Small Area Statistics (SAS) are made available to customers, on request, for the following standard areas:

Area	SAS	LBS
Great Britain and national levels	✓	✓
Standard Regions of England	✓	✓
Counties and Scottish Regions	✓	✓
Local authority districts	✓	✓
Regional and District Health Authorities in England and Wales	✓	✓
Health Boards in Scotland	✓	✓
Wards and Civil Parishes in England/Communities in Wales	✓	✓
Postcode sectors: (a) England and Wales	✓	
(b) Scotland	✓	✓
Parliamentary and European constituencies	✓	✓
Scottish regional electoral divisions and wards	✓	
Scottish New Towns, localities, inhabited islands and Civil Parishes	✓	
Enumeration Districts in England and Wales	✓	
Output Areas in Scotland	✓	

8.12 Abstracts of LBS and SAS may only be released for an area if it exceeds certain population thresholds, in order to preserve confidentiality. These thresholds are:

for LBS - 1,000 residents *and* 320 resident households;
for SAS - 50 residents *and* 16 resident households.
(see also paragraphs 1.33 and 1.38.)

8.13 The LBS/SAS will not be released for any area falling below these thresholds. The statistics for such suppressed areas are merged with those of a contiguous area (at the same level), provided that the resulting *amalgamated* total numbers of residents and households both exceed the corresponding threshold. In England and Wales, separate LBS or SAS will not be released for an area that has 'imported' statistics from a suppressed area in this way, but in the output an area that contains imported statistics is identified as such. In Scotland, in the final stages of creating Output Areas, provisional areas which do not pass the thresholds are amalgamated with a *predetermined* contiguous area. This neighbouring area is chosen, wherever possible, to be within the area of the same 1981 ED and within the same statutory boundary.

8.14 The contiguous area to be amalgamated with a suppressed area is generally that with the *fewest* number of people, including an area which itself may fall below the threshold. But other relevant local circumstances are taken into consideration; for example, amalgamations are constrained to areas within the same statutory boundaries wherever possible.

8.15 For any area suppressed at the LBS level, SAS may still be released if the minimum thresholds are exceeded.

Urban and rural areas

8.16 As in the 1981 Census, a selection of key Census statistics and derived variables will be published for specially defined *urban areas*, and for the rural remainders. An OPCS/GRO(S) *User Guide,* describing these areas, will be available in 1992.

Contiguous areas

8.17 Data are presented in some migration tables for aggregates of moves to (or from) an area from (or to) areas surrounding it, referred to as neighbouring areas or *contiguous areas.*

8.18 When data are given for a county or Scottish Region, the *contiguous counties/Regions* are those with a shared boundary with that *county* (or *Scottish Region*). When data are given for a district, then:

(a) *contiguous districts* are those districts sharing a boundary with the relevant *district;* whereas

(b) *contiguous counties (or Scottish Regions)* are those counties (or *Scottish Regions)* sharing any boundary with the *county* (or *Scottish Region)* in which the district is located.

See, for example Table 4 in the *Regional Migration (part 1)* volumes.

8.19 *Contiguous areas* are defined as all areas which share a section of land boundary, including those which touch at a point. Areas which are separated by water are included if there is a transport link (such as a bridge, tunnel or ferry) between the two areas. Areas which are separated by land belonging to a third area are not regarded as contiguous, no matter how close together the areas are.

8.20 A list of all contiguous areas for each county, Scottish Region and district, compiled in consultation with local authorities throughout Great Britain, will be published in a 1991 Census *User Guide* on geographic areas, to be issued early in 1992.

Maps

Map 1 Standard Regions and counties of England and Wales, and regions of Scotland

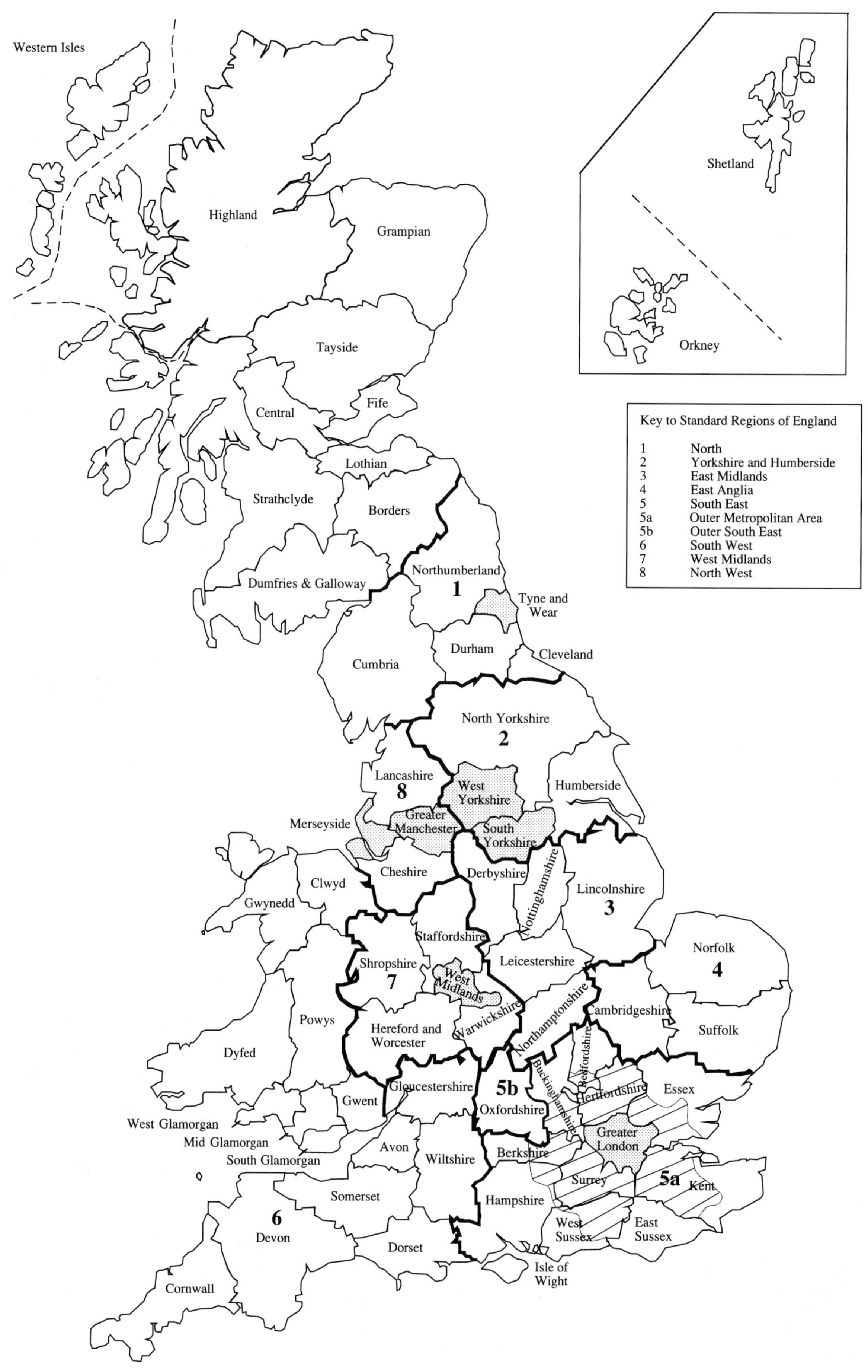

Map 2 Regions, Islands Areas and districts of Scotland

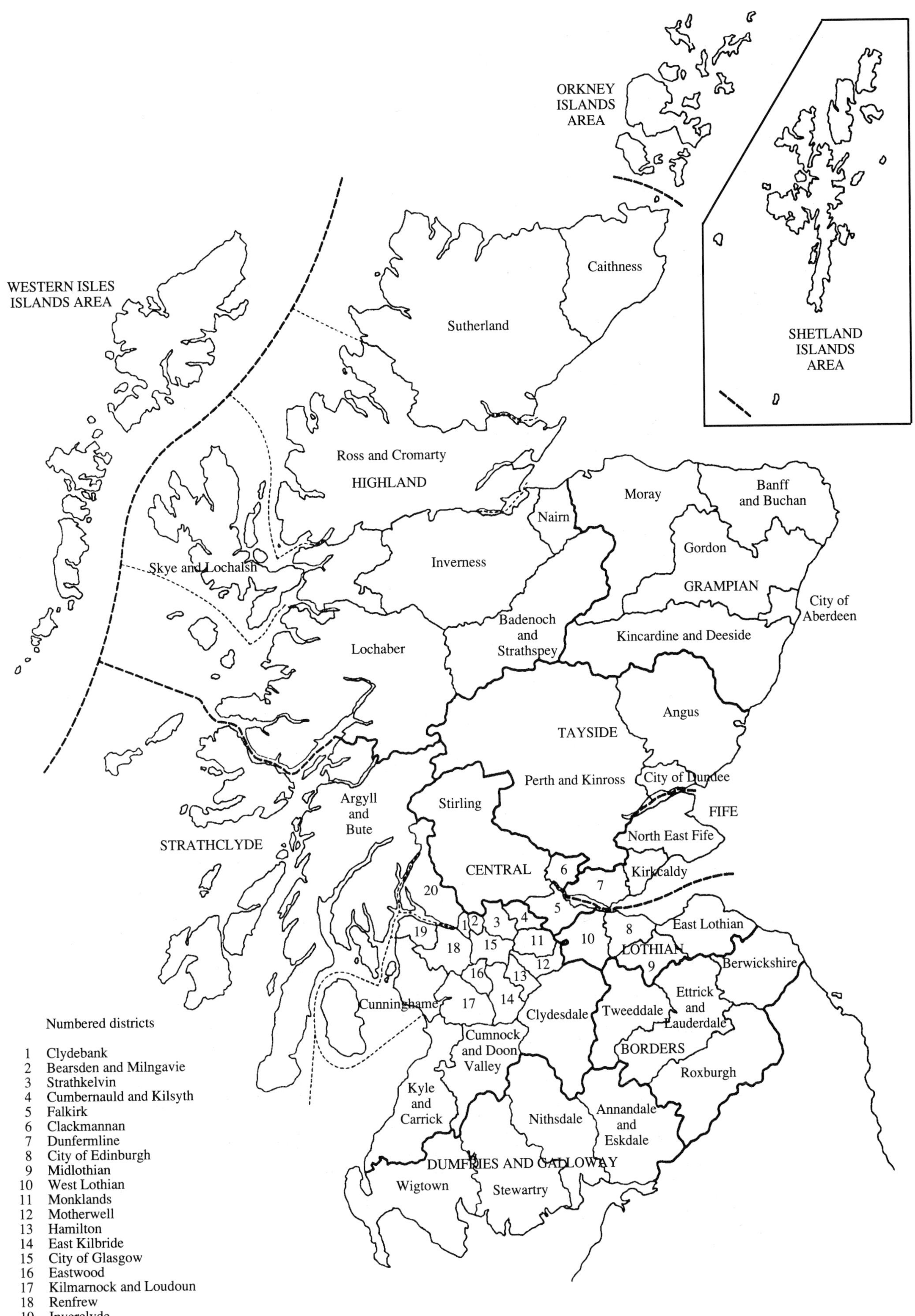

Map 3 Counties and districts of England and Wales

Great Yarmouth
Waveney
North Norfolk
NORFOLK
Broadland
Norwich
South Norfolk
Suffolk Coastal
Mid Suffolk
SUFFOLK
Ipswich
Babergh
Breckland
St Edmundsbury
Forest Heath
Kings Lynn and West Norfolk
East Cambridgeshire
Cambridge
South Cambridgeshire
Fenland
CAMBRIDGESHIRE
Huntingdonshire
Peterborough
South Holland
Boston
East Lindsey
LINCOLNSHIRE
North Kesteven
South Kesteven
Lincoln
West Lindsey
Tendring
Colchester
Maldon
Braintree
ESSEX
Chelmsford
Uttlesford
Rochford
Southend-on-Sea
Castle Point
Basildon
Brentwood
Thurrock
Harlow
Epping Forest
Broxbourne
Thanet
Dover
Canterbury
Shepway
Swale
Gillingham
Rochester upon Medway
Maidstone
KENT
Ashford
Gravesham
Tonbridge and Malling
Tunbridge Wells
Dartford
Sevenoaks
Hastings
Rother
Wealden
EAST SUSSEX
Eastbourne
Lewes
Brighton
Hove
Adur
Worthing
Arun
Chichester
WEST SUSSEX
Horsham
Mid Sussex
Crawley
Tandridge
Reigate and Banstead
Epsom and Ewell
Mole Valley
SURREY
Elmbridge
Spelthorne
Runnymede
Woking
Guildford
Waverley
Surrey Heath
Rushmoor
Hart
East Hampshire
Havant
Portsmouth
Gosport
Fareham
Winchester
HAMPSHIRE
Eastleigh
Southampton
Test Valley
Basingstoke and Deane
New Forest
Medina
South Wight
ISLE OF WIGHT
Christchurch
Bournemouth
Poole
Purbeck
East Dorset
North Dorset
DORSET
Weymouth & Portland
West Dorset
GREATER LONDON
Hertsmere
Watford
Three Rivers
St Albans
Welwyn Hatfield
HERTFORDSHIRE
East Hertfordshire
Stevenage
North Hertfordshire
Dacorum
Luton
South Bedfordshire
Mid Bedfordshire
North Bedfordshire
BEDFORDSHIRE
Milton Keynes
BUCKINGHAMSHIRE
Aylesbury Vale
Wycombe
Chiltern
South Bucks
Slough
Windsor and Maidenhead
Bracknell Forest
Wokingham
Reading
BERKSHIRE
Newbury
East Northamptonshire
Corby
Kettering
Wellingborough
Northampton
NORTHAMPTONSHIRE
Daventry
South Northamptonshire
Cherwell
Oxford
OXFORDSHIRE
South Oxfordshire
Vale of White Horse
West Oxfordshire
Rutland
Melton
Harborough
Oadby and Wigston
Leicester
LEICESTERSHIRE
Charnwood
Blaby
Hinckley and Bosworth
North West Leicestershire
Rugby
Nuneaton & Bedworth
North Warwickshire
Coventry
Warwick
WARWICKSHIRE
Stratford-on-Avon
Solihull
WEST MIDLANDS
Birmingham
Bassetlaw
NOTTINGHAMSHIRE
Newark and Sherwood
Rushcliffe
Gedling
Nottingham
Broxtowe
Mansfield
Ashfield
Bolsover
Rotherham
Sheffield
Chesterfield
North East Derbyshire
Amber Valley
Erewash
Derby
South Derbyshire
DERBYSHIRE
Derbyshire Dales
High Peak
Stockport
Macclesfield
Congleton
Staffordshire Moorlands
Stoke-on-Trent
Newcastle-under-Lyme
Stafford
STAFFORDSHIRE
East Staffordshire
Lichfield
Tamworth
Cannock Chase
South Staffordshire
Walsall
Sandwell
Dudley
Wolverhampton
Bromsgrove
Redditch
Wyre Forest
Worcester
Wychavon
Malvern Hills
HEREFORD AND WORCESTER
Leominster
Hereford
South Herefordshire
Tewkesbury
Cheltenham
Gloucester
Cotswold
GLOUCESTERSHIRE
Stroud
Forest of Dean
Thamesdown
North Wiltshire
Kennet
WILTSHIRE
West Wiltshire
Salisbury
Northavon
Kingswood
Bath
Bristol
AVON
Wansdyke
Woodspring
Mendip
SOMERSET
Sedgemoor
South Somerset
Taunton Deane
West Somerset
East Devon
Exeter
Mid Devon
Teignbridge
Torbay
North Devon
DEVON
West Devon
South Hams
Plymouth
Torridge
North Cornwall
CORNWALL
Caradon
Restormel
Carrick
Kerrier
Penwith
ISLES OF SCILLY
Warrington
Halton
Vale Royal
CHESHIRE
Crewe and Nantwich
Chester
Ellesmere Port & Neston
Wirral
The Wrekin
Bridgnorth
SHROPSHIRE
Shrewsbury and Atcham
North Shropshire
South Shropshire
Oswestry
Wrexham Maelor
Alyn & Deeside
Delyn
CLWYD
Glyndwr
Rhuddlan
Colwyn
Aberconwy
GWYNEDD
Meirionnydd
Arfon
Dwyfor
Ynys Môn Isle of Anglesey
Montgomeryshire
Radnorshire
POWYS
Brecknock
Monmouth
GWENT
Torfaen
Newport
Blaenau Gwent
Islwyn
Rhymney Valley
Cardiff
Merthyr Tydfil
Cynon Valley
Rhondda
Taff-Ely
Vale of Glamorgan
SOUTH GLAMORGAN
Ogwr
MID GLAMORGAN
Neath
Port Talbot
WEST GLAMORGAN
Lliw Valley
Swansea
Llanelli
Ceredigion
Dinefwr
DYFED
Carmarthen
South Pembrokeshire
Preseli Pembrokeshire
Havering
Barking & Dagenham
Redbridge
Waltham Forest
Newham
Greenwich
Bexley
Bromley
Lewisham
Tower Hamlets
Hackney
Islington
Haringey
Enfield
Camden
City of Westminster
City
Southwark
Lambeth
Croydon
Wandsworth
Merton
Sutton
Barnet
Brent
Harrow
Ealing
Hounslow
Richmond upon Thames
Kingston upon Thames
Hillingdon
a Kensington & Chelsea
b Hammersmith & Fulham

Map 4 Regional Health Authority areas of England

Map 5 Scottish Health Board areas

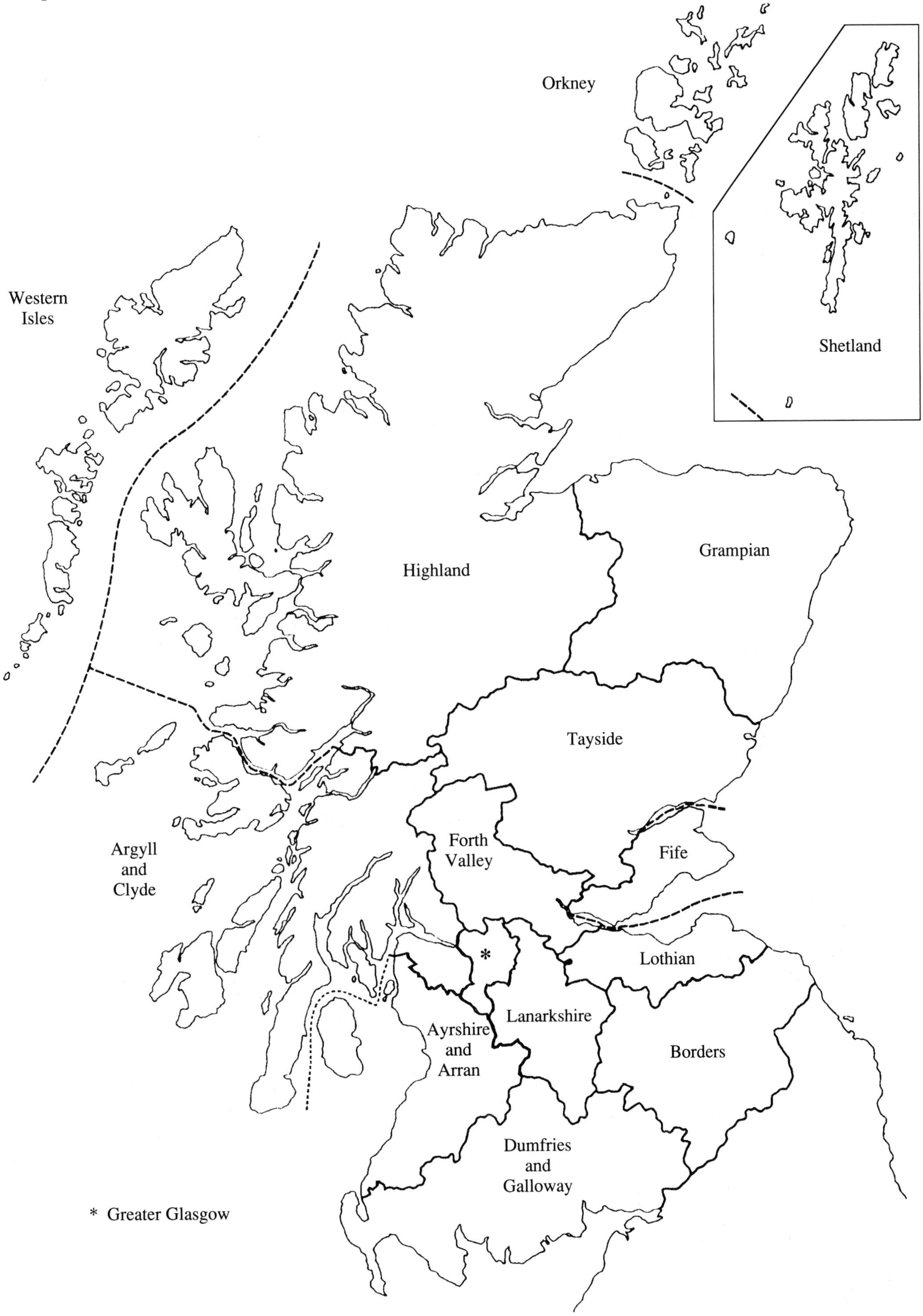

Orkney

Shetland

Western Isles

Highland

Grampian

Tayside

Argyll and Clyde

Forth Valley

Fife

Lothian

*

Lanarkshire

Ayrshire and Arran

Borders

Dumfries and Galloway

* Greater Glasgow

References

1 *The Census Order 1990 (*Statutory Instrument 1990 No. 243). HMSO, 1990. ISBN 0 11 003243 8.

2 *The Census Regulations 1990* (Statutory Instrument 1990 No. 307). HMSO, 1990. ISBN 0 11 003307 8.

3 *The Census (Scotland) Regulations 1990* (Statutory Instrument 1990 No. 326 (S.32)). HMSO, 1990. ISBN 0 11 003326 4.

4 OPCS. *1991 Census Preliminary Report for England and Wales.* HMSO, 1991. ISBN 0 11 691347 9.

5 GRO(S). *1991 Census Preliminary Report for Scotland.* HMSO, 1991. ISBN 0 11 494180 7.

6 *1991 Census of Population* (Cm 430). HMSO, 1988. ISBN 0 10 104302 3.

7 *1991 Census of Population: Confidentiality and Computing* (Cm 1447). HMSO, 1991. ISBN 0 10 114472 5.

7a The British Computer Society. *Review of Confidentiality Arrangements for the Processing of 1991 Census data: Report of the Supplementary Review.* OPCS, 1991.

8 OPCS. *1981 Census Definitions, Great Britain.* HMSO, 1981. ISBN 0 11 690788 6.

9 Robert, DHL. Dwelling stock estimates from the 1981 Census of Population. *Statistical News no. 49.* HMSO, 1980. ISBN 0 11 726059 2.

10 OPCS and Employment Department Group. *Standard Occupational Classification.*
Volume 1: *Structure and Definition of Major, Minor and Unit Groups.* HMSO, 1990. ISBN 0 11 691284 7.
Volume 2: *Coding Index.* HMSO, 1990. ISBN 0 11 691285 5.
Volume 3: *Social Classification and Coding Methodology.* HMSO, 1991. ISBN 0 11 691338 X.

11 OPCS. *Classification of Occupations 1980.* HMSO, 1980. ISBN 0 11 690728 2.

12 Department of Employment. *Classification of Occupations and Directory of Occupational Titles.* HMSO, 1972. SBN 11 390092.

13 Central Statistical Office. *Standard Industrial Classification, Revised 1980.* HMSO, 1979. ISBN 0 11 630764 1.

14 OPCS. *Evalution of the 1981 Census: the 10 per cent sample.* OPCS Monitor CEN 83/6. OPCS, 1983.

Annex A COUNTRY OF BIRTH CLASSIFICATION

Coded country of birth	Also including the following other countries, states, territories and dependencies
United Kingdom	
England	
Scotland	
Wales	
Northern Ireland	
United Kingdom (part not stated)	
Outside United Kingdom	
Irish Republic	
Channel Islands	
Isle of Man	
Ireland (part not stated)	
Old Commonwealth	
Australia	
Canada	
New Zealand	
New Commonwealth	
Africa	
Eastern Africa	
Kenya	
Malawi	
Tanzania	
Uganda	
Zambia	
Southern Africa	
Zimbabwe	
Botswana	*Lesotho, Swaziland*
Western Africa	
Gambia	
Ghana	
Nigeria	
Sierra Leone	

Coded country of birth	Also including the following other countries, states, territories and dependencies
New Commonwealth - continued	
Caribbean	
Barbados	
Jamaica	
Trinidad and Tobago	
Other independent states	*Antigua and Barbuda, Bahamas, Dominica, Grenada, Grenadines, St Kitts-Nevis, St Lucia, St Vincent*
Caribbean Dependent Territories	*Anguilla, Bermuda, Cayman Islands, Montserrat, Turks and Caicos Islands, Virgin Islands (British)*
West Indies	*Commonwealth West Indies - dependence/independence not stated (e.g. "West Indies", "Leeward Islands (British)", "Leeward Islands", "Windward Islands (British)", "Windward Islands")*
Belize	
Guyana	
Asia	
South Asia	
Bangladesh	
India	
Pakistan	
Sri Lanka	
South East Asia	
Hong Kong	
Malaysia	
Singapore	
Remainder of the New Commonwealth	
Cyprus	
Gibraltar	
Malta	*Gozo*
Mauritius	
Seychelles	
Other New Commonwealth	*Ascension Island, British Antarctic Territory, British Indian Ocean Territory, Brunei, Christmas Island, Cocos (Keeling) Islands, Cook Islands, Diego Garcia Islands, Falkland Islands, Gough Island, Heard Island, Kiribati, MacDonald Islands, Namibia, Nauru, Niue Island, Norfolk Island, Papua New Guinea, Pitcairn Island, Raratonga, Solomon Islands (British), South Georgia, South Sandwich Islands, St Helena, Tokelau Islands, Tonga, Tristan Da Cunha, Tuvalu, Vanuatu, Western Somoa*

Coded country of birth	Also including the following other countries, states, territories and dependencies
European Community	*Excluding United Kingdom and Ireland*
Belgium	
Denmark	*Greenland*
France	*Monaco*
Italy	*San Marino, Vatican City*
Luxembourg	
Netherlands	
Germany	
Greece	
Portugal	*Azores, Madeira*
Spain	*Canary Islands, Ceuta, Melilla*
Remainder of Europe	
Albania	
Austria	
Bulgaria	
Czechoslovakia	
Finland	
Hungary	
Norway	
Poland	
Romania	
Sweden	
Switzerland	*Liechtenstein*
Yugoslavia	
Other Europe	*Andorra, Faeroe Islands, Iceland*
Turkey	
USSR	
Africa	
Algeria	
Egypt	
Libya	
Morocco	
Tunisia	
South Africa, Republic of	
Other Africa	*Angola, Benin, Bioko, Burkina (Faso), Burundi, Cabinda, Cameroon, Cape Verde Islands, Central African Republic, Chad, Chafarinas, Comoros, Congo, Djibouti, Equatorial Guinea, Ethiopia, Gabon, Guinea, Guinea-Bissau, Ivory Coast, Liberia, Madagascar, Mali, Mauritania, Mayotte (Grande Terre and Pamanzi), Mozambique, Niger, Pagalu, Reunion, Rwanda, Sao Tome and Principe, Senegal, Somalia, Sudan, Togo, Walvis Bay, Zaire*

Coded country of birth	Also including the following other countries, states, territories and dependencies
America	
United States of America	
Caribbean	*Cuba, Dominican Republic, Guadeloupe, Haiti, Marie Galante Island, Martinique, Netherlands Antilles, Puerto Rico, St Barthelemy Island, St Croix Island, St Eustatius Island, St Martin Island, Virgin Islands (US), Windward Islands (Dutch), Windward Islands (French), Windward Islands (Portuguese)*
Central America	*Costa Rica, El Salvador, Guatemala, Honduras, Islas Revillagigedo, Mexico, Nicaragua, Panama*
Brazil	
Colombia	
Other South America	*Argentina, Bolivia, Chile, Easter Island, Ecuador, French Guiana, Galapagos Islands, Juan Fernandez Islands, Paraguay, Peru, Suriname, Uruguay, Venezuela*
Asia	
Middle East	
Iran	
Iraq	
Israel	
Jordan	
Lebanon	
Saudi Arabia	
Syria	
Other Middle East	*Bahrain, Kuwait, Oman, Qatar, South Yemen, United Arab Emirates, Yemen*
Rest of Asia	
China, Peoples Republic of	
Japan	
Burma (Myanmar, Union of)	
Philippines	
Taiwan	
Thailand	
Vietnam	
Other Asia	*Afghanistan, Bhutan, Cambodia, Indonesia, Kerguelen, Laos, Macao (Macau), Maldives, Mongolia, Nepal, North Korea, South Korea*
Rest of the World	*American Samoa, Federated States of Micronesia, Fiji, French Polynesia, French Southern and Antarctic Territories, Guam, Mariana Island (Northern), Marshall Islands, New Caledonia and Dependencies, Pacific Islands (French), Pacific Islands (USA), Palau, St Pierre and Miquelon, Tubai Islands, Wallis and Futuna Islands, At Sea, In the Air*
Elsewhere - no further details	*Africa (part not stated), East Africa (part not stated)*

Annex B FULL ETHNIC GROUP CLASSIFICATION

Code	Category
0	White
1	Black-Caribbean
2	Black-African
3	Indian
4	Pakistani
5	Bangladeshi
6	Chinese
	Black-Other: non-mixed origin
7	British
8	Caribbean Island, West Indies or Guyana
9	North African, Arab or Iranian
10	Other African countries
11	East African, Asian or Indo-Caribbean
12	Indian sub-continent
13	Other Asian
14	Other answers
	Black-Other: mixed origin
15	Black/White
16	Asian/White
17	Other mixed
	Other ethnic group: non-mixed origin
18	British - ethnic minority indicated
19	British - no ethnic minority indicated
20	Caribbean Island, West Indies or Guyana
21	North African, Arab or Iranian
22	Other African countries
23	East African, Asian or Indo-Caribbean
24	Indian sub-continent
25	Other Asian
26	Irish
27	Greek (including Greek Cypriot)
28	Turkish (including Turkish Cypriot)
29	Other European
30	Other answers
	Other ethnic group: mixed origin
31	Black/White
32	Asian/White
33	Mixed White
34	Other mixed

Annex C FAMILY UNIT CLASSIFICATION

Code	Family unit description	No. of persons in family	No. of generations in family	Type of family*
1	**Head of household only**	1	-	N
	All families which include the head of household as a parent or a member of a couple			
2	Head of household and son(s)/daughter(s)	2+	2	L
3	Head of household and grandchild(ren)	2+	2	L
4	Head of household and spouse	2	1	M
5	Head of household, spouse and son(s)/daughter(s)	3+	2	M
6	Head of household, spouse and grandchild(ren)	3+	2	M
7	Head of household and cohabitant	2	1	C
8	Head of household, cohabitant and son(s)/daughter(s) of head only	3+	2	C
9	Head of household, cohabitant and son(s)/daughter(s) of cohabitant only	3+	2	C
10	Head of household, cohabitant, child(ren) of head and child(ren) of cohabitant	4+	2	C
11	Head of household, cohabitant and grandchild(ren) of head	3+	2	C
57	Head of household, cohabitant, child(ren) of cohabitant and grand-child(ren) of head	4+	2	C
	Other families containing the head of household			
22	Head of household and one parent of head	2	2	L
23	Head of household, one parent of head and sibling(s) of head	3+	2	L
26	Head of household and both parents of head	3	2	M/C
27	Head of household, both parents of head and sibling(s) of head	4+	2	M/C
	Families containing persons related to the head of household			
12	Son or daughter	1	-	N
13	Son or daughter and grandchild(ren)	2+	2	L
14	Son or daughter and son- or daughter-in-law	2	1	M
15	Son or daughter, son- or daughter-in-law and grandchild(ren)	3+	2	M
16	Son or daughter and cohabitant of son or daughter	2	1	C
17	Son or daughter, cohabitant of son or daughter and grandchild(ren)	3+	2	C
18	Non-single son or daughter of cohabitant	1	-	N
19	Son- or daughter-in-law	1	-	N
20	Son- or daughter-in-law and grandchild(ren)	2+	2	L
21	Parent of head	1	-	N
24	One parent of head and sibling(s)	2+	2	L
25	Both parents of head	2	1	M/C
28	Both parents of head and sibling(s)	3	2	M/C
29	Parent-in-law	1	-	N
30	Parent-in-law and brother(s)/sister(s)-in-law	2+	2	L
31	Both parents-in-law	2	1	M/C
32	Both parents-in-law and brother(s)/sister(s)-in-law	3+	2	M/C
33	Brother or sister	1	-	N
34	Brother or sister and nephew(s)/niece(s)	2+	2	L
35	Brother or sister and brother/sister-in-law	2	1	M
36	Brother or sister, brother/sister-in-law and nephew(s)/niece(s)	3+	2	M
37	Brother- or sister-in-law	1	-	N
38	Brother- or sister-in-law and nephew(s)/niece(s)	2+	2	L
39	Grandchild	1	-	N

Code	Family unit description	No. of persons in family	No. of generations in family	Type of family*
40	Nephew or niece	1	-	N
41	Other relative	1	-	N
45	Other married couple related to head	2	1	M
46	Other cohabiting couple related to head	2	1	C
47	Other married couple (related to head) with child(ren)	3+	2	M
48	Other cohabiting couple (related to head) with child(ren)	3+	2	C
49	Other lone parent (related to head) with child(ren)	2+	2	L
	Families *not* related to head of household			
50	Married couple	2	1	M
51	Cohabiting couple	2	1	C
52	Married couple with child(ren)	3+	2	M
53	Cohabiting couple with child(ren)	3+	2	C
54	Lone parent with child(ren)	2+	2	L
42	Boarder/lodger	1	-	N
43	Joint head of household	1	-	N
44	Other unrelated person	1	-	N
	No family-households containing no persons aged 16 or over			
55	Households containing only one person aged under 16	1	-	N
56	Households containing more than one person aged under 16 years	2+	-	N
	Visitors			
58	All-visitor households (no residents)	1+	-	N
59	Visitors in a household with residents	1+	-	N
60	Visitor only (one person in a household with no other residents)	1	-	N

* L = Lone parent family; M = Married couple family; C = Cohabiting couple family; N = No-family person

Annex D STANDARD OCCUPATIONAL CLASSIFICATION MAJOR, SUB-MAJOR AND MINOR GROUPS (and number of unit codes)

1 Managers and administrators

1a Corporate managers and administrators

10 General managers and administrators in national and local government, large companies and organisations (4)
11 Production managers in manufacturing, construction, mining and energy industries (4)
12 Specialist managers (8)
13 Financial institution and office managers, civil service executive officers (4)
14 Managers in transport and storing (3)
15 Protective service officers (6)
19 Managers and administrators, not elsewhere classified (nec) (3)

1b Managers/proprietors in agriculture and services

16 Managers in farming, horticulture, forestry and fishing (2)
17 Managers and proprietors in service industries (10)

2 Professional occupations

2a Science and engineering professions

20 Natural scientists (4)
21 Engineers and technologists (10)

2b Health professions

22 Health professionals (5)

2c Education professions

23 Teaching professionals (7)

2d Other professions

24 Legal professionals (3)
25 Business and financial professionals (4)
26 Architects, town planners and surveyors (3)
27 Librarians and related professionals (2)
29 Professional occupations nec (4)

3 Associate professional and technical occupations

3a Science and engineering associate professions

30 Scientific technicians (6)
31 Draughtspersons, quantity and other surveyors (4)
32 Computer analysts, programmers (1)

3b Health associate professions

34 Health associate professionals (10)

3c Other associate professions

33 Ship and aircraft officers, air traffic planners and controllers (3)
35 Legal associate professionals (1)

3c Other associate professions - *continued*

36 Business and financial associate professionals (5)
37 Social welfare associate professionals (2)
38 Literary, artistic and sports professionals (8)
39 Associate professional and technical occupations nec (8)

4 Clerical and secretarial occupations

4a Clerical occupations

40 Administrative/clerical officers and assistants in civil service and local government (2)
41 Numerical clerks and cashiers (3)
42 Filing and records clerks (2)
43 Clerks, not otherwise specified (1)
44 Stores and dispatch clerks, storekeepers (2)
49 Clerical and secretarial occupations nec (2)

4b Secretarial occupations

45 Secretaries, personal assistants, typists and word processor operators (4)
46 Receptionists, telephonists and related occupations (4)

5 Craft and related occupations

5a Skilled construction trades

50 Construction trades (9)

5b Skilled engineering trades

51 Metal machining, fitting and instrument making trades (10)
52 Electrical/electronic trades (8)

5c Other skilled trades

53 Metal forming, welding and related trades (8)
54 Vehicle trades (5)
55 Textiles, garments and related trades (9)
56 Printing and related trades (5)
57 Woodworking trades (5)
58 Food preparation trades (3)
59 Other craft and related occupations nec (10)

6 Personal and protective service occupations

6a Protective service occupations

60 NCOs and other ranks, armed forces (2)
61 Security and protective service occupations (7)

6b Personal service occupations

62 Catering occupations (3)
63 Travel attendants and related occupations (2)
64 Health and related occupations (5)
65 Childcare and related occupations (4)
66 Hairdressers, beauticians and related occupations (2)
67 Domestic staff and related occupations (4)
69 Personal and protective service occupations nec (3)

STANDARD OCCUPATIONAL CLASSIFICATION MAJOR, SUB-MAJOR AND MINOR GROUPS (and number of unit codes) - *continued*

7 Sales occupations

7a Buyers, brokers and sales representatives

70 Buyers, brokers and related agents (4)
71 Sales representatives (2)

7b Other sales occupations

72 Sales assistants and check-out operators (3)
73 Mobile, market and door-to-door salespersons and agents (4)
79 Sales occupations nec (3)

8 Plant and machine operatives

8a Industrial plant stationary machine operators and assemblers

80 Food, drink and tobacco process operatives (4)
81 Textiles and tannery process operatives (5)
82 Chemicals, paper, plastics and related process operatives (8)
83 Metal making and treating process operatives (6)
84 Metal working process operatives (5)
85 Assemblers/lineworkers (3)
86 Other routine process operatives (6)
89 Machinery and plant operatives nec (10)

8b Drivers and mobile machinery operators

87 Road transport operatives (6)
88 Other transport and machinery operatives (9)

9 Other occupations

9a Other occupations in agriculture, forestry and fishing

90 Other occupations in agriculture, forestry and fishing (5)

9b Other elementary occupations

91 Other occupations in mining and manufacturing (5)
92 Other occupations in construction (6)
93 Other occupations in transport (6)
94 Other occupations in communication (2)
95 Other occupations in sales and services (10)
99 Other occupations nec (2)

Annex E SUMMARY OF INDUSTRY DIVISIONS, CLASSES, GROUPS AND ACTIVITY HEADINGS

Class	Group	Activity	
			DIVISION 0 AGRICULTURE, FORESTRY AND FISHING
01	010	0100	AGRICULTURE AND HORTICULTURE
02	020	0200	FORESTRY
03	030	0300	FISHING
			DIVISION 1 ENERGY AND WATER SUPPLY INDUSTRIES
11	111		COAL EXTRACTION AND MANUFACTURE OF SOLID FUELS
		1113	Deep coal mines
		1114	Opencast coal working
		1115	Manufacture of solid fuels
12	120	1200	COKE OVENS
13	130	1300	EXTRACTION OF MINERAL OIL AND NATURAL GAS
14	140		MINERAL OIL PROCESSING
		1401	Mineral oil refining
		1402	Other treatment of petroleum products (excluding petrochemical manufacture)
15	152	1520	NUCLEAR FUEL PRODUCTION
16			PRODUCTION AND DISTRIBUTION OF ELECTRICITY, GAS AND OTHER FORMS OF ENERGY
	161	1610	**Production and distribution of electricity**
	162	1620	**Public gas supply**
	163	1630	**Production and distribution of other forms of energy**
17	170	1700	WATER SUPPLY INDUSTRY
			DIVISION 2 EXTRACTION OF MINERALS AND ORES OTHER THAN FUELS; MANUFACTURE OF METALS, MINERAL PRODUCTS AND CHEMICALS
21	210	2100	EXTRACTION AND PREPARATION OF METALLIFEROUS ORES
22			METAL MANUFACTURING
	221	2210	**Iron and steel industry**
	222	2220	**Steel tubes**
	223		**Drawing, cold rolling and cold forming of steel**
		2234	Drawing and manufacture of steel wire and steel wire products
		2235	Other drawing, cold rolling and cold forming of steel
	224		**Non-ferrous metals industry**
		2245	Aluminium and aluminium alloys
		2246	Copper, brass and other copper alloys
		2247	Other non-ferrous metals and their alloys

SUMMARY OF INDUSTRY DIVISIONS, CLASSES, GROUPS AND ACTIVITY HEADINGS - *continued*

Class	Group	Activity	
			DIVISION 2 *(continued)*
23			EXTRACTION OF MINERALS, NOT ELSEWHERE SPECIFIED
	231	2310	**Extraction of stone, clay, sand and gravel**
	233	2330	**Salt extraction and refining**
	239	2396	**Extraction of other minerals, not elsewhere specified**
24			MANUFACTURE OF NON-METALLIC MINERAL PRODUCTS
	241	2410	**Structural clay products**
	242	2420	**Cement, lime and plaster**
	243		**Building products of concrete, cement or plaster**
		2436	Ready mixed concrete
		2437	Other building products of concrete, cement or plaster
	244	2440	**Asbestos goods**
	245	2450	**Working of stone and other non-metallic minerals, not elsewhere specified**
	246	2460	**Abrasive products**
	247		**Glass and glassware**
		2471	Flat glass
		2478	Glass containers
		2479	Other glass products
	248		**Refractory and ceramic goods**
		2481	Refractory goods
		2489	Ceramic goods
25			CHEMICAL INDUSTRY
	251		**Basic industrial chemicals**
		2511	Inorganic chemicals except industrial gases
		2512	Basic organic chemicals except specialised pharmaceutical chemicals
		2513	Fertilisers
		2514	Synthetic resins and plastics materials
		2515	Synthetic rubber
		2516	Dyestuffs and pigments
	255		**Paints, varnishes and printing ink**
		2551	Paints, varnishes and painters' fillings
		2552	Printing ink
	256		**Specialised chemical products mainly for industrial and agricultural purposes**
		2562	Formulated adhesives and sealants
		2563	Chemical treatment of oils and fats
		2564	Essential oils and flavouring materials
		2565	Explosives
		2567	Miscellaneous chemical products for industrial use
		2568	Formulated pesticides
		2569	Adhesive film, cloth and foil

Class	Group	Activity	
			DIVISION 2 *(continued)*
	257	2570	**Pharmaceutical products**
	258		**Soap and toilet preparations**
		2581	Soap and synthetic detergents
		2582	Perfumes, cosmetics and toilet preparations
	259		**Specialised chemical products mainly for household and office use**
		2591	Photographic materials and chemicals
		2599	Chemical products, not elsewhere specified
26	260	2600	PRODUCTION OF MAN-MADE FIBRES
			DIVISION 3 METAL GOODS, ENGINEERING AND VEHICLES INDUSTRIES
31			MANUFACTURE OF METAL GOODS, NOT ELSEWHERE SPECIFIED
	311		**Foundries**
		3111	Ferrous metal foundries
		3112	Non-ferrous metal foundries
	312	3120	**Forging, pressing and stamping**
	313		**Bolts, nuts, etc; springs; non precision chains; metals treatment**
		3137	Bolts, nuts, washers, rivets, springs and non-precision chains
		3138	Heat and surface treatment of metals, including sintering
	314	3142	**Metal doors, windows, etc**
	316		**Hand tools and finished metal goods**
		3161	Hand tools and implements
		3162	Cutlery, spoons, forks and similar tableware; razors
		3163	Metal storage vessels (mainly non-industrial)
		3164	Packaging products of metal
		3165	Domestic heating and cooking appliances (non-electrical)
		3166	Metal furniture and safes
		3167	Domestic and similar utensils of metal
		3169	Finished metal products, not elsewhere specified
32			MECHANICAL ENGINEERING
	320		**Industrial plant and steelwork**
		3204	Fabricated constructional steelwork
		3205	Boilers and process plant fabrications
	321		**Agricultural machinery and tractors**
		3211	Agricultural machinery
		3212	Wheeled tractors
	322		**Metal-working machine tools and engineers' tools**
		3221	Metal-working machine tools
		3222	Engineers' small tools
	323	3230	**Textile machinery**

SUMMARY OF INDUSTRY DIVISIONS, CLASSES, GROUPS AND ACTIVITY HEADINGS - *continued*

Class	Group	Activity	
			DIVISION 3 *(continued)*
	324		**Machinery for the food, chemical and related industries; process engineering contractors**
		3244	Food, drink and tobacco processing machinery; packaging and bottling machinery
		3245	Chemical industry machinery; furnaces and kilns; gas, water and waste treatment plant
		3246	Process engineering contractors
	325		**Mining machinery, construction and mechanical handling equipment**
		3251	Mining machinery
		3254	Construction and earth moving equipment
		3255	Mechanical lifting and handling equipment
	326		**Mechanical power transmission equipment**
		3261	Precision chains and other mechanical power transmission equipment
		3262	Ball, needle and roller bearings
	327		**Machinery for the printing, paper, wood, leather, rubber, glass and related industries; laundry and dry cleaning machinery**
		3275	Machinery for working wood, rubber, plastics, leather and making paper, glass, bricks and similar materials; laundry and dry cleaning machinery
		3276	Printing, bookbinding and paper goods machinery
	328		**Other machinery and mechanical equipment**
		3281	Internal combustion engines (except for road vehicles, wheeled tractors primarily for agricultural purposes and aircraft) and other prime movers
		3283	Compressors and fluid power equipment
		3284	Refrigerating machinery, space heating, ventilating and air conditioning equipment
		3285	Scales, weighing machinery and portable power tools
		3286	Other industrial and commercial machinery
		3287	Pumps
		3288	Industrial valves
		3289	Mechanical, marine and precision engineering, not elsewhere specified
	329	3290	**Ordnance, small arms and ammunition**
33	330		MANUFACTURE OF OFFICE MACHINERY AND DATA PROCESSING EQUIPMENT
		3301	Office machinery
		3302	Electronic data processing equipment
34			ELECTRICAL AND ELECTRONIC ENGINEERING
	341	3410	**Insulated wires and cables**
	342	3420	**Basic electrical equipment**
	343		**Electrical equipment for industrial use, and batteries and accumulators**
		3432	Batteries and accumulators
		3433	Alarms and signalling equipment
		3434	Electrical equipment for motor vehicles, cycles and aircraft
		3435	Electrical equipment for industrial use, not elsewhere specified

Class	Group	Activity	
			DIVISION 3 *(continued)*
	344		**Telecommunication equipment, electrical measuring equipment, electronic capital goods and passive electronic components**
		3441	Telegraph and telephone apparatus and equipment
		3442	Electrical instruments and control systems
		3443	Radio and electronic capital goods
		3444	Components other than active components, mainly for electronic equipment
	345		**Other electronic equipment**
		3452	Gramophone records and pre-recorded tapes
		3453	Active components and electronic sub-assemblies
		3454	Electronic consumer goods and other electronic equipment, not elsewhere specified
	346	3460	**Domestic-type electric appliances**
	347	3470	**Electric lamps and other electric lighting equipment**
	348	3480	**Electrical equipment installation**
35			MANUFACTURE OF MOTOR VEHICLES AND PARTS THEREOF
	351	3510	**Motor vehicles and their engines**
	352		**Motor vehicle bodies, trailers and caravans**
		3521	Motor vehicle bodies
		3522	Trailers and semi-trailers
		3523	Caravans
	353	3530	**Motor vehicle parts**
36			MANUFACTURE OF OTHER TRANSPORT EQUIPMENT
	361	3610	**Shipbuilding and repairing**
	362	3620	**Railway and tramway vehicles**
	363		**Cycles and motor cycles**
		3633	Motor cycles and parts
		3634	Pedal cycles and parts
	364	3640	**Aerospace equipment manufacturing and repairing**
	365	3650	**Other vehicles**
37			INSTRUMENT ENGINEERING
	371	3710	**Measuring, checking and precision instruments and apparatus**
	372	3720	**Medical and surgical equipment and orthopaedic appliances**
	373		**Optical precision instruments and photographic equipment**
		3731	Spectacles and unmounted lenses
		3732	Optical precision instruments
		3733	Photographic and cinematographic equipment
	374	3740	**Clocks, watches and other timing devices**

Class	Group	Activity	
			DIVISION 4 OTHER MANUFACTURING INDUSTRIES
41/42			FOOD, DRINK AND TOBACCO MANUFACTURING INDUSTRIES
	411		**Organic oils and fats (other than crude animal fats)**
		4115	Margarine and compound cooking fats
		4116	Processing organic oils and fats (other than crude animal fat production)
	412		**Slaughtering of animals and production of meat and by-products**
		4121	Slaughterhouses
		4122	Bacon curing and meat processing
		4123	Poultry slaughter and processing
		4126	Animal by-product processing
	413	4130	**Preparation of milk and milk products**
	414	4147	**Processing of fruit and vegetables**
	415	4150	**Fish processing**
	416	4160	**Grain milling**
	418	4180	**Starch**
	419		**Bread, biscuits and flour confectionery**
		4196	Bread and flour confectionery
		4197	Biscuits and crispbread
	420	4200	**Sugar and sugar by-products**
	421		**Ice cream, cocoa, chocolate and sugar confectionery**
		4213	Ice cream
		4214	Cocoa, chocolate and sugar confectionery
	422		**Animal feeding stuffs**
		4221	Compound animal feeds
		4222	Pet foods and non-compound animal feeds
	423	4239	**Miscellaneous foods**
	424	4240	**Spirit distilling and compounding**
	426	4261	**Wines, cider and perry**
	427	4270	**Brewing and malting**
	428	4283	**Soft drinks**
	429	4290	**Tobacco industry**
43			TEXTILE INDUSTRY
	431	4310	**Woollen and worsted industry**
	432		**Cotton and silk industries**
		4321	Spinning and doubling on the cotton system
		4322	Weaving of cotton, silk and man-made fibres

Class	Group	Activity	DIVISION 4 *(continued)*
	433	4336	**Throwing, texturing, etc of continuous filament yarn**
	434	4340	**Spinning and weaving of flax, hemp and ramie**
	435	4350	**Jute and polypropylene yarns and fabrics**
	436		**Hosiery and other knitted goods**
		4363	Hosiery and other weft knitted goods and fabrics
		4364	Warp knitted fabrics
	437	4370	**Textile finishing**
	438		**Carpets and other textile floor coverings**
		4384	Pile carpets, carpeting and rugs
		4385	Other carpets, carpeting, rugs and matting
	439		**Miscellaneous textiles**
		4395	Lace
		4396	Rope, twine and net
		4398	Narrow fabrics
		4399	Other miscellaneous textiles
44			MANUFACTURE OF LEATHER AND LEATHER GOODS
	441	4410	**Leather (tanning and dressing) and fellmongery**
	442	4420	**Leather goods**
45			FOOTWEAR AND CLOTHING INDUSTRIES
	451	4510	**Footwear**
	453		**Clothing, hats and gloves**
		4531	Weatherproof outerwear
		4532	Men's and boys' tailored outerwear
		4533	Women's and girls' tailored outerwear
		4534	Work clothing and men's and boys' jeans
		4535	Men's and boys' shirts, underwear and nightwear
		4536	Women's and girls' light outerwear, lingerie and infants' wear
		4537	Hats, caps and millinery
		4538	Gloves
		4539	Other dress industries
	455		**Household textiles and other made-up textiles**
		4555	Soft furnishings
		4556	Canvas goods, sacks and other made-up textiles
		4557	Household textiles
	456	4560	**Fur goods**

SUMMARY OF INDUSTRY DIVISIONS, CLASSES, GROUPS AND ACTIVITY HEADINGS - *continued*

Class	Group	Activity	
			DIVISION 4 *(continued)*
46			TIMBER AND WOODEN FURNITURE INDUSTRIES
	461	4610	**Sawmilling, planing, etc of wood**
	462	4620	**Manufacture of semi-finished wood products and further processing and treatment of wood**
	463	4630	**Builders' carpentry and joinery**
	464	4640	**Wooden containers**
	465	4650	**Other wooden articles (except furniture)**
	466		**Articles of cork and plaiting materials, brushes and brooms**
		4663	Brushes and brooms
		4664	Articles of cork and basketwear, wickerwork and other plaiting materials
	467		**Wooden and upholstered furniture and shop and office fittings**
		4671	Wooden and upholstered furniture
		4672	Shop and office fittings
47			MANUFACTURE OF PAPER AND PAPER PRODUCTS; PRINTING AND PUBLISHING
	471	4710	**Pulp, paper and board**
	472		**Conversion of paper and board**
		4721	Wall coverings
		4722	Household and personal hygiene products of paper
		4723	Stationery
		4724	Packaging products of paper and pulp
		4725	Packaging products of board
		4728	Other paper and board products
	475		**Printing and publishing**
		4751	Printing and publishing of newspapers
		4752	Printing and publishing of periodicals
		4753	Printing and publishing of books
		4754	Other printing and publishing
48			PROCESSING OF RUBBER AND PLASTICS
	481		**Rubber products**
		4811	Rubber tyres and inner tubes
		4812	Other rubber products
	482	4820	**Retreading and specialist repairing of rubber tyres**
	483		**Processing of plastics**
		4831	Plastic coated textile fabric
		4832	Plastics semi-manufactures
		4833	Plastics floorcoverings
		4834	Plastics building products
		4835	Plastics packaging products
		4836	Plastics products, not elsewhere specified

Class	Group	Activity	
			DIVISION 4 *(continued)*
49			OTHER MANUFACTURING INDUSTRIES
	491	4910	**Jewellery and coins**
	492	4920	**Musical instruments**
	493	4930	**Photographic and cinematographic processing laboratories**
	494		**Toys and sports goods**
		4941	Toys and games
		4942	Sports goods
	495		**Miscellaneous manufacturing industries**
		4954	Miscellaneous stationers' goods
		4959	Other manufacturers, not elsewhere specified
			DIVISION 5 CONSTRUCTION
50			CONSTRUCTION
			DIVISION 6 DISTRIBUTION, HOTELS AND CATERING; REPAIRS
61			WHOLESALE DISTRIBUTION (EXCEPT DEALING IN SCRAP AND WASTE MATERIALS)
	614 *(part)*	6148	**Wholesale distribution of motor vehicles and parts and accessories**
61 *(remainder)*			**Remainder of Wholesale distribution (except dealing in scrap and waste materials)**
62			DEALING IN SCRAP AND WASTE MATERIALS
63	630	6300	COMMISSION AGENTS
64/65			RETAIL DISTRIBUTION
	{ 651	6510	**Retail distribution of motor vehicles and parts**
	{ 652	6520	**Filling stations (motor fuel and lubricants)**
64/65 *(remainder)*			**Remainder of Retail distribution**

SUMMARY OF INDUSTRY DIVISIONS, CLASSES, GROUPS AND ACTIVITY HEADINGS - *continued*

Class	Group	Activity	
			DIVISION 6 *(continued)*
66			HOTELS AND CATERING
	661		**Restaurants, snack bars, cafes and other eating places**
		6611	Eating places supplying food for consumption on the premises
		6612	Take-away food shops
	662	6620	**Public houses and bars**
	663	6630	**Night clubs and licensed clubs**
	664	6640	**Canteens and messes**
	665	6650	**Hotel trade**
	667	6670	**Other tourist or short-stay accommodation**
67			REPAIR OF CONSUMER GOODS AND VEHICLES
	671	6710	**Repair and servicing of motor vehicles**
	672	6720	**Repair of footwear and leather goods**
	673	6730	**Repair of other consumer goods**
			DIVISION 7 TRANSPORT AND COMMUNICATION
71	710	7100	RAILWAYS
72			OTHER INLAND TRANSPORT
	721	7210	**Scheduled road passenger transport and urban railways**
	722	7220	**Other road passenger transport**
	723	7230	**Road haulage**
	726	7260	**Transport, not elsewhere specified**
74	740	7400	SEA TRANSPORT
75	750	7500	AIR TRANSPORT
76			SUPPORTING SERVICES TO TRANSPORT
	761	7610	**Supporting services to inland transport**
	763	7630	**Supporting services to sea transport**
	764	7640	**Supporting services to air transport**
77	770	7700	MISCELLANEOUS TRANSPORT SERVICES AND STORAGE, NOT ELSEWHERE SPECIFIED
79	790		POSTAL SERVICES AND TELECOMMUNICATIONS
		7901	Postal services
		7902	Telecommunications

Class	Group	Activity	
			DIVISION 8 BANKING, FINANCE, INSURANCE, BUSINESS SERVICES AND LEASING
81			BANKING AND FINANCE
	814	8140	**Banking and bill-discounting**
	815	8150	**Other financial institutions**
82	820	8200	INSURANCE, EXCEPT FOR COMPULSORY SOCIAL SECURITY
83			BUSINESS SERVICES
	831	8310	**Activities auxiliary to banking and finance**
	832	8320	**Activities auxiliary to insurance**
	834	8340	**House and estate agents**
	835	8350	**Legal services**
	836	8360	**Accountants, auditors, tax experts**
	837	8370	**Professional and technical services, not elsewhere specified**
	838	8380	**Advertising**
	839		**Business services**
		8394	Computer services
		8395	Business services, not elsewhere specified
		8396	Central offices, not allocable elsewhere
84			RENTING OF MOVABLES
	841	8410	**Hiring out agricultural and horticultural equipment**
	842	8420	**Hiring out construction machinery and equipment**
	843	8430	**Hiring out office machinery and furniture**
	846	8460	**Hiring out consumer goods**
	848	8480	**Hiring out transport equipment**
	849	8490	**Hiring out other movables**
85	850	8500	OWNING AND DEALING IN REAL ESTATE

SUMMARY OF INDUSTRY DIVISIONS, CLASSES, GROUPS AND ACTIVITY HEADINGS - *continued*

Class	Group	Activity	
			DIVISION 9 OTHER SERVICES
91			PUBLIC ADMINISTRATION, NATIONAL DEFENCE AND COMPULSORY SOCIAL SECURITY
	911		**National and local government services, not elsewhere specified**
		9111	National government service, not elsewhere specified
		9112	Local government service, not elsewhere specified
	912	9120	**Justice**
	913	9130	**Police**
	914	9140	**Fire services**
	915	9150	**National defence**
	919	9190	**Social security**
92			SANITARY SERVICES
	921		**Refuse disposal, sanitation and similar services**
		9211	Refuse disposal, street cleaning, fumigation, etc
		9212	Sewerage disposal
	923	9230	**Cleaning services**
93			EDUCATION
	931	9310 *(part)*	**Higher education - Universities**
		9310 *(part)*	**Higher education - Polytechnics**
		9310 *(remainder)*	**Higher education - remainder**
	932	9320 *(part)*	**School education - Maintained (nursery and primary and middle deemed primary)**
	932	9320 *(part)*	**School education - Non-maintained (nursery and primary and middle deemed primary)**
	932	9320 *(part)*	**School education - Maintained (secondary and middle deemed secondary)**
	932	9320 *(part)*	**School education - Non-maintained (secondary and middle deemed secondary)**
	932	9320 *(part)*	**School education - Maintained (special)**
	932	9320 *(remainder)*	**School education - Non-maintained (special)**
	933	9330	**Education, not elsewhere specified, and vocational training**
	936	9360	**Driving and flying schools**
94	940	9400	RESEARCH AND DEVELOPMENT
95			MEDICAL AND OTHER HEALTH SERVICES: VETERINARY SERVICES
	951	9510	**Hospitals, nursing homes, etc**
	952	9520	**Other medical care institutions**
	953	9530	**Medical practices**
	954	9540	**Dental practices**
	955	9550	**Agency and private midwives, nurses, etc**
	956	9560	**Veterinary practices and animal hospitals**

Class	Group	Activity	
			DIVISION 9 *(continued)*
96			OTHER SERVICES PROVIDED TO THE GENERAL PUBLIC
	961	9611	**Social welfare, charitable and community services**
	963	9631	**Trade unions, business and professional associations**
	966	9660	**Religious organisations and similar associations**
	969	9690	**Tourist offices and other community services**
97			RECREATIONAL SERVICES AND OTHER CULTURAL SERVICES
	971	9711	**Film production, distribution and exhibition**
	974	9741	**Radio and television services, theatres, etc**
	976	9760	**Authors, music composers and other own account artists, not elsewhere specified**
	977	9770	**Libraries, museums, art galleries, etc**
	979	9791	**Sport and other recreational services**
98			PERSONAL SERVICES
	981		**Laundries, dyers and dry cleaners**
		9811	Laundries
		9812	Dry cleaning and allied services
	982	9820	**Hair dressing and beauty parlours**
	989	9890	**Personal services, not elsewhere specified**
99	990	9900	DOMESTIC SERVICES
00	000	0000	DIPLOMATIC REPRESENTATION, INTERNATIONAL ORGANISATIONS, ALLIED ARMED FORCES

Annex F SOCIO-ECONOMIC GROUPS

1 Employers and managers in central and local government, industry, commerce, etc - large establishments

1.1 Employers in industry, commerce, etc.
Persons who employ others in non-agricultural enterprises employing 25 or more persons.

1.2 Managers in central and local government, industry, commerce, etc.
Persons who generally plan and supervise in non-agricultural enterprises employing 25 or more persons.

2 Employers and managers in industry, commerce, etc - small establishments

2.1 Employers in industry, commerce, etc - small establishments.
As in 1.1 but in establishments employing fewer than 25 persons.

2.2 Managers in industry, commerce, etc - small establishments.
As in 1.2 but in establishments employing fewer than 25 persons.

3 Professional workers - self-employed

Self-employed persons engaged in work normally requiring qualifications of university degree standard.

4 Professional workers - employees

Employees engaged in work normally requiring qualifications of university degree standard.

5 Intermediate non-manual workers

5.1 Ancillary workers and artists.
Employees engaged in non-manual occupations ancillary to the professions, not normally requiring qualifications of university degree standard; persons engaged in artistic work and not employing others therein. Self-employed nurses, medical auxiliaries, teachers, work study engineers and technicians are included.

5.2 Foremen and supervisors non-manual.
Employees (other than managers) engaged in occupations included in Group 6, who formally and immediately supervise others engaged in such occupations.

6 Junior non-manual workers

Employees, not exercising general planning or supervisory powers, engaged in clerical, sales and non-manual communications occupations, excluding those who have additional and formal supervisory functions (these are included in Group 5.2).

7 Personal service workers

Employees engaged in service occupations caring for food, drink, clothing and other personal needs.

8 Foremen and supervisors - manual

Employees (other than managers) who formally and immediately supervise others engaged in manual occupations, whether or not themselves engaged in such occupations.

9 Skilled manual workers

Employees engaged in manual occupations which require considerable and specific skills.

10 Semi-skilled manual workers

Employees engaged in manual occupations which require slight but specific skills.

11 Unskilled manual workers

Other employees engaged in manual occupations.

12 Own account workers (other than professional)

Self-employed persons engaged in any trade, personal service or manual occupation not normally requiring training of university degree standard and having no employees other than family workers.

13 Farmers - employers and managers

Persons who own, rent or manage farms, market gardens or forests, employing people other than family workers in the work of the enterprise.

14 Farmers - own account

Persons who own or rent farms, market gardens or forests and having no employees other than family workers.

15 Agricultural workers

Persons engaged in tending crops, animals, game or forests, or operating agricultural or forestry machinery.

16 Members of armed forces

17 Inadequately described and not stated occupations

Annex G CLASSIFICATION OF SUBJECT GROUPS

Code		Description
1		**Education**
1.1		Education, not elsewhere specified (nes)
1.2.1		Education with teacher training and other subjects
1.2.2		Education without teacher training but including other subjects
2		**Health, Medicine and Dentistry**
2.3.1		Pre-clinical studies
2.3.2		Clinical medicine
2.4.1		Pre-clinical dentistry
2.4.2		Dentistry nes
2.5		Pharmacy
2.6		Pharmacology
2.7.1		Nursing
2.7.2		Ophthalmic optics
2.7.3		Other studies allied to medicine and health
2.7.4		Combinations of health with Subject Groups 3-10
3		**Technology and Engineering**
3.8		Aeronautical engineering
3.9.1		Chemical engineering nes
3.9.2		Chemical technology
3.9.3		Fuel technology
3.10.1		Civil engineering nes
3.10.2		Building
3.11(a)	*	Electrical engineering
3.11(b)	*	Electronics and electronic engineering
3.12.1		Mechanical engineering nes
3.12.2		Agricultural engineering
3.12.3		Automobile engineering
3.12.4		Marine engineering
3.12.5		Naval architecture
3.13		Production and control engineering (including manufacturing technology)
3.14		Mining
3.15		Metallurgy
3.16		General and other engineering subjects (including combinations of engineering subjects)
3.17		Surveying
3.18.1		General technology and manufacture nes
3.18.2		Clothing and footwear
3.18.3		Food technology and manufacture
3.18.4		Printing and book production
3.18.5		Textile technology and manufacture
3.19		Combinations of technology with Subject Groups 4-10

* OPCS sub division

Code	Description
4	**Agriculture, Forestry, and Veterinary Studies**
4.20	Agriculture
4.21	Agricultural biology
4.22	Agricultural chemistry
4.23	Forestry
4.24.1	Veterinary studies nes
4.24.2	Combinations of agricultural subjects with Subject Groups 5-10
5	**Science (including Mathematics and Applied Sciences)**
5.25	Biology
5.26	Botany
5.27	Zoology
5.28	Physiology and anatomy
5.29	Biochemistry
5.30	Combinations of biological sciences
5.31.1	Mathematics nes
5.31.2	Dynamics, applied dynamics, thermo-dynamics
5.31.3	Computer science
5.31.4	Statistics
5.32	Mathematics/physics
5.33	Physics
5.34	Chemistry
5.35	Geology
5.36	Environmental studies (other than geology)
5.37	Combinations of physical sciences (other than mathematics/physics)
5.38	Biology with physical sciences
5.39	Combinations of science with Subject Groups 6-10 (except the philosophy/ physiology/psychology - PPP degrees)
6	**Social, Administrative and Business Studies**
6.40.1	Management studies nes
6.40.2	Business and commerce
6.40.3	Secretarial studies
6.41	Economics
6.42	Geography
6.43	Accountancy (including banking and insurance)
6.44	Government and public administration
6.45	Law
6.46	Psychology (including PPP degrees)
6.47	Sociology
6.48	Social anthropology
6.49	Combinations of social studies
6.50	Combinations of social studies with Subject Groups 7-10 (excluding archaeology/anthropology)

Code	Description
7	**Vocational (including Architecture and other professional studies)**
7.51	Architecture
7.52	Town and country planning
7.53.1	Catering and institutional management nes
7.53.2	Home economics
7.54.1	Vocational studies nes
7.54.2	Librarianship and information science
7.54.3	Nautical subjects
7.54.4	Transport
7.54.5	Wholesale and retail trades
7.54.6	Combinations of vocational subjects within Group 7
7.54.7	Combinations of vocational subjects with Subject Groups 8-10
8	**Language (Literature and Area) Studies**
8.55	English
8.56	Celtic language (Welsh and other)
8.57	French (language and studies)
8.58	French/German
8.59	German (language and studies)
8.60	Hispanic languages (and studies)
8.61	Other West European languages and studies (including combinations of West European languages other than French/German)
8.62	Russian (language and studies)
8.63	Slavonic and East European languages and studies other than Russian (including combinations of these languages)
8.64	Chinese (language and area studies)
8.65	Oriental, Asian and African languages and studies other than Chinese (including combinations of these languages)
8.66	Classical studies (including combinations of classics with philosophy)
8.67	Other language studies and combinations of subjects within the group (excluding those such as French/German, separately allowed for)
8.68	Languages with arts (excluding classics/ philosophy and archaeology/ancient history)

Code	Description
9	**Arts (other than languages and performing arts)**
9.69	History
9.70	Archaeology
9.71	Philosophy
9.72	Theology
9.76	Arts, general (where subject content is not specified and combinations within Groups 9 and 10)
10	**Music, Drama and Visual Arts**
10.73	Art and design
10.74	Drama
10.75.1	Music nes
10.75.2	Combinations with art and design, drama and music

Appendices

1991 Census England

H form for Private Households

For office use

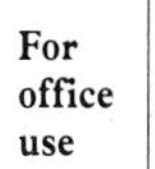

To the Head or Joint Heads or members of the Household aged 16 or over

Please complete this form for all members of the household, including children, and have it ready for collection on Monday 22nd April. Your census enumerator will call to collect it then or soon afterwards and will help you with the form if you have any difficulties. The enclosed leaflet explains why the Census is necessary and how the information is used.

Completion of the form is compulsory under the Census Act 1920. If you refuse to complete it, or give false information, you may have to pay a fine of up to £400.

Your answers will be treated in strict confidence and used only to produce statistics. Names and addresses will not be put into the computer; only the postcode will be entered. The forms will be kept securely within my Office and treated as confidential for 100 years.

Anyone using or disclosing Census information improperly will be liable to prosecution. For example, it would be improper for you to pass on to someone else information which you had been given in confidence by a visitor to enable you to complete the Census form.

If any member of the household aged 16 or over does not wish you, or another member of the household, to see their information, please ask the enumerator for an individual form with an envelope.

After completing the form, please sign the declaration on the last page.

Thank you for your co-operation.

P J Wormald
Registrar General
Office of Population Censuses and Surveys
PO Box 100 Fareham PO16 0AL
Telephone: 0329 844444

Please read these instructions before filling in this form

A Household:

A household comprises either one person living alone or a group of people (not necessarily related) living at the same address with common housekeeping — that is, sharing at least one meal a day or sharing a living room or sitting room.

People staying temporarily with the household are included.

- ► If there is more than one household in this building, answer for your household only.
- ► First answer questions **H1 and H2** on **this page** and **H3 to H5** on the **back page** about your household and the rooms which it occupies.
- ► When you have answered the household questions, answer the questions on the **inside pages** about each member of your household.
- ► If a member of the household is completing an Individual form please still enter their name and answer questions 5 and 6 on this form.
- ► Then complete **Panel B** and **Panel C** on the back page.
- ► ***Answer each question by ticking the appropriate box or boxes ☑ where they are provided.***
- ► ***Please use ink or ballpoint pen.***

To be completed by the Enumerator

Census District ☐ **Enumeration District** ☐ Form Number ☐

Name ☐

Address ☐

Postcode ☐☐☐☐ ☐☐☐ **ABS** ☐

H1 Rooms

Please count the number of rooms your household has for its **own** use.

Do not count: small kitchens, under 2 metres (6 feet 6 inches) wide
bathrooms
toilets

Do count: living rooms
bedrooms
kitchens at least 2 metres (6 feet 6 inches) wide
all other rooms in your accommodation

The total number of rooms is ☐

Panel A

To be completed by the Enumerator and amended, if necessary, by the person(s) signing this form.

Tick one box to show the type of accommodation which this household occupies.

A caravan or other mobile or temporary structure ☐ 1

A whole house or bungalow that is
- detached ☐ 2
- semi-detached ☐ 3
- terraced (include end of terrace) ☐ 4

The whole of a purpose built flat or maisonette
- in a commercial building (for example in an office building or hotel or over a shop) ☐ 5
- in a block of flats or tenement ☐ 6

Part of a converted or shared house, bungalow or flat
- separate entrance into the building ☐ 7
- shared entrance into the building ☐ 8

H2 Accommodation

If box 7 or box 8 in Panel A is ticked, tick one box below to show the type of accommodation which your household occupies.

A one roomed flatlet
with private bath or shower, WC and kitchen facilities. ☐ 1

One room or bedsit, not self-contained
(to move from your room to bathroom, WC or kitchen facilities you have to use a hall, landing or stairway open to other household(s)). ☐ 2

A self-contained flat or accommodation with 2 or more rooms,
having bath or shower, WC and kitchen facilities all behind its own private door. ☐ 3

2 or more rooms, not self-contained
(to move between rooms or to bathroom, WC or kitchen facilities you have to use a hall, landing or stairway open to other household(s)). ☐ 4

Please turn to the back page and answer questions H3 to H5 ►

		Person No. 1	Person No. 2
1-3	**Name, sex and date of birth of people to be included**	**Name and surname**	**Name and surname**
	Important: please read the notes before answering the questions. In answering the rest of the questions please include: ► every person who spends census night (21-22 April) in this household, **including anyone staying temporarily**. ► any other people who are usually members of the household but on census night are absent on holiday, at school or college, or for any other reason, even if they are being included on another census form elsewhere. ► anyone who arrives here on Monday 22nd April who was in Great Britain on the Sunday and who has not been included as present on another census form. ► any newly born baby born before the 22nd April, even if still in hospital. If not yet given a name, write BABY and the surname. **Write the names in BLOCK CAPITALS starting with the head or a joint head of household.**	**Sex** Male ☐ 1 Female ☐ 2 **Date of birth** Day Month Year	**Sex** Male ☐ 1 Female ☐ 2 **Date of birth** Day Month Year
4	**Marital status** On the 21st April what is the person's marital status? If separated but not divorced, please tick 'Married (first marriage)' or 'Re-married' as appropriate. Please tick one box.	Single (never married) ☐ 1 Married (first marriage) ☐ 2 Re-married ☐ 3 Divorced (decree absolute) ☐ 4 Widowed ☐ 5	Single (never married) ☐ 1 Married (first marriage) ☐ 2 Re-married ☐ 3 Divorced (decree absolute) ☐ 4 Widowed ☐ 5
5	**Relationship in household** Please tick the box which indicates the relationship of each person to the person in the first column. A step child or adopted child should be included as the son or daughter of the step or adoptive parent. Write in relationship of 'Other relative' — for example, father, daughter-in-law, niece, uncle, cousin. Write in position in household of an 'Unrelated' person for example, boarder, housekeeper, friend, flatmate, foster child.		**Relationship to Person No.1** Husband or wife ☐ 1 Living together as a couple ☐ 2 Son or daughter ☐ 3 Other relative ☐ *please specify* Unrelated ☐ *please specify*
6	**Whereabouts on night of 21-22 April 1991** Please tick the appropriate box to indicate where the person was on the night of 21-22 April 1991.	At this address, out on night work or travelling to this address ☐ 0 Elsewhere in England, Scotland or Wales ☐ 1 Outside Great Britain ☐ 2	At this address, out on night work or travelling to this address ☐ 0 Elsewhere in England, Scotland or Wales ☐ 1 Outside Great Britain ☐ 2
7	**Usual address** If the person usually lives here, please tick 'This address'. If not, tick 'Elsewhere' and write in the person's usual address. For students and children away from home during term time, the home address should be taken as the usual address. For any person who lives away from home for part of the week, the home address should be taken as the usual address. Any person who is not a permanent member of the household should be asked what he or she considers to be his or her usual address.	This address ☐ 1 Elsewhere ☐ If elsewhere, please write the person's usual address and postcode below in BLOCK CAPITALS Post-code	This address ☐ 1 Elsewhere ☐ If elsewhere, please write the person's usual address and postcode below in BLOCK CAPITALS Post-code
8	**Term time address of students and schoolchildren** If not a student or schoolchild, please tick first box. For a student or schoolchild who lives here during term time, tick 'This address'. If he or she does not live here during term time, tick 'Elsewhere' and write in the current or most recent term time address.	Not a student or schoolchild ☐ This address ☐ 1 Elsewhere ☐ If elsewhere, please write the term time address and postcode below in BLOCK CAPITALS Post-code	Not a student or schoolchild ☐ This address ☐ 1 Elsewhere ☐ If elsewhere, please write the term time address and postcode below in BLOCK CAPITALS Post-code

Person No. 3	**Person No. 4**	**Person No. 5**	**Person No. 6**
Name and surname ☐	**Name and surname** ☐	**Name and surname** ☐	**Name and surname** ☐
Sex Male ☐ 1 Female ☐ 2	**Sex** Male ☐ 1 Female ☐ 2	**Sex** Male ☐ 1 Female ☐ 2	**Sex** Male ☐ 1 Female ☐ 2
Date of birth Day ☐ Month ☐ Year ☐	**Date of birth** Day ☐ Month ☐ Year ☐	**Date of birth** Day ☐ Month ☐ Year ☐	**Date of birth** Day ☐ Month ☐ Year ☐
Single (never married) ☐ 1 Married (first marriage) ☐ 2 Re-married ☐ 3 Divorced (decree absolute) ☐ 4 Widowed ☐ 5	Single (never married) ☐ 1 Married (first marriage) ☐ 2 Re-married ☐ 3 Divorced (decree absolute) ☐ 4 Widowed ☐ 5	Single (never married) ☐ 1 Married (first marriage) ☐ 2 Re-married ☐ 3 Divorced (decree absolute) ☐ 4 Widowed ☐ 5	Single (never married) ☐ 1 Married (first marriage) ☐ 2 Re-married ☐ 3 Divorced (decree absolute) ☐ 4 Widowed ☐ 5
Relationship to Person No.1 Husband or wife ☐ 1 Living together as a couple ☐ 2 Son or daughter ☐ 3 Other relative ☐ *please specify* ☐ Unrelated ☐ *please specify* ☐	**Relationship to Person No.1** Husband or wife ☐ 1 Living together as a couple ☐ 2 Son or daughter ☐ 3 Other relative ☐ *please specify* ☐ Unrelated ☐ *please specify* ☐	**Relationship to Person No.1** Husband or wife ☐ 1 Living together as a couple ☐ 2 Son or daughter ☐ 3 Other relative ☐ *please specify* ☐ Unrelated ☐ *please specify* ☐	**Relationship to Person No.1** Husband or wife ☐ 1 Living together as a couple ☐ 2 Son or daughter ☐ 3 Other relative ☐ *please specify* ☐ Unrelated ☐ *please specify* ☐
At this address, out on night work or travelling to this address ☐ 0 Elsewhere in England, Scotland or Wales ☐ 1 Outside Great Britain ☐ 2	At this address, out on night work or travelling to this address ☐ 0 Elsewhere in England, Scotland or Wales ☐ 1 Outside Great Britain ☐ 2	At this address, out on night work or travelling to this address ☐ 0 Elsewhere in England, Scotland or Wales ☐ 1 Outside Great Britain ☐ 2	At this address, out on night work or travelling to this address ☐ 0 Elsewhere in England, Scotland or Wales ☐ 1 Outside Great Britain ☐ 2
This address ☐ 1 Elsewhere ☐ If elsewhere, please write the person's usual address and postcode below in BLOCK CAPITALS ☐ Post-code ☐	This address ☐ 1 Elsewhere ☐ If elsewhere, please write the person's usual address and postcode below in BLOCK CAPITALS ☐ Post-code ☐	This address ☐ 1 Elsewhere ☐ If elsewhere, please write the person's usual address and postcode below in BLOCK CAPITALS ☐ Post-code ☐	This address ☐ 1 Elsewhere ☐ If elsewhere, please write the person's usual address and postcode below in BLOCK CAPITALS ☐ Post-code ☐
Not a student or schoolchild ☐ This address ☐ 1 Elsewhere ☐ If elsewhere, please write the term time address and postcode below in BLOCK CAPITALS ☐ Post-code ☐	Not a student or schoolchild ☐ This address ☐ 1 Elsewhere ☐ If elsewhere, please write the term time address and postcode below in BLOCK CAPITALS ☐ Post-code ☐	Not a student or schoolchild ☐ This address ☐ 1 Elsewhere ☐ If elsewhere, please write the term time address and postcode below in BLOCK CAPITALS ☐ Post-code ☐	Not a student or schoolchild ☐ This address ☐ 1 Elsewhere ☐ If elsewhere, please write the term time address and postcode below in BLOCK CAPITALS ☐ Post-code ☐

Please turn over ►

1-3	Name, sex and date of birth of people to be included	Person No. 1	Person No. 2
	Important: please read the notes before answering the questions. In answering the rest of the questions please include: ► every person who spends census night (21-22 April) in this household, **including anyone staying temporarily**. ► any other people who are usually members of the household but on census night are absent on holiday, at school or college, or for any other reason, even if they are being included on another census form elsewhere. ► anyone who arrives here on Monday 22nd April who was in Great Britain on the Sunday and who has not been included as present on another census form. ► any newly born baby born before the 22nd April, even if still in hospital. If not yet given a name, write BABY and the surname. **Write the names in BLOCK CAPITALS starting with the head or a joint head of household.**	**Name and surname** **Sex** Male ☐ 1 Female ☐ 2 **Date of birth** Day Month Year	**Name and surname** **Sex** Male ☐ 1 Female ☐ 2 **Date of birth** Day Month Year
9	**Usual address one year ago** If the person's usual address one year ago (on the 21st April 1990) was the same as his or her current usual address (given in answer to question 7), please tick 'Same'. If not, tick 'Different' and write in the usual address one year ago. If everyone on the form has moved from the same address, please write the address in full for the first person and indicate with an arrow that this applies to the other people on the form. For a child born since the 21st April 1990, tick the 'Child under one' box.	Same as question 7 ☐ 1 Different ☐ Child under one ☐ 3 If different, please write the person's address and postcode on the 21st April 1990 below in BLOCK CAPITALS Post-code	Same as question 7 ☐ 1 Different ☐ Child under one ☐ 3 If different, please write the person's address and postcode on the 21st April 1990 below in BLOCK CAPITALS Post-code
10	**Country of birth** Please tick the appropriate box. If the 'Elsewhere' box is ticked, please write in the present name of the country in which the birthplace is now situated.	England ☐ 1 Scotland ☐ 2 Wales ☐ 3 Northern Ireland ☐ 4 Irish Republic ☐ 5 Elsewhere ☐ If elsewhere, please write in the present name of the country	England ☐ 1 Scotland ☐ 2 Wales ☐ 3 Northern Ireland ☐ 4 Irish Republic ☐ 5 Elsewhere ☐ If elsewhere, please write in the present name of the country
11	**Ethnic group** Please tick the appropriate box. If the person is descended from more than one ethnic or racial group, please tick the group to which the person considers he/she belongs, or tick the 'Any other ethnic group' box and describe the person's ancestry in the space provided.	White ☐ 0 Black-Caribbean ☐ 1 Black-African ☐ 2 Black-Other ☐ *please describe* Indian ☐ 3 Pakistani ☐ 4 Bangladeshi ☐ 5 Chinese ☐ 6 Any other ethnic group ☐ *please describe*	White ☐ 0 Black-Caribbean ☐ 1 Black-African ☐ 2 Black-Other ☐ *please describe* Indian ☐ 3 Pakistani ☐ 4 Bangladeshi ☐ 5 Chinese ☐ 6 Any other ethnic group ☐ *please describe*
12	**Long-term illness** Does the person have any long-term illness, health problem or handicap which limits his/her daily activities or the work he/she can do? **Include problems which are due to old age.**	Yes, has a health problem which limits activities ☐ 1 Has no such health problem ☐ 2	Yes, has a health problem which limits activities ☐ 1 Has no such health problem ☐ 2

Person No. 3

Name and surname

Sex Male ☐ 1 Female ☐ 2

Date of birth Day Month Year

Same as question 7 ☐ 1
Different ☐
Child under one ☐ 3

If different, please write the person's address and postcode on the 21st April 1990 below in BLOCK CAPITALS

Post-code

England ☐ 1
Scotland ☐ 2
Wales ☐ 3
Northern Ireland ☐ 4
Irish Republic ☐ 5
Elsewhere ☐

If elsewhere, please write in the present name of the country

White ☐ 0
Black-Caribbean ☐ 1
Black-African ☐ 2
Black-Other ☐
please describe

Indian ☐ 3
Pakistani ☐ 4
Bangladeshi ☐ 5
Chinese ☐ 6
Any other ethnic group ☐
please describe

Yes, has a health problem which limits activities ☐ 1
Has no such health problem ☐ 2

Person No. 4

Name and surname

Sex Male ☐ 1 Female ☐ 2

Date of birth Day Month Year

Same as question 7 ☐ 1
Different ☐
Child under one ☐ 3

If different, please write the person's address and postcode on the 21st April 1990 below in BLOCK CAPITALS

Post-code

England ☐ 1
Scotland ☐ 2
Wales ☐ 3
Northern Ireland ☐ 4
Irish Republic ☐ 5
Elsewhere ☐

If elsewhere, please write in the present name of the country

White ☐ 0
Black-Caribbean ☐ 1
Black-African ☐ 2
Black-Other ☐
please describe

Indian ☐ 3
Pakistani ☐ 4
Bangladeshi ☐ 5
Chinese ☐ 6
Any other ethnic group ☐
please describe

Yes, has a health problem which limits activities ☐ 1
Has no such health problem ☐ 2

Person No. 5

Name and surname

Sex Male ☐ 1 Female ☐ 2

Date of birth Day Month Year

Same as question 7 ☐ 1
Different ☐
Child under one ☐ 3

If different, please write the person's address and postcode on the 21st April 1990 below in BLOCK CAPITALS

Post-code

England ☐ 1
Scotland ☐ 2
Wales ☐ 3
Northern Ireland ☐ 4
Irish Republic ☐ 5
Elsewhere ☐

If elsewhere, please write in the present name of the country

White ☐ 0
Black-Caribbean ☐ 1
Black-African ☐ 2
Black-Other ☐
please describe

Indian ☐ 3
Pakistani ☐ 4
Bangladeshi ☐ 5
Chinese ☐ 6
Any other ethnic group ☐
please describe

Yes, has a health problem which limits activities ☐ 1
Has no such health problem ☐ 2

Person No. 6

Name and surname

Sex Male ☐ 1 Female ☐ 2

Date of birth Day Month Year

Same as question 7 ☐ 1
Different ☐
Child under one ☐ 3

If different, please write the person's address and postcode on the 21st April 1990 below in BLOCK CAPITALS

Post-code

England ☐ 1
Scotland ☐ 2
Wales ☐ 3
Northern Ireland ☐ 4
Irish Republic ☐ 5
Elsewhere ☐

If elsewhere, please write in the present name of the country

White ☐ 0
Black-Caribbean ☐ 1
Black-African ☐ 2
Black-Other ☐
please describe

Indian ☐ 3
Pakistani ☐ 4
Bangladeshi ☐ 5
Chinese ☐ 6
Any other ethnic group ☐
please describe

Yes, has a health problem which limits activities ☐ 1
Has no such health problem ☐ 2

Please turn over ►

1-3 Name, sex and date of birth of people to be included

Important: please read the notes before answering the questions.

In answering the rest of the questions please include:

- every person who spends census night (21-22 April) in this household, **including anyone staying temporarily**.
- any other people who are usually members of the household but on census night are absent on holiday, at school or college, or for any other reason, even if they are being included on another census form elsewhere.
- anyone who arrives here on Monday 22nd April who was in Great Britain on the Sunday and who has not been included as present on another census form.
- any newly born baby born before the 22nd April, even if still in hospital. If not yet given a name, write BABY and the surname.

Write the names in BLOCK CAPITALS starting with the head or a joint head of household.

Person No. 1	Person No. 2
Name and surname ☐	**Name and surname** ☐
Sex Male ☐ 1 Female ☐ 2	**Sex** Male ☐ 1 Female ☐ 2
Date of birth Day ☐ Month ☐ Year ☐	**Date of birth** Day ☐ Month ☐ Year ☐

Answers to the remaining questions are not required for any person under 16 years of age (born after 21st April 1975)

13 Whether working, retired, looking after the home etc last week

Which of these things was the person doing **last week**?

Please read carefully right through the list and **tick all the descriptions that apply**.

Casual or temporary work should be counted at boxes 1, 2, 3 or 4. Also tick boxes 1, 2, 3 or 4 if the person had a job last week but was off sick, on holiday, temporarily laid off or on strike.

Boxes 1, 2, 3 and 4 refer to work for pay or profit but not to unpaid work except in a family business.

Working for an employer is **part time** (box 2) if the hours worked, excluding any overtime and mealbreaks, are usually 30 hours or less per week.

Include any person wanting a job but prevented from looking by holiday or temporary sickness.

Do not count training given or paid for by an employer.

Person No. 1	Person No. 2
Was working for an employer full time (more than 30 hours a week) ☐ 1	Was working for an employer full time (more than 30 hours a week) ☐ 1
Was working for an employer part time (one hour or more a week) ☐ 2	Was working for an employer part time (one hour or more a week) ☐ 2
Was self-employed, employing other people ☐ 3	Was self-employed, employing other people ☐ 3
Was self-employed, not employing other people ☐ 4	Was self-employed, not employing other people ☐ 4
Was on a government employment or training scheme ☐ 5	Was on a government employment or training scheme ☐ 5
Was waiting to start a job he/she had already accepted ☐ 6	Was waiting to start a job he/she had already accepted ☐ 6
Was unemployed and looking for a job ☐ 7	Was unemployed and looking for a job ☐ 7
Was at school or in other full time education ☐ 8	Was at school or in other full time education ☐ 8
Was unable to work because of long term sickness or disability ☐ 9	Was unable to work because of long term sickness or disability ☐ 9
Was retired from paid work ☐ 10	Was retired from paid work ☐ 10
Was looking after the home or family ☐ 11	Was looking after the home or family ☐ 11
Other ☐ *please specify*	Other ☐ *please specify*

Person No. 3	Person No. 4	Person No. 5	Person No. 6
Name and surname	**Name and surname**	**Name and surname**	**Name and surname**
Sex Male ☐ 1 Female ☐ 2	**Sex** Male ☐ 1 Female ☐ 2	**Sex** Male ☐ 1 Female ☐ 2	**Sex** Male ☐ 1 Female ☐ 2
Date of birth Day Month Year	**Date of birth** Day Month Year	**Date of birth** Day Month Year	**Date of birth** Day Month Year

Answers to the remaining questions are not required for any person under 16 years of age (born after 21st April 1975)

Person No. 3	Person No. 4	Person No. 5	Person No. 6
Was working for an employer full time (more than 30 hours a week) ☐ 1	Was working for an employer full time (more than 30 hours a week) ☐ 1	Was working for an employer full time (more than 30 hours a week) ☐ 1	Was working for an employer full time (more than 30 hours a week) ☐ 1
Was working for an employer part time (one hour or more a week) ☐ 2	Was working for an employer part time (one hour or more a week) ☐ 2	Was working for an employer part time (one hour or more a week) ☐ 2	Was working for an employer part time (one hour or more a week) ☐ 2
Was self-employed, employing other people ☐ 3	Was self-employed, employing other people ☐ 3	Was self-employed, employing other people ☐ 3	Was self-employed, employing other people ☐ 3
Was self-employed, not employing other people ☐ 4	Was self-employed, not employing other people ☐ 4	Was self-employed, not employing other people ☐ 4	Was self-employed, not employing other people ☐ 4
Was on a government employment or training scheme ☐ 5	Was on a government employment or training scheme ☐ 5	Was on a government employment or training scheme ☐ 5	Was on a government employment or training scheme ☐ 5
Was waiting to start a job he/she had already accepted ☐ 6	Was waiting to start a job he/she had already accepted ☐ 6	Was waiting to start a job he/she had already accepted ☐ 6	Was waiting to start a job he/she had already accepted ☐ 6
Was unemployed and looking for a job ☐ 7	Was unemployed and looking for a job ☐ 7	Was unemployed and looking for a job ☐ 7	Was unemployed and looking for a job ☐ 7
Was at school or in other full time education ☐ 8	Was at school or in other full time education ☐ 8	Was at school or in other full time education ☐ 8	Was at school or in other full time education ☐ 8
Was unable to work because of long term sickness or disability ☐ 9	Was unable to work because of long term sickness or disability ☐ 9	Was unable to work because of long term sickness or disability ☐ 9	Was unable to work because of long term sickness or disability ☐ 9
Was retired from paid work ☐ 10	Was retired from paid work ☐ 10	Was retired from paid work ☐ 10	Was retired from paid work ☐ 10
Was looking after the home or family ☐ 11	Was looking after the home or family ☐ 11	Was looking after the home or family ☐ 11	Was looking after the home or family ☐ 11
Other ☐ *please specify*	Other ☐ *please specify*	Other ☐ *please specify*	Other ☐ *please specify*

Please turn over ►

1-3 Name, sex and date of birth of people to be included

Important: please read the notes before answering the questions.

In answering the rest of the questions please include:

- every person who spends census night (21-22 April) in this household, **including anyone staying temporarily**.
- any other people who are usually members of the household but on census night are absent on holiday, at school or college, or for any other reason, even if they are being included on another census form elsewhere.
- anyone who arrives here on Monday 22nd April who was in Great Britain on the Sunday and who has not been included as present on another census form.
- any newly born baby born before the 22nd April, even if still in hospital. If not yet given a name, write BABY and the surname.

Write the names in BLOCK CAPITALS starting with the head or a joint head of household.

Person No. 1	Person No. 2
Name and surname	**Name and surname**
Sex Male ☐ 1 Female ☐ 2	**Sex** Male ☐ 1 Female ☐ 2
Date of birth Day Month Year	**Date of birth** Day Month Year

Please read A below, tick the box that applies and follow the instruction by the box ticked.

	Person No. 1	Person No. 2
A Did the person have a paid job last week (any of the boxes 1, 2, 3 or 4 ticked at question 13)?	YES ☐ Answer questions 14, 15, 16, 17 and 18 about the main job last week, then go on to question 19 NO ☐ Answer B	YES ☐ Answer questions 14, 15, 16, 17 and 18 about the main job last week, then go on to question 19 NO ☐ Answer B
B Has the person had a paid job within the last 10 years?	YES ☐ Answer questions 14, 15 and 16 about the most recent job, then go on to question 19 NO ☐ Go on to question 19	YES ☐ Answer questions 14, 15 and 16 about the most recent job, then go on to question 19 NO ☐ Go on to question 19

14 Hours worked per week

How many hours per week does or did the person usually work in his or her main job?

Do not count overtime or meal breaks.

Person No. 1	Person No. 2
Number of hours worked per week ☐	Number of hours worked per week ☐

15 Occupation

Please give the full title of the person's present or last job and describe the main things he/she does or did in the job.

At a, give the full title by which the job is known, for example: 'packing machinist'; 'poultry processor'; 'jig and tool fitter'; 'supervisor of typists'; 'accounts clerk'; rather than general titles like 'machinist'; 'process worker'; 'supervisor' or 'clerk'. Give rank or grade if the person has one.

At b, write down the main things the person actually does or did in the job. If possible ask him/her to say what these things are and write them down.

Armed Forces — enter 'commissioned officer' or 'other rank' as appropriate at **a,** and leave **b** blank.

Civil Servants — give grade at **a** and discipline or specialism, for example: 'electrical engineer'; 'accountant'; 'chemist'; 'administrator' at **b.**

Person No. 1	Person No. 2
a Full job title	**a** Full job title
b Main things done in job	**b** Main things done in job

16 Name and business of employer (if self-employed give the name and nature of the person's business)

At a, please give the name of the employer. Give the trading name if one is used. Do not use abbreviations.

At b, describe clearly what the employer (or the person if self-employed) makes or does (or did).

Armed Forces — write 'Armed Forces' at **a** and leave **b** blank. For a member of the Armed Forces of a country other than the UK — add the name of the country.

Civil Servants — give name of Department at **a** and write 'Government Department' at **b.**

Local Government Officers — give name of employing authority at **a** and department in which employed at **b.**

Person No. 1	Person No. 2
a Name of employer	**a** Name of employer
b Description of employer's business	**b** Description of employer's business

Person No. 3	Person No. 4	Person No. 5	Person No. 6
Name and surname	Name and surname	Name and surname	Name and surname
Sex Male ☐ 1 Female ☐ 2	Sex Male ☐ 1 Female ☐ 2	Sex Male ☐ 1 Female ☐ 2	Sex Male ☐ 1 Female ☐ 2
Date of birth Day Month Year	Date of birth Day Month Year	Date of birth Day Month Year	Date of birth Day Month Year

This will tell you which questions to answer for each person.

Person No. 3	Person No. 4	Person No. 5	Person No. 6
YES ☐ Answer questions 14, 15, 16, 17 and 18 about the main job last week, then go on to question 19 NO ☐ Answer B	YES ☐ Answer questions 14, 15, 16, 17 and 18 about the main job last week, then go on to question 19 NO ☐ Answer B	YES ☐ Answer questions 14, 15, 16, 17 and 18 about the main job last week, then go on to question 19 NO ☐ Answer B	YES ☐ Answer questions 14, 15, 16, 17 and 18 about the main job last week, then go on to question 19 NO ☐ Answer B
YES ☐ Answer questions 14, 15 and 16 about the most recent job, then go on to question 19 NO ☐ Go on to question 19	YES ☐ Answer questions 14, 15 and 16 about the most recent job, then go on to question 19 NO ☐ Go on to question 19	YES ☐ Answer questions 14, 15 and 16 about the most recent job, then go on to question 19 NO ☐ Go on to question 19	YES ☐ Answer questions 14, 15 and 16 about the most recent job, then go on to question 19 NO ☐ Go on to question 19
Number of hours worked per week ☐	Number of hours worked per week ☐	Number of hours worked per week ☐	Number of hours worked per week ☐
a Full job title	**a** Full job title	**a** Full job title	**a** Full job title
b Main things done in job	**b** Main things done in job	**b** Main things done in job	**b** Main things done in job
a Name of employer	**a** Name of employer	**a** Name of employer	**a** Name of employer
b Description of employer's business	**b** Description of employer's business	**b** Description of employer's business	**b** Description of employer's business

Please turn over ►

1-3 Name, sex and date of birth of people to be included

Important: please read the notes before answering the questions.

In answering the rest of the questions please include:

- ► every person who spends census night (21-22 April) in this household, **including anyone staying temporarily**.
- ► any other people who are usually members of the household but on census night are absent on holiday, at school or college, or for any other reason, even if they are being included on another census form elsewhere.
- ► anyone who arrives here on Monday 22nd April who was in Great Britain on the Sunday and who has not been included as present on another census form.
- ► any newly born baby born before the 22nd April, even if still in hospital. If not yet given a name, write BABY and the surname.

17 Address of place of work

Please give the full address of the person's place of work.

For a person employed on a site for a long period, give the address of the site.

For a person not working regularly at one place who reports daily to a depot or other fixed address, give that address.

For a person not reporting daily to a fixed address, tick box 1.

For a person working mainly at home, tick box 2.

Armed Forces — leave blank.

18 Daily journey to work

Please tick the appropriate box to show how the longest part, by distance, of the person's daily journey to work is normally made.

For a person using different means of transport on different days, show the means most often used.

Car or van includes three-wheeled cars and motor caravans.

19 Degrees, professional and vocational qualifications

Has the person obtained any qualifications after reaching the age of 18 such as:

-degrees, diplomas, HNC, HND,

-nursing qualifications,

-teaching qualifications (see * below),

-graduate or corporate membership of professional institutions,

-other professional, educational or vocational qualifications?

Do not count qualifications normally obtained at school such as GCE, CSE, GCSE, SCE and school certificates.

If box 2 is ticked, write in all qualifications even if they are not relevant to the person's present job or if the person is not working.

Please list the qualifications in the order in which they were obtained.

If more than three, please enter in a spare column and link with an arrow.

*For a person with **school teaching qualifications**, give the full title of the qualification, such as 'Certificate of Education' and the subject(s) which the person is qualified to teach. The subject 'education' should then only be shown if the course had no other subject specialisation.

Person No. 1

Name and surname

Sex Male ☐ 1 Female ☐ 2

Date of birth Day Month Year

Please write full address and postcode of workplace below in BLOCK CAPITALS

Post-code

No fixed place ☐ 1
Mainly at home ☐ 2

British Rail train ☐ 1
Underground, tube, metro ☐ 2
Bus, minibus or coach (public or private) ☐ 3
Motor cycle, scooter, moped ☐ 4
Driving a car or van ☐ 5
Passenger in car or van ☐ 6
Pedal cycle ☐ 7
On foot ☐ 8
Other ☐ 9 *please specify*

Works mainly at home ☐ 0

NO — no such qualifications ☐ 1
YES — give details ☐ 2

1 Title
Subject(s)
Year
Institution

2 Title
Subject(s)
Year
Institution

3 Title
Subject(s)
Year
Institution

Person No. 2

Name and surname

Sex Male ☐ 1 Female ☐ 2

Date of birth Day Month Year

Please write full address and postcode of workplace below in BLOCK CAPITALS

Post-code

No fixed place ☐ 1
Mainly at home ☐ 2

British Rail train ☐ 1
Underground, tube, metro ☐ 2
Bus, minibus or coach (public or private) ☐ 3
Motor cycle, scooter, moped ☐ 4
Driving a car or van ☐ 5
Passenger in car or van ☐ 6
Pedal cycle ☐ 7
On foot ☐ 8
Other ☐ 9 *please specify*

Works mainly at home ☐ 0

NO — no such qualifications ☐ 1
YES — give details ☐ 2

1 Title
Subject(s)
Year
Institution

2 Title
Subject(s)
Year
Institution

3 Title
Subject(s)
Year
Institution

Person No. 3	Person No. 4	Person No. 5	Person No. 6
Name and surname	**Name and surname**	**Name and surname**	**Name and surname**
Sex Male ☐ 1 Female ☐ 2	**Sex** Male ☐ 1 Female ☐ 2	**Sex** Male ☐ 1 Female ☐ 2	**Sex** Male ☐ 1 Female ☐ 2
Date of birth Day Month Year	**Date of birth** Day Month Year	**Date of birth** Day Month Year	**Date of birth** Day Month Year
Please write full address and postcode of workplace below in BLOCK CAPITALS	Please write full address and postcode of workplace below in BLOCK CAPITALS	Please write full address and postcode of workplace below in BLOCK CAPITALS	Please write full address and postcode of workplace below in BLOCK CAPITALS
Post-code	Post-code	Post-code	Post-code
No fixed place ☐ 1	No fixed place ☐ 1	No fixed place ☐ 1	No fixed place ☐ 1
Mainly at home ☐ 2	Mainly at home ☐ 2	Mainly at home ☐ 2	Mainly at home ☐ 2
British Rail train ☐ 1	British Rail train ☐ 1	British Rail train ☐ 1	British Rail train ☐ 1
Underground, tube, metro ☐ 2	Underground, tube, metro ☐ 2	Underground, tube, metro ☐ 2	Underground, tube, metro ☐ 2
Bus, minibus or coach (public or private) ☐ 3	Bus, minibus or coach (public or private) ☐ 3	Bus, minibus or coach (public or private) ☐ 3	Bus, minibus or coach (public or private) ☐ 3
Motor cycle, scooter, moped ☐ 4	Motor cycle, scooter, moped ☐ 4	Motor cycle, scooter, moped ☐ 4	Motor cycle, scooter, moped ☐ 4
Driving a car or van ☐ 5	Driving a car or van ☐ 5	Driving a car or van ☐ 5	Driving a car or van ☐ 5
Passenger in car or van ☐ 6	Passenger in car or van ☐ 6	Passenger in car or van ☐ 6	Passenger in car or van ☐ 6
Pedal cycle ☐ 7	Pedal cycle ☐ 7	Pedal cycle ☐ 7	Pedal cycle ☐ 7
On foot ☐ 8	On foot ☐ 8	On foot ☐ 8	On foot ☐ 8
Other ☐ 9 *please specify*	Other ☐ 9 *please specify*	Other ☐ 9 *please specify*	Other ☐ 9 *please specify*
Works mainly at home ☐ 0	Works mainly at home ☐ 0	Works mainly at home ☐ 0	Works mainly at home ☐ 0
NO — no such qualifications ☐ 1	NO — no such qualifications ☐ 1	NO — no such qualifications ☐ 1	NO — no such qualifications ☐ 1
YES — give details ☐ 2	YES — give details ☐ 2	YES — give details ☐ 2	YES — give details ☐ 2
1 Title	1 Title	1 Title	1 Title
Subject(s)	Subject(s)	Subject(s)	Subject(s)
Year	Year	Year	Year
Institution	Institution	Institution	Institution
2 Title	2 Title	2 Title	2 Title
Subject(s)	Subject(s)	Subject(s)	Subject(s)
Year	Year	Year	Year
Institution	Institution	Institution	Institution
3 Title	3 Title	3 Title	3 Title
Subject(s)	Subject(s)	Subject(s)	Subject(s)
Year	Year	Year	Year
Institution	Institution	Institution	Institution

Please turn over and complete Panels B and C ►

H3 Tenure

Please tick the box which best describes how you and your household occupy your accommodation.

If buying by stages from a Council, Housing Association or New Town (under shared ownership, co-ownership or equity sharing scheme), answer as an owner-occupier at box 1.

If your accommodation is occupied by lease originally granted for, or extended to, more than 21 years, answer as an owner-occupier. For shorter leases, answer 'By renting'.

A private landlord may be a person or a company or another organisation not mentioned at 3, 4, 5 or 6 above.

As an owner-occupier:

- -buying the property through mortgage or loan ☐ 1
- -owning the property outright (no loan) ☐ 2

By renting, rent free or by lease:

- -with a job, farm, shop or other business ☐ 3
- -from a local authority (Council) ☐ 4
- -from a New Town Development Corporation (or Commission) or from a Housing Action Trust ☐ 5
- -from a housing association or charitable trust ☐ 6
- -from a private landlord, furnished ☐ 7
- -from a private landlord, unfurnished ☐ 8

In some other way:

- -please give details below ☐

H4 Amenities

Does your household — that is, you and any people who usually live here with you — **have the use of:**

a A bath or shower?

- **Yes** — for use only by this household ☐ 1
- **Yes** — for use also by another household ☐ 2
- **No** — no bath or shower available ☐ 3

b A flush toilet (WC) with entrance inside the building?

- **Yes** — for use only by this household ☐ 0
- **Yes** — for use also by another household ☐ 1
- **No** — flush toilet with outside entrance only ☐ 2
- **No** — no flush toilet indoors or outdoors ☐ 3

c Central heating in living rooms and bedrooms (including night storage heaters, warm air or under-floor heating), whether actually used or not?

- **Yes** — all living rooms and bedrooms centrally heated ☐ 1
- **Yes** — some (not all) living rooms and bedrooms centrally heated ☐ 2
- **No** — no living rooms or bedrooms centrally heated ☐ 3

H5 Cars and vans

Please tick the appropriate box to indicate the number of cars and vans normally available for use by you or members of your household (other than visitors).

Include any car or van provided by employers if normally available for use by you or members of your household, but **exclude** vans used only for carrying goods.

- None ☐ 0
- One ☐ 1
- Two ☐ 2
- Three or more ☐ 3

◄ **Please turn to the first inside page**

Panel B

Was there anyone else (such as a visitor) here on the night of 21-22 April whom you have not included because there was no room on the form? No ☐ Yes ☐

If **yes** ticked, please ask the Enumerator for another form.

Have you left anyone out because you were not sure whether they should be included on the form? No ☐ Yes ☐

If **yes** ticked, please give their names and the reason why you were not sure about including them.

Name

Reason

Name

Reason

Name

Reason

Panel C

Before you sign the form, will you please check:

- ► that all questions which should have been answered have been answered for every member of your household
- ► that you have included everyone who spent the night of 21-22 April in your household
- ► that you have included everyone who usually lives here but was away from home on the night of 21-22 April
- ► that no visitors, boarders or newly born children, even if still in hospital, have been missed

It would help the Enumerator to be able to telephone you if there is a query on, or an omission from, your form.

If you have no objection, please write your telephone number here.

Telephone number

Declaration

This form is correctly completed to the best of my knowledge and belief.

Signature(s)

Date **April 1991**

1991 Census Scotland

H form for Private Households

For office use ☐ 1 ☐ 2 ☐ 3

To the Head or Joint Heads or members of the Household aged 16 or over

Please complete this form for all members of the household, including children, and have it ready for collection on Monday 22nd April. Your census enumerator will call to collect it then or soon afterwards and will help you with the form if you have any difficulties. The enclosed leaflet explains why the Census is necessary and how the information is used.

Completion of the form is compulsory under the Census Act 1920. If you refuse to complete it, or give false information, you may have to pay a fine of up to £400.

Your answers will be treated in strict confidence and used only to produce statistics. Names and addresses will not be put into the computer; only the postcode will be entered. The forms will be kept securely within my Office and treated as confidential for 100 years.

Anyone using or disclosing Census information improperly will be liable to prosecution. For example, it would be improper for you to pass on to someone else information which you had been given in confidence by a visitor to enable you to complete the Census form.

If any member of the household aged 16 or over does not wish you, or another member of the household, to see their information, please ask the enumerator for an individual form with an envelope.

After completing the form, please sign the declaration on the last page.

Thank you for your co-operation.

CM Glennie
Registrar General for Scotland
Ladywell House, Ladywell Road, Edinburgh EH12 7TF
Telephone: 031-316 4172

To be completed by the Enumerator

Census District	Enumeration District	Form Number

Name

Address

Postcode ☐☐☐☐ ■ ☐☐ ABS ☐

Panel A
To be completed by the Enumerator and amended, if necessary, by the person(s) signing this form.

Tick one box to show the type of accommodation which this household occupies.

A caravan or other mobile or temporary structure ☐ 1

A whole house or bungalow that is
- detached ☐ 2
- semi-detached ☐ 3
- terraced (include end of terrace) ☐ 4

The whole of a purpose built flat or maisonette
- in a commercial building (for example in an office building or hotel or over a shop) ☐ 5
- in a block of flats or tenement ☐ 6

Part of a converted or shared house, bungalow or flat
- separate entrance into the building ☐ 7
- shared entrance into the building ☐ 8

Please read these instructions before filling in this form

A Household:

A household comprises either one person living alone or a group of people (not necessarily related) living at the same address with common housekeeping — that is, sharing at least one meal a day or sharing a living room or sitting room.

People staying temporarily with the household are included.

► If there is more than one household in this building, answer for your household only.

► First answer questions **H1, HL and H2** on **this page** and **H3 to H5** on the **back page** about your household and the rooms which it occupies.

► When you have answered the household questions, answer the questions on the **inside pages** about each member of your household.

► If a member of the household is completing an Individual form please still enter their name and answer questions 5 and 6 on this form.

► Then complete **Panel B** and **Panel C** on the back page.

► ***Answer each question by ticking the appropriate box or boxes ☑ where they are provided.***

► ***Please use ink or ballpoint pen.***

H1 Rooms

Please count the number of rooms your household has for its **own** use.

Do not count: small kitchens, under 2 metres (6 feet 6 inches) wide
bathrooms
toilets

Do count: living rooms
bedrooms
kitchens at least 2 metres (6 feet 6 inches) wide
all other rooms in your accommodation

The total number of rooms is ☐

HL Floor level of household's living accommodation

Which is the lowest floor on which any of your household's living accommodation is situated?
Tick box **B** or **G** or write number of floor

- Basement ☐ **B**
- Ground floor ☐ **G**
- Floor number ☐

H2 Accommodation
If box 7 or box 8 in Panel A is ticked, tick one box below to show the type of accommodation which your household occupies.

A one roomed flatlet
with private bath or shower, WC and kitchen facilities. ☐ 1

One room or bedsit, not self-contained
(to move from your room to bathroom, WC or kitchen facilities you have to use a hall, landing or stairway open to other household(s)). ☐ 2

A self-contained flat or accommodation with 2 or more rooms,
having bath or shower, WC and kitchen facilities all behind its own private door. ☐ 3

2 or more rooms, not self-contained
(to move between rooms or to bathroom, WC or kitchen facilities you have to use a hall, landing or stairway open to other household(s)). ☐ 4

Please turn to the back page and answer questions H3 to H5 ►

1-3 Name, sex and date of birth of people to be included

Important: please read the notes before answering the questions.

In answering the rest of the questions please include:

- ► every person who spends census night (21-22 April) in this household, **including anyone staying temporarily**.
- ► any other people who are usually members of the household but on census night are absent on holiday, at school or college, or for any other reason, even if they are being included on another census form elsewhere.
- ► anyone who arrives here on Monday 22nd April who was in Great Britain on the Sunday and who has not been included as present on another census form.
- ► any newly born baby born before the 22nd April, even if still in hospital. If not yet given a name, write BABY and the surname.

Write the names in BLOCK CAPITALS starting with the head or a joint head of household.

	Person No. 1	Person No. 2
Name and surname		
Sex	Male ☐ 1 / Female ☐ 2	Male ☐ 1 / Female ☐ 2
Date of birth	Day ☐ Month ☐ Year ☐	Day ☐ Month ☐ Year ☐

4 Marital status

On the 21st April what is the person's marital status?
If separated but not divorced, please tick 'Married (first marriage)' or 'Re-married' as appropriate.
Please tick one box.

Person No. 1	Person No. 2
Single (never married) ☐ 1	Single (never married) ☐ 1
Married (first marriage) ☐ 2	Married (first marriage) ☐ 2
Re-married ☐ 3	Re-married ☐ 3
Divorced ☐ 4	Divorced ☐ 4
Widowed ☐ 5	Widowed ☐ 5

5 Relationship in household

Please tick the box which indicates the relationship of each person to the person in the first column.

A step child or adopted child should be included as the son or daughter of the step or adoptive parent.

Write in relationship of 'Other relative' — for example, father, daughter-in-law, niece, uncle, cousin.

Write in position in household of an 'Unrelated' person for example, boarder, housekeeper, friend, flatmate, foster child.

Relationship to Person No.1 (Person No. 2)

- Husband or wife ☐ 1
- Living together as a couple ☐ 2
- Son or daughter ☐ 3
- Other relative ☐ *please specify* ____
- Unrelated ☐ *please specify* ____

6 Whereabouts on night of 21-22 April 1991

Please tick the appropriate box to indicate where the person was on the night of 21-22 April 1991.

Person No. 1	Person No. 2
At this address, out on night work or travelling to this address ☐ 0	At this address, out on night work or travelling to this address ☐ 0
Elsewhere in England, Scotland or Wales ☐ 1	Elsewhere in England, Scotland or Wales ☐ 1
Outside Great Britain ☐ 2	Outside Great Britain ☐ 2

7 Usual address

If the person usually lives here, please tick 'This address'. If not, tick 'Elsewhere' and write in the person's usual address.

For students and children away from home during term time, the home address should be taken as the usual address.

For any person who lives away from home for part of the week, the home address should be taken as the usual address.

Any person who is not a permanent member of the household should be asked what he or she considers to be his or her usual address.

Person No. 1	Person No. 2
This address ☐ 1	This address ☐ 1
Elsewhere ☐	Elsewhere ☐
If elsewhere, please write the person's usual address and postcode below in BLOCK CAPITALS	If elsewhere, please write the person's usual address and postcode below in BLOCK CAPITALS
Post-code	Post-code

8 Term time address of students and schoolchildren

If not a student or schoolchild, please tick first box.

For a student or schoolchild who lives here during term time, tick 'This address'.

If he or she does not live here during term time, tick 'Elsewhere' and write in the current or most recent term time address.

Person No. 1	Person No. 2
Not a student or schoolchild ☐	Not a student or schoolchild ☐
This address ☐ 1	This address ☐ 1
Elsewhere ☐	Elsewhere ☐
If elsewhere, please write the term time address and postcode below in BLOCK CAPITALS	If elsewhere, please write the term time address and postcode below in BLOCK CAPITALS
Post-code	Post-code

	Person No. 3	Person No. 4	Person No. 5	Person No. 6
Name and surname				
Sex	Male ☐ 1 Female ☐ 2	Male ☐ 1 Female ☐ 2	Male ☐ 1 Female ☐ 2	Male ☐ 1 Female ☐ 2
Date of birth	Day Month Year	Day Month Year	Day Month Year	Day Month Year
	Single (never married) ☐ 1 Married (first marriage) ☐ 2 Re-married ☐ 3 Divorced ☐ 4 Widowed ☐ 5	Single (never married) ☐ 1 Married (first marriage) ☐ 2 Re-married ☐ 3 Divorced ☐ 4 Widowed ☐ 5	Single (never married) ☐ 1 Married (first marriage) ☐ 2 Re-married ☐ 3 Divorced ☐ 4 Widowed ☐ 5	Single (never married) ☐ 1 Married (first marriage) ☐ 2 Re-married ☐ 3 Divorced ☐ 4 Widowed ☐ 5
Relationship to Person No.1	Husband or wife ☐ 1 Living together as a couple ☐ 2 Son or daughter ☐ 3 Other relative ☐ *please specify* Unrelated ☐ *please specify*	Husband or wife ☐ 1 Living together as a couple ☐ 2 Son or daughter ☐ 3 Other relative ☐ *please specify* Unrelated ☐ *please specify*	Husband or wife ☐ 1 Living together as a couple ☐ 2 Son or daughter ☐ 3 Other relative ☐ *please specify* Unrelated ☐ *please specify*	Husband or wife ☐ 1 Living together as a couple ☐ 2 Son or daughter ☐ 3 Other relative ☐ *please specify* Unrelated ☐ *please specify*
	At this address, out on night work or travelling to this address ☐ 0 Elsewhere in England, Scotland or Wales ☐ 1 Outside Great Britain ☐ 2	At this address, out on night work or travelling to this address ☐ 0 Elsewhere in England, Scotland or Wales ☐ 1 Outside Great Britain ☐ 2	At this address, out on night work or travelling to this address ☐ 0 Elsewhere in England, Scotland or Wales ☐ 1 Outside Great Britain ☐ 2	At this address, out on night work or travelling to this address ☐ 0 Elsewhere in England, Scotland or Wales ☐ 1 Outside Great Britain ☐ 2
	This address ☐ 1 Elsewhere ☐ If elsewhere, please write the person's usual address and postcode below in BLOCK CAPITALS Post-code	This address ☐ 1 Elsewhere ☐ If elsewhere, please write the person's usual address and postcode below in BLOCK CAPITALS Post-code	This address ☐ 1 Elsewhere ☐ If elsewhere, please write the person's usual address and postcode below in BLOCK CAPITALS Post-code	This address ☐ 1 Elsewhere ☐ If elsewhere, please write the person's usual address and postcode below in BLOCK CAPITALS Post-code
	Not a student or schoolchild ☐ This address ☐ 1 Elsewhere ☐ If elsewhere, please write the term time address and postcode below in BLOCK CAPITALS Post-code	Not a student or schoolchild ☐ This address ☐ 1 Elsewhere ☐ If elsewhere, please write the term time address and postcode below in BLOCK CAPITALS Post-code	Not a student or schoolchild ☐ This address ☐ 1 Elsewhere ☐ If elsewhere, please write the term time address and postcode below in BLOCK CAPITALS Post-code	Not a student or schoolchild ☐ This address ☐ 1 Elsewhere ☐ If elsewhere, please write the term time address and postcode below in BLOCK CAPITALS Post-code

Please turn over ►

1-3 Name, sex and date of birth of people to be included

Important: please read the notes before answering the questions.

In answering the rest of the questions please include:

- every person who spends census night (21-22 April) in this household, **including anyone staying temporarily.**
- any other people who are usually members of the household but on census night are absent on holiday, at school or college, or for any other reason, even if they are being included on another census form elsewhere.
- anyone who arrives here on Monday 22nd April who was in Great Britain on the Sunday and who has not been included as present on another census form.
- any newly born baby born before the 22nd April, even if still in hospital. If not yet given a name, write BABY and the surname.

Write the names in BLOCK CAPITALS starting with the head or a joint head of household.

Person No. 1	Person No. 2
Name and surname	**Name and surname**
Sex Male ☐ 1 Female ☐ 2	**Sex** Male ☐ 1 Female ☐ 2
Date of birth Day Month Year	**Date of birth** Day Month Year

9 Usual address one year ago

If the person's usual address one year ago (on the 21st April 1990) was the same as his or her current usual address (given in answer to question 7), please tick 'Same'. If not, tick 'Different' and write in the usual address one year ago.

If everyone on the form has moved from the same address, please write the address in full for the first person and indicate with an arrow that this applies to the other people on the form.

For a child born since the 21st April 1990, tick the 'Child under one' box.

Person No. 1	Person No. 2
Same as question 7 ☐ 1 Different ☐ Child under one ☐ 3	Same as question 7 ☐ 1 Different ☐ Child under one ☐ 3
If different, please write the person's address and postcode on the 21st April 1990 below in BLOCK CAPITALS	If different, please write the person's address and postcode on the 21st April 1990 below in BLOCK CAPITALS
Post-code	Post-code

10 Country of birth

Please tick the appropriate box.

If the 'Elsewhere' box is ticked, please write in the present name of the country in which the birthplace is now situated.

Person No. 1	Person No. 2
England ☐ 1 Scotland ☐ 2 Wales ☐ 3 Northern Ireland ☐ 4 Irish Republic ☐ 5 Elsewhere ☐	England ☐ 1 Scotland ☐ 2 Wales ☐ 3 Northern Ireland ☐ 4 Irish Republic ☐ 5 Elsewhere ☐
If elsewhere, please write in the present name of the country	If elsewhere, please write in the present name of the country

11 Ethnic group

Please tick the appropriate box.

If the person is descended from more than one ethnic or racial group, please tick the group to which the person considers he/she belongs, or tick the 'Any other ethnic group' box and describe the person's ancestry in the space provided.

Person No. 1	Person No. 2
White ☐ 0 Black-Caribbean ☐ 1 Black-African ☐ 2 Black-Other ☐ *please describe*	White ☐ 0 Black-Caribbean ☐ 1 Black-African ☐ 2 Black-Other ☐ *please describe*
Indian ☐ 3 Pakistani ☐ 4 Bangladeshi ☐ 5 Chinese ☐ 6 Any other ethnic group ☐ *please describe*	Indian ☐ 3 Pakistani ☐ 4 Bangladeshi ☐ 5 Chinese ☐ 6 Any other ethnic group ☐ *please describe*

12 Long-term illness

Does the person have any long-term illness, health problem or handicap which limits his/her daily activities or the work he/she can do?

Include problems which are due to old age.

Person No. 1	Person No. 2
Yes, has a health problem which limits activities ☐ 1	Yes, has a health problem which limits activities ☐ 1
Has no such health problem ☐ 2	Has no such health problem ☐ 2

Person No. 3

Name and surname

Sex Male ☐ 1
Female ☐ 2

Date of birth
Day Month Year

Person No. 4

Name and surname

Sex Male ☐ 1
Female ☐ 2

Date of birth
Day Month Year

Person No. 5

Name and surname

Sex Male ☐ 1
Female ☐ 2

Date of birth
Day Month Year

Person No. 6

Name and surname

Sex Male ☐ 1
Female ☐ 2

Date of birth
Day Month Year

Same as question 7 ☐ 1
Different ☐
Child under one ☐ 3

If different, please write the person's address and postcode on the 21st April 1990 below in BLOCK CAPITALS

Post-code

England ☐ 1
Scotland ☐ 2
Wales ☐ 3
Northern Ireland ☐ 4
Irish Republic ☐ 5
Elsewhere ☐

If elsewhere, please write in the present name of the country

White ☐ 0
Black-Caribbean ☐ 1
Black-African ☐ 2
Black-Other ☐
please describe

Indian ☐ 3
Pakistani ☐ 4
Bangladeshi ☐ 5
Chinese ☐ 6
Any other ethnic group ☐
please describe

Yes, has a health problem which limits activities ☐ 1
Has no such health problem ☐ 2

Same as question 7 ☐ 1
Different ☐
Child under one ☐ 3

If different, please write the person's address and postcode on the 21st April 1990 below in BLOCK CAPITALS

Post-code

England ☐ 1
Scotland ☐ 2
Wales ☐ 3
Northern Ireland ☐ 4
Irish Republic ☐ 5
Elsewhere ☐

If elsewhere, please write in the present name of the country

White ☐ 0
Black-Caribbean ☐ 1
Black-African ☐ 2
Black-Other ☐
please describe

Indian ☐ 3
Pakistani ☐ 4
Bangladeshi ☐ 5
Chinese ☐ 6
Any other ethnic group ☐
please describe

Yes, has a health problem which limits activities ☐ 1
Has no such health problem ☐ 2

Same as question 7 ☐ 1
Different ☐
Child under one ☐ 3

If different, please write the person's address and postcode on the 21st April 1990 below in BLOCK CAPITALS

Post-code

England ☐ 1
Scotland ☐ 2
Wales ☐ 3
Northern Ireland ☐ 4
Irish Republic ☐ 5
Elsewhere ☐

If elsewhere, please write in the present name of the country

White ☐ 0
Black-Caribbean ☐ 1
Black-African ☐ 2
Black-Other ☐
please describe

Indian ☐ 3
Pakistani ☐ 4
Bangladeshi ☐ 5
Chinese ☐ 6
Any other ethnic group ☐
please describe

Yes, has a health problem which limits activities ☐ 1
Has no such health problem ☐ 2

Same as question 7 ☐ 1
Different ☐
Child under one ☐ 3

If different, please write the person's address and postcode on the 21st April 1990 below in BLOCK CAPITALS

Post-code

England ☐ 1
Scotland ☐ 2
Wales ☐ 3
Northern Ireland ☐ 4
Irish Republic ☐ 5
Elsewhere ☐

If elsewhere, please write in the present name of the country

White ☐ 0
Black-Caribbean ☐ 1
Black-African ☐ 2
Black-Other ☐
please describe

Indian ☐ 3
Pakistani ☐ 4
Bangladeshi ☐ 5
Chinese ☐ 6
Any other ethnic group ☐
please describe

Yes, has a health problem which limits activities ☐ 1
Has no such health problem ☐ 2

Please turn over ►

1-3 **Name, sex and date of birth of people to be included**

Important: please read the notes before answering the questions.

In answering the rest of the questions please include:

- every person who spends census night (21-22 April) in this household, **including anyone staying temporarily**.
- any other people who are usually members of the household but on census night are absent on holiday, at school or college, or for any other reason, even if they are being included on another census form elsewhere.
- anyone who arrives here on Monday 22nd April who was in Great Britain on the Sunday and who has not been included as present on another census form.
- any newly born baby born before the 22nd April, even if still in hospital. If not yet given a name, write BABY and the surname.

Write the names in BLOCK CAPITALS starting with the head or a joint head of household.

Person No. 1	Person No. 2
Name and surname ☐	**Name and surname** ☐
Sex Male ☐ 1 / Female ☐ 2	**Sex** Male ☐ 1 / Female ☐ 2
Date of birth Day ☐ Month ☐ Year ☐	**Date of birth** Day ☐ Month ☐ Year ☐

This question is for all persons aged 3 or over (born before 22nd April 1988)

G **Scottish Gaelic**

Can the person speak, read or write Scottish Gaelic?

Please tick the appropriate box(es)

Person No. 1	Person No. 2
Can speak Gaelic ☐ 1	Can speak Gaelic ☐ 1
Can read Gaelic ☐ 2	Can read Gaelic ☐ 2
Can write Gaelic ☐ 4	Can write Gaelic ☐ 4
Does not know Gaelic ☐ 0	Does not know Gaelic ☐ 0

Answers to the remaining questions are not required for any person under 16 years of age (born after 21st April 1975)

13 **Whether working, retired, looking after the home etc last week**

Which of these things was the person doing **last week**?

Please read carefully right through the list and **tick all the descriptions that apply**.

Casual or temporary work should be counted at boxes 1, 2, 3 or 4. Also tick boxes 1, 2, 3 or 4 if the person had a job last week but was off sick, on holiday, temporarily laid off or on strike.

Boxes 1, 2, 3 and 4 refer to work for pay or profit but not to unpaid work except in a family business.

Working for an employer is **part time** (box 2) if the hours worked, excluding any overtime and mealbreaks, are usually 30 hours or less per week.

Include any person wanting a job but prevented from looking by holiday or temporary sickness.

Do not count training given or paid for by an employer.

Person No. 1	Person No. 2
Was working for an employer full time (more than 30 hours a week) ☐ 1	Was working for an employer full time (more than 30 hours a week) ☐ 1
Was working for an employer part time (one hour or more a week) ☐ 2	Was working for an employer part time (one hour or more a week) ☐ 2
Was self-employed, employing other people ☐ 3	Was self-employed, employing other people ☐ 3
Was self-employed, not employing other people ☐ 4	Was self-employed, not employing other people ☐ 4
Was on a government employment or training scheme ☐ 5	Was on a government employment or training scheme ☐ 5
Was waiting to start a job he/she had already accepted ☐ 6	Was waiting to start a job he/she had already accepted ☐ 6
Was unemployed and looking for a job ☐ 7	Was unemployed and looking for a job ☐ 7
Was at school or in other full time education ☐ 8	Was at school or in other full time education ☐ 8
Was unable to work because of long term sickness or disability ☐ 9	Was unable to work because of long term sickness or disability ☐ 9
Was retired from paid work ☐ 10	Was retired from paid work ☐ 10
Was looking after the home or family ☐ 11	Was looking after the home or family ☐ 11
Other ☐ *please specify*	Other ☐ *please specify*

Person No. 3	Person No. 4	Person No. 5	Person No. 6
Name and surname	**Name and surname**	**Name and surname**	**Name and surname**
Sex Male ☐ 1 Female ☐ 2	**Sex** Male ☐ 1 Female ☐ 2	**Sex** Male ☐ 1 Female ☐ 2	**Sex** Male ☐ 1 Female ☐ 2
Date of birth Day Month Year	**Date of birth** Day Month Year	**Date of birth** Day Month Year	**Date of birth** Day Month Year

This question is for all persons aged 3 or over (born before 22nd April 1988)

Person No. 3	Person No. 4	Person No. 5	Person No. 6
Can speak Gaelic ☐ 1	Can speak Gaelic ☐ 1	Can speak Gaelic ☐ 1	Can speak Gaelic ☐ 1
Can read Gaelic ☐ 2	Can read Gaelic ☐ 2	Can read Gaelic ☐ 2	Can read Gaelic ☐ 2
Can write Gaelic ☐ 4	Can write Gaelic ☐ 4	Can write Gaelic ☐ 4	Can write Gaelic ☐ 4
Does not know Gaelic ☐ 0	Does not know Gaelic ☐ 0	Does not know Gaelic ☐ 0	Does not know Gaelic ☐ 0

Answers to the remaining questions are not required for any person under 16 years of age (born after 21st April 1975)

Person No. 3	Person No. 4	Person No. 5	Person No. 6
Was working for an employer full time (more than 30 hours a week) ☐ 1	Was working for an employer full time (more than 30 hours a week) ☐ 1	Was working for an employer full time (more than 30 hours a week) ☐ 1	Was working for an employer full time (more than 30 hours a week) ☐ 1
Was working for an employer part time (one hour or more a week) ☐ 2	Was working for an employer part time (one hour or more a week) ☐ 2	Was working for an employer part time (one hour or more a week) ☐ 2	Was working for an employer part time (one hour or more a week) ☐ 2
Was self-employed, employing other people ☐ 3	Was self-employed, employing other people ☐ 3	Was self-employed, employing other people ☐ 3	Was self-employed, employing other people ☐ 3
Was self-employed, not employing other people ☐ 4	Was self-employed, not employing other people ☐ 4	Was self-employed, not employing other people ☐ 4	Was self-employed, not employing other people ☐ 4
Was on a government employment or training scheme ☐ 5	Was on a government employment or training scheme ☐ 5	Was on a government employment or training scheme ☐ 5	Was on a government employment or training scheme ☐ 5
Was waiting to start a job he/she had already accepted ☐ 6	Was waiting to start a job he/she had already accepted ☐ 6	Was waiting to start a job he/she had already accepted ☐ 6	Was waiting to start a job he/she had already accepted ☐ 6
Was unemployed and looking for a job ☐ 7	Was unemployed and looking for a job ☐ 7	Was unemployed and looking for a job ☐ 7	Was unemployed and looking for a job ☐ 7
Was at school or in other full time education ☐ 8	Was at school or in other full time education ☐ 8	Was at school or in other full time education ☐ 8	Was at school or in other full time education ☐ 8
Was unable to work because of long term sickness or disability ☐ 9	Was unable to work because of long term sickness or disability ☐ 9	Was unable to work because of long term sickness or disability ☐ 9	Was unable to work because of long term sickness or disability ☐ 9
Was retired from paid work ☐ 10	Was retired from paid work ☐ 10	Was retired from paid work ☐ 10	Was retired from paid work ☐ 10
Was looking after the home or family ☐ 11	Was looking after the home or family ☐ 11	Was looking after the home or family ☐ 11	Was looking after the home or family ☐ 11
Other ☐ *please specify*	Other ☐ *please specify*	Other ☐ *please specify*	Other ☐ *please specify*

Please turn over ►

1-3 Name, sex and date of birth of people to be included

Important: please read the notes before answering the questions.

In answering the rest of the questions please include:

- every person who spends census night (21-22 April) in this household, **including anyone staying temporarily**.
- any other people who are usually members of the household but on census night are absent on holiday, at school or college, or for any other reason, even if they are being included on another census form elsewhere.
- anyone who arrives here on Monday 22nd April who was in Great Britain on the Sunday and who has not been included as present on another census form.
- any newly born baby born before the 22nd April, even if still in hospital. If not yet given a name, write BABY and the surname.

Write the names in BLOCK CAPITALS starting with the head or a joint head of household.

Person No. 1	Person No. 2
Name and surname	**Name and surname**
Sex Male ☐ 1 Female ☐ 2	**Sex** Male ☐ 1 Female ☐ 2
Date of birth Day Month Year	**Date of birth** Day Month Year

Please read A below, tick the box that applies and follow the instruction by the box ticked.

	Person No. 1	Person No. 2
A Did the person have a paid job last week (any of the boxes 1, 2, 3 or 4 ticked at question 13)?	YES ☐ Answer questions 14, 15, 16, 17 and 18 about the main job last week, then go on to question 19 NO ☐ Answer B	YES ☐ Answer questions 14, 15, 16, 17 and 18 about the main job last week, then go on to question 19 NO ☐ Answer B
B Has the person had a paid job within the last 10 years?	YES ☐ Answer questions 14, 15 and 16 about the most recent job, then go on to question 19 NO ☐ Go on to question 19	YES ☐ Answer questions 14, 15 and 16 about the most recent job, then go on to question 19 NO ☐ Go on to question 19

14 Hours worked per week

How many hours per week does or did the person usually work in his or her main job?

Do not count overtime or meal breaks.

Person No. 1	Person No. 2
Number of hours worked per week ☐	Number of hours worked per week ☐

15 Occupation

Please give the full title of the person's present or last job and describe the main things he/she does or did in the job.

At a, give the full title by which the job is known, for example: 'packing machinist'; 'poultry processor'; 'jig and tool fitter'; 'supervisor of typists'; 'accounts clerk'; rather than general titles like 'machinist'; 'process worker'; 'supervisor' or 'clerk'. Give rank or grade if the person has one.

At b, write down the main things the person actually does or did in the job. If possible ask him/her to say what these things are and write them down.

Armed Forces — enter 'commissioned officer' or 'other rank' as appropriate at **a**, and leave **b** blank.

Civil Servants — give grade at **a** and discipline or specialism, for example: 'electrical engineer'; 'accountant'; 'chemist'; 'administrator' at **b**.

Person No. 1	Person No. 2
a Full job title	**a** Full job title
b Main things done in job	**b** Main things done in job

16 Name and business of employer (if self-employed give the name and nature of the person's business)

At a, please give the name of the employer. Give the trading name if one is used. Do not use abbreviations.

At b, describe clearly what the employer (or the person if self-employed) makes or does (or did).

Armed Forces — write 'Armed Forces' at **a** and leave **b** blank. For a member of the Armed Forces of a country other than the UK — add the name of the country.

Civil Servants — give name of Department at **a** and write 'Government Department' at **b**.

Local Government Officers — give name of employing authority at **a** and department in which employed at **b**.

Person No. 1	Person No. 2
a Name of employer	**a** Name of employer
b Description of employer's business	**b** Description of employer's business

Person No. 3	Person No. 4	Person No. 5	Person No. 6
Name and surname	**Name and surname**	**Name and surname**	**Name and surname**
Sex Male ☐ 1 Female ☐ 2	**Sex** Male ☐ 1 Female ☐ 2	**Sex** Male ☐ 1 Female ☐ 2	**Sex** Male ☐ 1 Female ☐ 2
Date of birth Day Month Year	**Date of birth** Day Month Year	**Date of birth** Day Month Year	**Date of birth** Day Month Year

This will tell you which questions to answer for each person.

YES ☐ Answer questions 14, 15, 16, 17 and 18 about the main job last week, then go on to question 19 NO ☐ Answer B	YES ☐ Answer questions 14, 15, 16, 17 and 18 about the main job last week, then go on to question 19 NO ☐ Answer B	YES ☐ Answer questions 14, 15, 16, 17 and 18 about the main job last week, then go on to question 19 NO ☐ Answer B	YES ☐ Answer questions 14, 15, 16, 17 and 18 about the main job last week, then go on to question 19 NO ☐ Answer B
YES ☐ Answer questions 14, 15 and 16 about the most recent job, then go on to question 19 NO ☐ Go on to question 19	YES ☐ Answer questions 14, 15 and 16 about the most recent job, then go on to question 19 NO ☐ Go on to question 19	YES ☐ Answer questions 14, 15 and 16 about the most recent job, then go on to question 19 NO ☐ Go on to question 19	YES ☐ Answer questions 14, 15 and 16 about the most recent job, then go on to question 19 NO ☐ Go on to question 19
Number of hours worked per week	Number of hours worked per week	Number of hours worked per week	Number of hours worked per week
a Full job title	**a** Full job title	**a** Full job title	**a** Full job title
b Main things done in job	**b** Main things done in job	**b** Main things done in job	**b** Main things done in job
a Name of employer	**a** Name of employer	**a** Name of employer	**a** Name of employer
b Description of employer's business	**b** Description of employer's business	**b** Description of employer's business	**b** Description of employer's business

Please turn over ►

	Question	Person No. 1	Person No. 2
1-3	**Name, sex and date of birth of people to be included** **Important:** please read the notes before answering the questions. In answering the rest of the questions please include: ► every person who spends census night (21-22 April) in this household, **including anyone staying temporarily**. ► any other people who are usually members of the household but on census night are absent on holiday, at school or college, or for any other reason, even if they are being included on another census form elsewhere. ► anyone who arrives here on Monday 22nd April who was in Great Britain on the Sunday and who has not been included as present on another census form. ► any newly born baby born before the 22nd April, even if still in hospital. If not yet given a name, write BABY and the surname. **Write the names in BLOCK CAPITALS starting with the head or a joint head of household.**	**Name and surname** **Sex** Male ☐ 1 Female ☐ 2 **Date of birth** Day Month Year	**Name and surname** **Sex** Male ☐ 1 Female ☐ 2 **Date of birth** Day Month Year
17	**Address of place of work** Please give the full address of the person's place of work. For a person employed on a site for a long period, give the address of the site. For a person employed on an offshore installation, write 'offshore installation'. For a person not working regularly at one place who reports daily to a depot or other fixed address, give that address. For a person not reporting daily to a fixed address, tick box 1. For a person working mainly at home, tick box 2. **Armed Forces** — leave blank.	Please write full address and postcode of workplace below in BLOCK CAPITALS Post-code No fixed place ☐ 1 Mainly at home ☐ 2	Please write full address and postcode of workplace below in BLOCK CAPITALS Post-code No fixed place ☐ 1 Mainly at home ☐ 2
18	**Daily journey to work** Please tick the appropriate box to show how the longest part, by distance, of the person's daily journey to work is normally made. For a person using different means of transport on different days, show the means most often used. Car or van includes three-wheeled cars and motor caravans.	British Rail train ☐ 1 Underground, tube, metro ☐ 2 Bus, minibus or coach (public or private) ☐ 3 Motor cycle, scooter, moped ☐ 4 Driving a car or van ☐ 5 Passenger in car or van ☐ 6 Pedal cycle ☐ 7 On foot ☐ 8 Other ☐ 9 *please specify* Works mainly at home ☐ 0	British Rail train ☐ 1 Underground, tube, metro ☐ 2 Bus, minibus or coach (public or private) ☐ 3 Motor cycle, scooter, moped ☐ 4 Driving a car or van ☐ 5 Passenger in car or van ☐ 6 Pedal cycle ☐ 7 On foot ☐ 8 Other ☐ 9 *please specify* Works mainly at home ☐ 0
19	**Degrees, professional and vocational qualifications** Has the person obtained any qualifications after reaching the age of 18 such as: -degrees, diplomas, HNC, HND, -nursing qualifications, -teaching qualifications (see * below), -graduate or corporate membership of professional institutions, -other professional, educational or vocational qualifications? Do not count qualifications normally obtained at school such as GCE, CSE, GCSE, SCE and school certificates. If box 2 is ticked, write in all qualifications even if they are not relevant to the person's present job or if the person is not working. Please list the qualifications in the order in which they were obtained. If more than three, please enter in a spare column and link with an arrow. *For a person with **school teaching qualifications**, give the full title of the qualification, such as 'Certificate of Education' and the subject(s) which the person is qualified to teach. The subject 'education' should then only be shown if the course had no other subject specialisation.	NO — no such qualifications ☐ 1 YES — give details ☐ 2 1 Title Subject(s) Year Institution 2 Title Subject(s) Year Institution 3 Title Subject(s) Year Institution	NO — no such qualifications ☐ 1 YES — give details ☐ 2 1 Title Subject(s) Year Institution 2 Title Subject(s) Year Institution 3 Title Subject(s) Year Institution

Person No. 3

Name and surname

Sex Male ☐ 1 Female ☐ 2

Date of birth
Day Month Year

Please write full address and postcode of workplace below in BLOCK CAPITALS

Post-code

No fixed place ☐ 1
Mainly at home ☐ 2

British Rail train ☐ 1
Underground, tube, metro ☐ 2
Bus, minibus or coach (public or private) ☐ 3
Motor cycle, scooter, moped ☐ 4
Driving a car or van ☐ 5
Passenger in car or van ☐ 6
Pedal cycle ☐ 7
On foot ☐ 8
Other ☐ 9
please specify

Works mainly at home ☐ 0

NO — no such qualifications ☐ 1
YES — give details ☐ 2

1 Title
Subject(s)
Year
Institution

2 Title
Subject(s)
Year
Institution

3 Title
Subject(s)
Year
Institution

Person No. 4

Name and surname

Sex Male ☐ 1 Female ☐ 2

Date of birth
Day Month Year

Please write full address and postcode of workplace below in BLOCK CAPITALS

Post-code

No fixed place ☐ 1
Mainly at home ☐ 2

British Rail train ☐ 1
Underground, tube, metro ☐ 2
Bus, minibus or coach (public or private) ☐ 3
Motor cycle, scooter, moped ☐ 4
Driving a car or van ☐ 5
Passenger in car or van ☐ 6
Pedal cycle ☐ 7
On foot ☐ 8
Other ☐ 9
please specify

Works mainly at home ☐ 0

NO — no such qualifications ☐ 1
YES — give details ☐ 2

1 Title
Subject(s)
Year
Institution

2 Title
Subject(s)
Year
Institution

3 Title
Subject(s)
Year
Institution

Person No. 5

Name and surname

Sex Male ☐ 1 Female ☐ 2

Date of birth
Day Month Year

Please write full address and postcode of workplace below in BLOCK CAPITALS

Post-code

No fixed place ☐ 1
Mainly at home ☐ 2

British Rail train ☐ 1
Underground, tube, metro ☐ 2
Bus, minibus or coach (public or private) ☐ 3
Motor cycle, scooter, moped ☐ 4
Driving a car or van ☐ 5
Passenger in car or van ☐ 6
Pedal cycle ☐ 7
On foot ☐ 8
Other ☐ 9
please specify

Works mainly at home ☐ 0

NO — no such qualifications ☐ 1
YES — give details ☐ 2

1 Title
Subject(s)
Year
Institution

2 Title
Subject(s)
Year
Institution

3 Title
Subject(s)
Year
Institution

Person No. 6

Name and surname

Sex Male ☐ 1 Female ☐ 2

Date of birth
Day Month Year

Please write full address and postcode of workplace below in BLOCK CAPITALS

Post-code

No fixed place ☐ 1
Mainly at home ☐ 2

British Rail train ☐ 1
Underground, tube, metro ☐ 2
Bus, minibus or coach (public or private) ☐ 3
Motor cycle, scooter, moped ☐ 4
Driving a car or van ☐ 5
Passenger in car or van ☐ 6
Pedal cycle ☐ 7
On foot ☐ 8
Other ☐ 9
please specify

Works mainly at home ☐ 0

NO — no such qualifications ☐ 1
YES — give details ☐ 2

1 Title
Subject(s)
Year
Institution

2 Title
Subject(s)
Year
Institution

3 Title
Subject(s)
Year
Institution

Please turn over and complete Panels B and C ►

H3 Tenure

Please tick the box which best describes how you and your household occupy your accommodation.

If buying by stages from a Council, Housing Association, New Town or Scottish Homes (under shared ownership, co-ownership or equity sharing scheme), answer as an owner-occupier at box 1.

As an owner-occupier:

- -buying the property through mortgage or loan ☐ 1
- -owning the property outright (no loan) ☐ 2

By renting, rent free or by lease:

If your accommodation is occupied by lease originally granted for, or extended to, more than 20 years, answer as an owner-occupier.
For shorter leases, answer 'By renting'.

- -with a job, farm, shop or other business ☐ 3
- -from a local authority (Council) ☐ 4
- -from a New Town Development Corporation ☐ 5
- -from Scottish Homes ☐ 0
- -from a housing association or charitable trust ☐ 6

A private landlord may be a person or a company or another organisation not mentioned at 3, 4, 5, 0 or 6 above.

- -from a private landlord, furnished ☐ 7
- -from a private landlord, unfurnished ☐ 8

In some other way:

- -please give details below ☐

H4 Amenities

Does your household — that is, you and any people who usually live here with you — **have the use of:**

a A bath or shower?

- **Yes** — for use only by this household ☐ 1
- **Yes** — for use also by another household ☐ 2
- **No** — no bath or shower available ☐ 3

b A flush toilet (WC) with entrance inside the building?

- **Yes** — for use only by this household ☐ 0
- **Yes** — for use also by another household ☐ 1
- **No** — flush toilet with outside entrance only ☐ 2
- **No** — no flush toilet indoors or outdoors ☐ 3

c Central heating in living rooms and bedrooms (including night storage heaters, warm air or under-floor heating), whether actually used or not?

- **Yes** — all living rooms and bedrooms centrally heated ☐ 1
- **Yes** — some (not all) living rooms and bedrooms centrally heated ☐ 2
- **No** — no living rooms or bedrooms centrally heated ☐ 3

H5 Cars and vans

Please tick the appropriate box to indicate the number of cars and vans normally available for use by you or members of your household (other than visitors).

Include any car or van provided by employers if normally available for use by you or members of your household, but **exclude** vans used only for carrying goods.

- None ☐ 0
- One ☐ 1
- Two ☐ 2
- Three or more ☐ 3

◄ **Please turn to the first inside page**

Panel B

Was there anyone else (such as a visitor) here on the night of 21-22 April whom you have not included because there was no room on the form? No ☐ Yes ☐

If **yes** ticked, please ask the Enumerator for another form.

Have you left anyone out because you were not sure whether they should be included on the form? No ☐ Yes ☐

If **yes** ticked, please give their names and the reason why you were not sure about including them.

Name

Reason

Name

Reason

Name

Reason

Panel C

Before you sign the form, will you please check:

- ► that all questions which should have been answered have been answered for every member of your household
- ► that you have included everyone who spent the night of 21-22 April in your household
- ► that you have included everyone who usually lives here but was away from home on the night of 21-22 April
- ► that no visitors, boarders or newly born children, even if still in hospital, have been missed

It would help the Enumerator to be able to telephone you if there is a query on, or an omission from, your form.

If you have no objection, please write your telephone number here.

Telephone number

Declaration

This form is correctly completed to the best of my knowledge and belief.

Signature(s)

Date **April 1991**

1991 Census Wales

W form for Private Households

This form is available in English and Welsh. If you have not received the version you require, please telephone 0329 844444

Mae'r ffurflen hon ar gael yn Gymraeg ac yn Saesneg. Os na chawsoch y fersiwn y mae ei eisiau arnoch, ffoniwch 0329 844444

For office use ☐ 1 ☐ 2 ☐ 3

To the Head or Joint Heads or members of the Household aged 16 or over

Please complete this form for all members of the household, including children, and have it ready for collection on Monday 22nd April. Your census enumerator will call to collect it then or soon afterwards and will help you with the form if you have any difficulties. The enclosed leaflet explains why the Census is necessary and how the information is used.

Completion of the form is compulsory under the Census Act 1920. If you refuse to complete it, or give false information, you may have to pay a fine of up to £400.

Your answers will be treated in strict confidence and used only to produce statistics. Names and addresses will not be put into the computer; only the postcode will be entered. The forms will be kept securely within my Office and treated as confidential for 100 years.

Anyone using or disclosing Census information improperly will be liable to prosecution. For example, it would be improper for you to pass on to someone else information which you had been given in confidence by a visitor to enable you to complete the Census form.

If any member of the household aged 16 or over does not wish you, or another member of the household, to see their information, please ask the enumerator for an individual form with an envelope.

After completing the form, please sign the declaration on the last page.

Thank you for your co-operation.

P J Wormald
Registrar General
Office of Population Censuses and Surveys
PO Box 100 Fareham PO16 0AL
Telephone: 0329 844444

Please read these instructions before filling in this form

A Household:

A household comprises either one person living alone or a group of people (not necessarily related) living at the same address with common housekeeping — that is, sharing at least one meal a day or sharing a living room or sitting room.

People staying temporarily with the household are included.

- ▶ If there is more than one household in this building, answer for your household only.
- ▶ First answer questions **H1 and H2** on **this page** and **H3 to H5** on the **back page** about your household and the rooms which it occupies.
- ▶ When you have answered the household questions, answer the questions on the **inside pages** about each member of your household.
- ▶ If a member of the household is completing an Individual form please still enter their name and answer questions 5 and 6 on this form.
- ▶ Then complete **Panel B** and **Panel C** on the back page.
- ▶ ***Answer each question by ticking the appropriate box or boxes ☑ where they are provided.***
- ▶ ***Please use ink or ballpoint pen.***

To be completed by the Enumerator

Census District ☐ **Enumeration District** ☐ Form Number ☐

Name

Address

Postcode ☐☐☐☐☐☐☐☐ **ABS** ☐

H1 Rooms

Please count the number of rooms your household has for its **own** use.

Do not count: small kitchens, under 2 metres (6 feet 6 inches) wide
bathrooms
toilets

Do count: living rooms
bedrooms
kitchens at least 2 metres (6 feet 6 inches) wide
all other rooms in your accommodation

The total number of rooms is ☐

Panel A
To be completed by the Enumerator and amended, if necessary, by the person(s) signing this form.

Tick one box to show the type of accommodation which this household occupies.

A caravan or other mobile or temporary structure ☐ 1

A whole house or bungalow that is
- detached ☐ 2
- semi-detached ☐ 3
- terraced (include end of terrace) ☐ 4

The whole of a purpose built flat or maisonette
- in a commercial building (for example in an office building or hotel or over a shop) ☐ 5
- in a block of flats or tenement ☐ 6

Part of a converted or shared house, bungalow or flat
- separate entrance into the building ☐ 7
- shared entrance into the building ☐ 8

H2 Accommodation
If box 7 or box 8 in Panel A is ticked, tick one box below to show the type of accommodation which your household occupies.

A one roomed flatlet
with private bath or shower, WC and kitchen facilities. ☐ 1

One room or bedsit, not self-contained
(to move from your room to bathroom, WC or kitchen facilities you have to use a hall, landing or stairway open to other household(s)). ☐ 2

A self-contained flat or accommodation with 2 or more rooms,
having bath or shower, WC and kitchen facilities all behind its own private door. ☐ 3

2 or more rooms, not self-contained
(to move between rooms or to bathroom, WC or kitchen facilities you have to use a hall, landing or stairway open to other household(s)). ☐ 4

Please turn to the back page and answer questions H3 to H5 ▶

1-3 Name, sex and date of birth of people to be included

Important: please read the notes before answering the questions.

In answering the rest of the questions please include:

- every person who spends census night (21-22 April) in this household, **including anyone staying temporarily**.
- any other people who are usually members of the household but on census night are absent on holiday, at school or college, or for any other reason, even if they are being included on another census form elsewhere.
- anyone who arrives here on Monday 22nd April who was in Great Britain on the Sunday and who has not been included as present on another census form.
- any newly born baby born before the 22nd April, even if still in hospital. If not yet given a name, write BABY and the surname.

Write the names in BLOCK CAPITALS starting with the head or a joint head of household.

	Person No. 1	Person No. 2
Name and surname	☐	☐
Sex	Male ☐ 1 Female ☐ 2	Male ☐ 1 Female ☐ 2
Date of birth	Day ☐ Month ☐ Year ☐	Day ☐ Month ☐ Year ☐

4 Marital status

On the 21st April what is the person's marital status?
If separated but not divorced, please tick 'Married (first marriage)' or 'Re-married' as appropriate.
Please tick one box.

Person No. 1	Person No. 2
Single (never married) ☐ 1 Married (first marriage) ☐ 2 Re-married ☐ 3 Divorced (decree absolute) ☐ 4 Widowed ☐ 5	Single (never married) ☐ 1 Married (first marriage) ☐ 2 Re-married ☐ 3 Divorced (decree absolute) ☐ 4 Widowed ☐ 5

5 Relationship in household

Please tick the box which indicates the relationship of each person to the person in the first column.

A step child or adopted child should be included as the son or daughter of the step or adoptive parent.

Write in relationship of 'Other relative' — for example, father, daughter-in-law, niece, uncle, cousin.

Write in position in household of an 'Unrelated' person for example, boarder, housekeeper, friend, flatmate, foster child.

Person No. 2
Relationship to Person No.1 Husband or wife ☐ 1 Living together as a couple ☐ 2 Son or daughter ☐ 3 Other relative ☐ *please specify* ☐ Unrelated ☐ *please specify* ☐

6 Whereabouts on night of 21-22 April 1991

Please tick the appropriate box to indicate where the person was on the night of 21-22 April 1991.

Person No. 1	Person No. 2
At this address, out on night work or travelling to this address ☐ 0 Elsewhere in England, Scotland or Wales ☐ 1 Outside Great Britain ☐ 2	At this address, out on night work or travelling to this address ☐ 0 Elsewhere in England, Scotland or Wales ☐ 1 Outside Great Britain ☐ 2

7 Usual address

If the person usually lives here, please tick 'This address'. If not, tick 'Elsewhere' and write in the person's usual address.

For students and children away from home during term time, the home address should be taken as the usual address.

For any person who lives away from home for part of the week, the home address should be taken as the usual address.

Any person who is not a permanent member of the household should be asked what he or she considers to be his or her usual address.

Person No. 1	Person No. 2
This address ☐ 1 Elsewhere ☐ If elsewhere, please write the person's usual address and postcode below in BLOCK CAPITALS ☐ Post-code ☐	This address ☐ 1 Elsewhere ☐ If elsewhere, please write the person's usual address and postcode below in BLOCK CAPITALS ☐ Post-code ☐

8 Term time address of students and schoolchildren

If not a student or schoolchild, please tick first box.

For a student or schoolchild who lives here during term time, tick 'This address'.

If he or she does not live here during term time, tick 'Elsewhere' and write in the current or most recent term time address.

Person No. 1	Person No. 2
Not a student or schoolchild ☐ This address ☐ 1 Elsewhere ☐ If elsewhere, please write the term time address and postcode below in BLOCK CAPITALS ☐ Post-code ☐	Not a student or schoolchild ☐ This address ☐ 1 Elsewhere ☐ If elsewhere, please write the term time address and postcode below in BLOCK CAPITALS ☐ Post-code ☐

Person No. 3

Name and surname

Sex Male ☐ 1 Female ☐ 2

Date of birth
Day Month Year

Person No. 4

Name and surname

Sex Male ☐ 1 Female ☐ 2

Date of birth
Day Month Year

Person No. 5

Name and surname

Sex Male ☐ 1 Female ☐ 2

Date of birth
Day Month Year

Person No. 6

Name and surname

Sex Male ☐ 1 Female ☐ 2

Date of birth
Day Month Year

Single (never married) ☐ 1
Married (first marriage) ☐ 2
Re-married ☐ 3
Divorced (decree absolute) ☐ 4
Widowed ☐ 5

Relationship to Person No.1
Husband or wife ☐ 1
Living together as a couple ☐ 2
Son or daughter ☐ 3
Other relative ☐ *please specify*

Unrelated ☐ *please specify*

At this address, out on night work or travelling to this address ☐ 0
Elsewhere in England, Scotland or Wales ☐ 1
Outside Great Britain ☐ 2

This address ☐ 1
Elsewhere ☐
If elsewhere, please write the person's usual address and postcode below in BLOCK CAPITALS

Post-code

Not a student or schoolchild ☐
This address ☐ 1
Elsewhere ☐
If elsewhere, please write the term time address and postcode below in BLOCK CAPITALS

Post-code

(The above questions are printed identically in each of the four columns for Persons No. 3, 4, 5 and 6.)

Please turn over ►

1-3 Name, sex and date of birth of people to be included

Important: please read the notes before answering the questions.

In answering the rest of the questions please include:

- every person who spends census night (21-22 April) in this household, **including anyone staying temporarily**.
- any other people who are usually members of the household but on census night are absent on holiday, at school or college, or for any other reason, even if they are being included on another census form elsewhere.
- anyone who arrives here on Monday 22nd April who was in Great Britain on the Sunday and who has not been included as present on another census form.
- any newly born baby born before the 22nd April, even if still in hospital. If not yet given a name, write BABY and the surname.

Write the names in BLOCK CAPITALS starting with the head or a joint head of household.

Person No. 1	Person No. 2
Name and surname	**Name and surname**
Sex Male ☐ 1 Female ☐ 2	**Sex** Male ☐ 1 Female ☐ 2
Date of birth Day Month Year	**Date of birth** Day Month Year

9 Usual address one year ago

If the person's usual address one year ago (on the 21st April 1990) was the same as his or her current usual address (given in answer to question 7), please tick 'Same'. If not, tick 'Different' and write in the usual address one year ago.

If everyone on the form has moved from the same address, please write the address in full for the first person and indicate with an arrow that this applies to the other people on the form.

For a child born since the 21st April 1990, tick the 'Child under one' box.

Person No. 1	Person No. 2
Same as question 7 ☐ 1	Same as question 7 ☐ 1
Different ☐	Different ☐
Child under one ☐ 3	Child under one ☐ 3
If different, please write the person's address and postcode on the 21st April 1990 below in BLOCK CAPITALS	If different, please write the person's address and postcode on the 21st April 1990 below in BLOCK CAPITALS
Post-code	Post-code

10 Country of birth

Please tick the appropriate box.

If the 'Elsewhere' box is ticked, please write in the present name of the country in which the birthplace is now situated.

Person No. 1	Person No. 2
England ☐ 1	England ☐ 1
Scotland ☐ 2	Scotland ☐ 2
Wales ☐ 3	Wales ☐ 3
Northern Ireland ☐ 4	Northern Ireland ☐ 4
Irish Republic ☐ 5	Irish Republic ☐ 5
Elsewhere ☐	Elsewhere ☐
If elsewhere, please write in the present name of the country	If elsewhere, please write in the present name of the country

11 Ethnic group

Please tick the appropriate box.

If the person is descended from more than one ethnic or racial group, please tick the group to which the person considers he/she belongs, or tick the 'Any other ethnic group' box and describe the person's ancestry in the space provided.

Person No. 1	Person No. 2
White ☐ 0	White ☐ 0
Black-Caribbean ☐ 1	Black-Caribbean ☐ 1
Black-African ☐ 2	Black-African ☐ 2
Black-Other ☐ *please describe*	Black-Other ☐ *please describe*
Indian ☐ 3	Indian ☐ 3
Pakistani ☐ 4	Pakistani ☐ 4
Bangladeshi ☐ 5	Bangladeshi ☐ 5
Chinese ☐ 6	Chinese ☐ 6
Any other ethnic group ☐ *please describe*	Any other ethnic group ☐ *please describe*

12 Long-term illness

Does the person have any long-term illness, health problem or handicap which limits his/her daily activities or the work he/she can do?

Include problems which are due to old age.

Person No. 1	Person No. 2
Yes, has a health problem which limits activities ☐ 1	Yes, has a health problem which limits activities ☐ 1
Has no such health problem ☐ 2	Has no such health problem ☐ 2

Person No. 3	**Person No. 4**	**Person No. 5**	**Person No. 6**
Name and surname	Name and surname	Name and surname	Name and surname
Sex Male ☐ 1 Female ☐ 2	**Sex** Male ☐ 1 Female ☐ 2	**Sex** Male ☐ 1 Female ☐ 2	**Sex** Male ☐ 1 Female ☐ 2
Date of birth Day Month Year	**Date of birth** Day Month Year	**Date of birth** Day Month Year	**Date of birth** Day Month Year

Same as question 7 ☐ 1 Different ☐ Child under one ☐ 3 If different, please write the person's address and postcode on the 21st April 1990 below in BLOCK CAPITALS Post-code	Same as question 7 ☐ 1 Different ☐ Child under one ☐ 3 If different, please write the person's address and postcode on the 21st April 1990 below in BLOCK CAPITALS Post-code	Same as question 7 ☐ 1 Different ☐ Child under one ☐ 3 If different, please write the person's address and postcode on the 21st April 1990 below in BLOCK CAPITALS Post-code	Same as question 7 ☐ 1 Different ☐ Child under one ☐ 3 If different, please write the person's address and postcode on the 21st April 1990 below in BLOCK CAPITALS Post-code
England ☐ 1 Scotland ☐ 2 Wales ☐ 3 Northern Ireland ☐ 4 Irish Republic ☐ 5 Elsewhere ☐ If elsewhere, please write in the present name of the country	England ☐ 1 Scotland ☐ 2 Wales ☐ 3 Northern Ireland ☐ 4 Irish Republic ☐ 5 Elsewhere ☐ If elsewhere, please write in the present name of the country	England ☐ 1 Scotland ☐ 2 Wales ☐ 3 Northern Ireland ☐ 4 Irish Republic ☐ 5 Elsewhere ☐ If elsewhere, please write in the present name of the country	England ☐ 1 Scotland ☐ 2 Wales ☐ 3 Northern Ireland ☐ 4 Irish Republic ☐ 5 Elsewhere ☐ If elsewhere, please write in the present name of the country
White ☐ 0 Black-Caribbean ☐ 1 Black-African ☐ 2 Black-Other ☐ *please describe* Indian ☐ 3 Pakistani ☐ 4 Bangladeshi ☐ 5 Chinese ☐ 6 Any other ethnic group ☐ *please describe*	White ☐ 0 Black-Caribbean ☐ 1 Black-African ☐ 2 Black-Other ☐ *please describe* Indian ☐ 3 Pakistani ☐ 4 Bangladeshi ☐ 5 Chinese ☐ 6 Any other ethnic group ☐ *please describe*	White ☐ 0 Black-Caribbean ☐ 1 Black-African ☐ 2 Black-Other ☐ *please describe* Indian ☐ 3 Pakistani ☐ 4 Bangladeshi ☐ 5 Chinese ☐ 6 Any other ethnic group ☐ *please describe*	White ☐ 0 Black-Caribbean ☐ 1 Black-African ☐ 2 Black-Other ☐ *please describe* Indian ☐ 3 Pakistani ☐ 4 Bangladeshi ☐ 5 Chinese ☐ 6 Any other ethnic group ☐ *please describe*
Yes, has a health problem which limits activities ☐ 1 Has no such health problem ☐ 2	Yes, has a health problem which limits activities ☐ 1 Has no such health problem ☐ 2	Yes, has a health problem which limits activities ☐ 1 Has no such health problem ☐ 2	Yes, has a health problem which limits activities ☐ 1 Has no such health problem ☐ 2

Please turn over ►

1-3 **Name, sex and date of birth of people to be included**

Important: please read the notes before answering the questions.

In answering the rest of the questions please include:

- every person who spends census night (21-22 April) in this household, **including anyone staying temporarily**.
- any other people who are usually members of the household but on census night are absent on holiday, at school or college, or for any other reason, even if they are being included on another census form elsewhere.
- anyone who arrives here on Monday 22nd April who was in Great Britain on the Sunday and who has not been included as present on another census form.
- any newly born baby born before the 22nd April, even if still in hospital. If not yet given a name, write BABY and the surname.

Write the names in BLOCK CAPITALS starting with the head or a joint head of household.

	Person No. 1	Person No. 2
Name and surname		
Sex	Male ☐ 1 Female ☐ 2	Male ☐ 1 Female ☐ 2
Date of birth	Day Month Year	Day Month Year

This question is for all persons aged 3 or over (born before 22nd April 1988)

W **Welsh language**

Does the person speak, read or write Welsh?

Please tick the appropriate box(es)

Person No. 1	Person No. 2
Speaks Welsh ☐ 1	Speaks Welsh ☐ 1
Reads Welsh ☐ 2	Reads Welsh ☐ 2
Writes Welsh ☐ 4	Writes Welsh ☐ 4
Does not speak, read or write Welsh ☐ 0	Does not speak, read or write Welsh ☐ 0

Answers to the remaining questions are not required for any person under 16 years of age (born after 21st April 1975)

13 **Whether working, retired, looking after the home etc last week**

Which of these things was the person doing **last week**?

Please read carefully right through the list and **tick all the descriptions that apply**.

Casual or temporary work should be counted at boxes 1, 2, 3 or 4. Also tick boxes 1, 2, 3 or 4 if the person had a job last week but was off sick, on holiday, temporarily laid off or on strike.

Boxes 1, 2, 3 and 4 refer to work for pay or profit but not to unpaid work except in a family business.

Working for an employer is **part time** (box 2) if the hours worked, excluding any overtime and mealbreaks, are usually 30 hours or less per week.

Include any person wanting a job but prevented from looking by holiday or temporary sickness.

Do not count training given or paid for by an employer.

Person No. 1	Person No. 2
Was working for an employer full time (more than 30 hours a week) ☐ 1	Was working for an employer full time (more than 30 hours a week) ☐ 1
Was working for an employer part time (one hour or more a week) ☐ 2	Was working for an employer part time (one hour or more a week) ☐ 2
Was self-employed, employing other people ☐ 3	Was self-employed, employing other people ☐ 3
Was self-employed, not employing other people ☐ 4	Was self-employed, not employing other people ☐ 4
Was on a government employment or training scheme ☐ 5	Was on a government employment or training scheme ☐ 5
Was waiting to start a job he/she had already accepted ☐ 6	Was waiting to start a job he/she had already accepted ☐ 6
Was unemployed and looking for a job ☐ 7	Was unemployed and looking for a job ☐ 7
Was at school or in other full time education ☐ 8	Was at school or in other full time education ☐ 8
Was unable to work because of long term sickness or disability ☐ 9	Was unable to work because of long term sickness or disability ☐ 9
Was retired from paid work ☐ 10	Was retired from paid work ☐ 10
Was looking after the home or family ☐ 11	Was looking after the home or family ☐ 11
Other ☐ *please specify*	Other ☐ *please specify*

Person No. 3	Person No. 4	Person No. 5	Person No. 6
Name and surname	Name and surname	Name and surname	Name and surname
Sex Male ☐ 1 Female ☐ 2	Sex Male ☐ 1 Female ☐ 2	Sex Male ☐ 1 Female ☐ 2	Sex Male ☐ 1 Female ☐ 2
Date of birth Day Month Year	Date of birth Day Month Year	Date of birth Day Month Year	Date of birth Day Month Year

This question is for all persons aged 3 or over (born before 22nd April 1988)

Speaks Welsh ☐ 1	Speaks Welsh ☐ 1	Speaks Welsh ☐ 1	Speaks Welsh ☐ 1
Reads Welsh ☐ 2	Reads Welsh ☐ 2	Reads Welsh ☐ 2	Reads Welsh ☐ 2
Writes Welsh ☐ 4	Writes Welsh ☐ 4	Writes Welsh ☐ 4	Writes Welsh ☐ 4
Does not speak, read or write Welsh ☐ 0	Does not speak, read or write Welsh ☐ 0	Does not speak, read or write Welsh ☐ 0	Does not speak, read or write Welsh ☐ 0

Answers to the remaining questions are not required for any person under 16 years of age (born after 21st April 1975)

Was working for an employer full time (more than 30 hours a week) ☐ 1	Was working for an employer full time (more than 30 hours a week) ☐ 1	Was working for an employer full time (more than 30 hours a week) ☐ 1	Was working for an employer full time (more than 30 hours a week) ☐ 1
Was working for an employer part time (one hour or more a week) ☐ 2	Was working for an employer part time (one hour or more a week) ☐ 2	Was working for an employer part time (one hour or more a week) ☐ 2	Was working for an employer part time (one hour or more a week) ☐ 2
Was self-employed, employing other people ☐ 3	Was self-employed, employing other people ☐ 3	Was self-employed, employing other people ☐ 3	Was self-employed, employing other people ☐ 3
Was self-employed, not employing other people ☐ 4	Was self-employed, not employing other people ☐ 4	Was self-employed, not employing other people ☐ 4	Was self-employed, not employing other people ☐ 4
Was on a government employment or training scheme ☐ 5	Was on a government employment or training scheme ☐ 5	Was on a government employment or training scheme ☐ 5	Was on a government employment or training scheme ☐ 5
Was waiting to start a job he/she had already accepted ☐ 6	Was waiting to start a job he/she had already accepted ☐ 6	Was waiting to start a job he/she had already accepted ☐ 6	Was waiting to start a job he/she had already accepted ☐ 6
Was unemployed and looking for a job ☐ 7	Was unemployed and looking for a job ☐ 7	Was unemployed and looking for a job ☐ 7	Was unemployed and looking for a job ☐ 7
Was at school or in other full time education ☐ 8	Was at school or in other full time education ☐ 8	Was at school or in other full time education ☐ 8	Was at school or in other full time education ☐ 8
Was unable to work because of long term sickness or disability ☐ 9	Was unable to work because of long term sickness or disability ☐ 9	Was unable to work because of long term sickness or disability ☐ 9	Was unable to work because of long term sickness or disability ☐ 9
Was retired from paid work ☐ 10	Was retired from paid work ☐ 10	Was retired from paid work ☐ 10	Was retired from paid work ☐ 10
Was looking after the home or family ☐ 11	Was looking after the home or family ☐ 11	Was looking after the home or family ☐ 11	Was looking after the home or family ☐ 11
Other ☐ *please specify*	Other ☐ *please specify*	Other ☐ *please specify*	Other ☐ *please specify*

Please turn over ►

1-3 Name, sex and date of birth of people to be included	Person No. 1	Person No. 2
Important: please read the notes before answering the questions. In answering the rest of the questions please include: ► every person who spends census night (21-22 April) in this household, **including anyone staying temporarily**. ► any other people who are usually members of the household but on census night are absent on holiday, at school or college, or for any other reason, even if they are being included on another census form elsewhere. ► anyone who arrives here on Monday 22nd April who was in Great Britain on the Sunday and who has not been included as present on another census form. ► any newly born baby born before the 22nd April, even if still in hospital. If not yet given a name, write BABY and the surname. **Write the names in BLOCK CAPITALS starting with the head or a joint head of household.**	**Name and surname** ☐ **Sex** Male ☐ 1 Female ☐ 2 **Date of birth** Day ☐ Month ☐ Year ☐	**Name and surname** ☐ **Sex** Male ☐ 1 Female ☐ 2 **Date of birth** Day ☐ Month ☐ Year ☐

Please read A below, tick the box that applies and follow the instruction by the box ticked.

	Person No. 1	Person No. 2
A Did the person have a paid job last week (any of the boxes 1, 2, 3 or 4 ticked at question 13)?	YES ☐ Answer questions 14, 15, 16, 17 and 18 about the main job last week, then go on to question 19 NO ☐ Answer B	YES ☐ Answer questions 14, 15, 16, 17 and 18 about the main job last week, then go on to question 19 NO ☐ Answer B
B Has the person had a paid job within the last 10 years?	YES ☐ Answer questions 14, 15 and 16 about the most recent job, then go on to question 19 NO ☐ Go on to question 19	YES ☐ Answer questions 14, 15 and 16 about the most recent job, then go on to question 19 NO ☐ Go on to question 19
14 Hours worked per week How many hours per week does or did the person usually work in his or her main job? **Do not count** overtime or meal breaks.	Number of hours worked per week ☐	Number of hours worked per week ☐
15 Occupation Please give the full title of the person's present or last job and describe the main things he/she does or did in the job. **At a,** give the full title by which the job is known, for example: 'packing machinist'; 'poultry processor'; 'jig and tool fitter'; 'supervisor of typists'; 'accounts clerk'; rather than general titles like 'machinist'; 'process worker'; 'supervisor' or 'clerk'. Give rank or grade if the person has one. **At b,** write down the main things the person actually does or did in the job. If possible ask him/her to say what these things are and write them down. **Armed Forces** — enter 'commissioned officer' or 'other rank' as appropriate at **a,** and leave **b** blank. **Civil Servants** — give grade at **a** and discipline or specialism, for example: 'electrical engineer'; 'accountant'; 'chemist'; 'administrator' at **b**.	**a** Full job title **b** Main things done in job	**a** Full job title **b** Main things done in job
16 Name and business of employer (if self-employed give the name and nature of the person's business) **At a,** please give the name of the employer. Give the trading name if one is used. Do not use abbreviations. **At b,** describe clearly what the employer (or the person if self-employed) makes or does (or did). **Armed Forces** — write 'Armed Forces' at **a** and leave **b** blank. For a member of the Armed Forces of a country other than the UK — add the name of the country. **Civil Servants** — give name of Department at **a** and write 'Government Department' at **b**. **Local Government Officers** — give name of employing authority at **a** and department in which employed at **b**.	**a** Name of employer **b** Description of employer's business	**a** Name of employer **b** Description of employer's business

Person No. 3	Person No. 4	Person No. 5	Person No. 6
Name and surname	Name and surname	Name and surname	Name and surname
Sex Male ☐ 1 Female ☐ 2	**Sex** Male ☐ 1 Female ☐ 2	**Sex** Male ☐ 1 Female ☐ 2	**Sex** Male ☐ 1 Female ☐ 2
Date of birth Day Month Year	**Date of birth** Day Month Year	**Date of birth** Day Month Year	**Date of birth** Day Month Year

This will tell you which questions to answer for each person.

Person No. 3	Person No. 4	Person No. 5	Person No. 6
YES ☐ Answer questions 14, 15, 16, 17 and 18 about the main job last week, then go on to question 19	YES ☐ Answer questions 14, 15, 16, 17 and 18 about the main job last week, then go on to question 19	YES ☐ Answer questions 14, 15, 16, 17 and 18 about the main job last week, then go on to question 19	YES ☐ Answer questions 14, 15, 16, 17 and 18 about the main job last week, then go on to question 19
NO ☐ Answer B	NO ☐ Answer B	NO ☐ Answer B	NO ☐ Answer B
YES ☐ Answer questions 14, 15 and 16 about the most recent job, then go on to question 19	YES ☐ Answer questions 14, 15 and 16 about the most recent job, then go on to question 19	YES ☐ Answer questions 14, 15 and 16 about the most recent job, then go on to question 19	YES ☐ Answer questions 14, 15 and 16 about the most recent job, then go on to question 19
NO ☐ Go on to question 19	NO ☐ Go on to question 19	NO ☐ Go on to question 19	NO ☐ Go on to question 19
Number of hours worked per week ☐	Number of hours worked per week ☐	Number of hours worked per week ☐	Number of hours worked per week ☐
a Full job title	**a** Full job title	**a** Full job title	**a** Full job title
b Main things done in job	**b** Main things done in job	**b** Main things done in job	**b** Main things done in job
a Name of employer	**a** Name of employer	**a** Name of employer	**a** Name of employer
b Description of employer's business	**b** Description of employer's business	**b** Description of employer's business	**b** Description of employer's business

Please turn over ►

1-3 Name, sex and date of birth of people to be included

Important: please read the notes before answering the questions.

In answering the rest of the questions please include:

- ► every person who spends census night (21-22 April) in this household, **including anyone staying temporarily**.
- ► any other people who are usually members of the household but on census night are absent on holiday, at school or college, or for any other reason, even if they are being included on another census form elsewhere.
- ► anyone who arrives here on Monday 22nd April who was in Great Britain on the Sunday and who has not been included as present on another census form.
- ► any newly born baby born before the 22nd April, even if still in hospital. If not yet given a name, write BABY and the surname.

Write the names in BLOCK CAPITALS starting with the head or a joint head of household.

Person No. 1	Person No. 2
Name and surname	**Name and surname**
Sex Male ☐ 1 Female ☐ 2	**Sex** Male ☐ 1 Female ☐ 2
Date of birth Day Month Year	**Date of birth** Day Month Year

17 Address of place of work

Please give the full address of the person's place of work.

For a person employed on a site for a long period, give the address of the site.

For a person not working regularly at one place who reports daily to a depot or other fixed address, give that address.

For a person not reporting daily to a fixed address, tick box 1.

For a person working mainly at home, tick box 2.

Armed Forces — leave blank.

Person No. 1	Person No. 2
Please write full address and postcode of workplace below in BLOCK CAPITALS	Please write full address and postcode of workplace below in BLOCK CAPITALS
Post-code	Post-code
No fixed place ☐ 1	No fixed place ☐ 1
Mainly at home ☐ 2	Mainly at home ☐ 2

18 Daily journey to work

Please tick the appropriate box to show how the longest part, by distance, of the person's daily journey to work is normally made.

For a person using different means of transport on different days, show the means most often used.

Car or van includes three-wheeled cars and motor caravans.

Person No. 1	Person No. 2
British Rail train ☐ 1	British Rail train ☐ 1
Underground, tube, metro ☐ 2	Underground, tube, metro ☐ 2
Bus, minibus or coach (public or private) ☐ 3	Bus, minibus or coach (public or private) ☐ 3
Motor cycle, scooter, moped ☐ 4	Motor cycle, scooter, moped ☐ 4
Driving a car or van ☐ 5	Driving a car or van ☐ 5
Passenger in car or van ☐ 6	Passenger in car or van ☐ 6
Pedal cycle ☐ 7	Pedal cycle ☐ 7
On foot ☐ 8	On foot ☐ 8
Other ☐ 9 *please specify*	Other ☐ 9 *please specify*
Works mainly at home ☐ 0	Works mainly at home ☐ 0

19 Degrees, professional and vocational qualifications

Has the person obtained any qualifications after reaching the age of 18 such as:

-degrees, diplomas, HNC, HND,

-nursing qualifications,

-teaching qualifications (see * below),

-graduate or corporate membership of professional institutions,

-other professional, educational or vocational qualifications?

Do not count qualifications normally obtained at school such as GCE, CSE, GCSE, SCE and school certificates.

If box 2 is ticked, write in all qualifications even if they are not relevant to the person's present job or if the person is not working.

Please list the qualifications in the order in which they were obtained.

If more than three, please enter in a spare column and link with an arrow.

*For a person with **school teaching qualifications**, give the full title of the qualification, such as 'Certificate of Education' and the subject(s) which the person is qualified to teach. The subject 'education' should then only be shown if the course had no other subject specialisation.

Person No. 1	Person No. 2
NO — no such qualifications ☐ 1	NO — no such qualifications ☐ 1
YES — give details ☐ 2	YES — give details ☐ 2
1 Title	1 Title
Subject(s)	Subject(s)
Year	Year
Institution	Institution
2 Title	2 Title
Subject(s)	Subject(s)
Year	Year
Institution	Institution
3 Title	3 Title
Subject(s)	Subject(s)
Year	Year
Institution	Institution

Person No. 3

Name and surname

Sex Male ☐ 1
Female ☐ 2

Date of birth
Day Month Year

Please write full address and postcode of workplace below in BLOCK CAPITALS

Post-code

No fixed place ☐ 1
Mainly at home ☐ 2

British Rail train ☐ 1
Underground, tube, metro ☐ 2
Bus, minibus or coach (public or private) ☐ 3
Motor cycle, scooter, moped ☐ 4
Driving a car or van ☐ 5
Passenger in car or van ☐ 6
Pedal cycle ☐ 7
On foot ☐ 8
Other ☐ 9
please specify

Works mainly at home ☐ 0

NO — no such qualifications ☐ 1
YES — give details ☐ 2

1 Title
Subject(s)
Year
Institution

2 Title
Subject(s)
Year
Institution

3 Title
Subject(s)
Year
Institution

Person No. 4

Name and surname

Sex Male ☐ 1
Female ☐ 2

Date of birth
Day Month Year

Please write full address and postcode of workplace below in BLOCK CAPITALS

Post-code

No fixed place ☐ 1
Mainly at home ☐ 2

British Rail train ☐ 1
Underground, tube, metro ☐ 2
Bus, minibus or coach (public or private) ☐ 3
Motor cycle, scooter, moped ☐ 4
Driving a car or van ☐ 5
Passenger in car or van ☐ 6
Pedal cycle ☐ 7
On foot ☐ 8
Other ☐ 9
please specify

Works mainly at home ☐ 0

NO — no such qualifications ☐ 1
YES — give details ☐ 2

1 Title
Subject(s)
Year
Institution

2 Title
Subject(s)
Year
Institution

3 Title
Subject(s)
Year
Institution

Person No. 5

Name and surname

Sex Male ☐ 1
Female ☐ 2

Date of birth
Day Month Year

Please write full address and postcode of workplace below in BLOCK CAPITALS

Post-code

No fixed place ☐ 1
Mainly at home ☐ 2

British Rail train ☐ 1
Underground, tube, metro ☐ 2
Bus, minibus or coach (public or private) ☐ 3
Motor cycle, scooter, moped ☐ 4
Driving a car or van ☐ 5
Passenger in car or van ☐ 6
Pedal cycle ☐ 7
On foot ☐ 8
Other ☐ 9
please specify

Works mainly at home ☐ 0

NO — no such qualifications ☐ 1
YES — give details ☐ 2

1 Title
Subject(s)
Year
Institution

2 Title
Subject(s)
Year
Institution

3 Title
Subject(s)
Year
Institution

Person No. 6

Name and surname

Sex Male ☐ 1
Female ☐ 2

Date of birth
Day Month Year

Please write full address and postcode of workplace below in BLOCK CAPITALS

Post-code

No fixed place ☐ 1
Mainly at home ☐ 2

British Rail train ☐ 1
Underground, tube, metro ☐ 2
Bus, minibus or coach (public or private) ☐ 3
Motor cycle, scooter, moped ☐ 4
Driving a car or van ☐ 5
Passenger in car or van ☐ 6
Pedal cycle ☐ 7
On foot ☐ 8
Other ☐ 9
please specify

Works mainly at home ☐ 0

NO — no such qualifications ☐ 1
YES — give details ☐ 2

1 Title
Subject(s)
Year
Institution

2 Title
Subject(s)
Year
Institution

3 Title
Subject(s)
Year
Institution

Please turn over and complete Panels B and C ►

H3 Tenure

Please tick the box which best describes how you and your household occupy your accommodation.

If buying by stages from a Council, Housing Association or New Town (under shared ownership, co-ownership or equity sharing scheme), answer as an owner-occupier at box 1.

As an owner-occupier:

-buying the property through mortgage or loan ☐ 1

-owning the property outright (no loan) ☐ 2

By renting, rent free or by lease:

If your accommodation is occupied by lease originally granted for, or extended to, more than 21 years, answer as an owner-occupier. For shorter leases, answer 'By renting'.

-with a job, farm, shop or other business ☐ 3

-from a local authority (Council) ☐ 4

-from a New Town Development Corporation (or Commission) or from a Housing Action Trust ☐ 5

-from a housing association or charitable trust ☐ 6

A private landlord may be a person or a company or another organisation not mentioned at 3, 4, 5 or 6 above.

-from a private landlord, furnished ☐ 7

-from a private landlord, unfurnished ☐ 8

In some other way:

-please give details below ☐

H4 Amenities

Does your household — that is, you and any people who usually live here with you — **have the use of:**

a A bath or shower?

Yes — for use only by this household ☐ 1

Yes — for use also by another household ☐ 2

No — no bath or shower available ☐ 3

b A flush toilet (WC) with entrance inside the building?

Yes — for use only by this household ☐ 0

Yes — for use also by another household ☐ 1

No — flush toilet with outside entrance only ☐ 2

No — no flush toilet indoors or outdoors ☐ 3

c Central heating in living rooms and bedrooms (including night storage heaters, warm air or under-floor heating), whether actually used or not?

Yes — all living rooms and bedrooms centrally heated ☐ 1

Yes — some (not all) living rooms and bedrooms centrally heated ☐ 2

No — no living rooms or bedrooms centrally heated ☐ 3

H5 Cars and vans

Please tick the appropriate box to indicate the number of cars and vans normally available for use by you or members of your household (other than visitors).

Include any car or van provided by employers if normally available for use by you or members of your household, but **exclude** vans used only for carrying goods.

None ☐ 0

One ☐ 1

Two ☐ 2

Three or more ☐ 3

◀ **Please turn to the first inside page**

Panel B

Was there anyone else (such as a visitor) here on the night of 21-22 April whom you have not included because there was no room on the form? No ☐ Yes ☐

If **yes** ticked, please ask the Enumerator for another form.

Have you left anyone out because you were not sure whether they should be included on the form? No ☐ Yes ☐

If **yes** ticked, please give their names and the reason why you were not sure about including them.

Name

Reason

Name

Reason

Name

Reason

Panel C

Before you sign the form, will you please check:

- ▶ that all questions which should have been answered have been answered for every member of your household
- ▶ that you have included everyone who spent the night of 21-22 April in your household
- ▶ that you have included everyone who usually lives here but was away from home on the night of 21-22 April
- ▶ that no visitors, boarders or newly born children, even if still in hospital, have been missed

It would help the Enumerator to be able to telephone you if there is a query on, or an omission from, your form.

If you have no objection, please write your telephone number here.

Telephone number

Declaration

This form is correctly completed to the best of my knowledge and belief.

Signature(s)

Date **April 1991**

1991 Census England

I form for making an individual return

Please complete this form and have it ready for collection on Monday 22nd April.

Completion of the form is compulsory under the Census Act 1920. If you refuse to complete it, or give false information, you may have to pay a fine of up to 400.

Your answers will be treated in strict confidence and used only to produce statistics. Names and addresses will not be put into the computer; only the postcode will be entered. The forms will be kept securely within my Office and treated as confidential for 100 years.

Anyone using or disclosing Census information improperly will be liable to prosecution.

After completing the form, please sign the declaration on the last page.

Thank you for your co-operation.

P J Wormald
Registrar General

Office of Population Censuses and Surveys
PO Box 100
Fareham PO16 0AL

Telephone 0329 844444

To be completed by the Enumerator

Census District

Enumeration District

Form Number

Serial Number

To be completed by the Manager, Commanding Officer, Chief Resident Officer, or other person in charge of the establishment or vessel.

Name of Establishment

Address

Postcode

To be completed by or for the Individual

Please answer question by ticking the appropriate box or boxes ☑ where they are provided.
Please use ink or ballpoint pen.

1 **Name**

Please write in your name and surname (BLOCK CAPITALS). For a baby who has not yet been given a name, write BABY and the surname.

2 **Sex**

Please tick the appropriate box.

Male ☐ 1
Female ☐ 2

3 **Date of birth**

Please write in the day, month and year of birth.

Day | Month | Year

4 **Marital status**

On the 21st April what is your marital status?

If separated but not divorced, please tick 'Married (first marriage)' or 'Re-married' as appropriate.

Please tick one box.

Single (never married) ☐ 1
Married (first marriage) ☐ 2
Re-married ☐ 3
Divorced (decree absolute) ☐ 4
Widowed ☐ 5

5 **Position in establishment**

Please write in your position in this establishment. For example, write 'Guest'; 'Patient'; 'Inmate'; 'Staff'; 'Student'; 'Boarder'.
If you are completing the form in a private household, your relationship to the person making the return for the rest of the household should be stated.

6 **Whereabouts on night of 21-22 April 1991**

Not applicable to this form

7 **Usual address**

If you usually live here, please tick 'This address'.
If not, tick 'Elsewhere' and write in your usual address.

If you are a student or a schoolchild away from home during term time, your home address should be taken as your usual address.

If you live away from home for part of the week, your home address should be taken as your usual address.

This address ☐ 1
Elsewhere ☐

If elsewhere, please write your usual address and postcode below in BLOCK CAPITALS

Post-code

Please turn over ▶

8 **Term time address of students and schoolchildren**

If not a student or schoolchild, please tick first box.

If you are a student or schoolchild and you live here during term time, tick 'This address'.

If you do not live here during term time, tick 'Elsewhere' and write in the current or most recent term time address.

Not a student or schoolchild ☐
This address ☐ 1
Elsewhere ☐

If elsewhere, please write your term time address and postcode below in BLOCK CAPITALS

Postcode

9 **Usual address one year ago**

If your usual address one year ago (on the 21st April 1990) was the same as your current usual address (given in answer to question 7), please tick 'Same'. If not, tick 'Different' and write in your usual address one year ago.

For a child born since the 21st April 1990, tick the 'Child under one' box.

Same as Question 7 ☐ 1
Different ☐
Child under one ☐ 3

If different, please write your address and postcode on the 21st April 1990 below in BLOCK CAPITALS

Postcode

10 **Country of birth**

Please tick the appropriate box.

If the 'Elsewhere' box is ticked, please write in the present name of the country in which your birthplace is now situated.

England ☐ 1
Scotland ☐ 2
Wales ☐ 3
Northern Ireland ☐ 4
Irish Republic ☐ 5
Elsewhere ☐

If elsewhere, please write in the present name of the country

11 **Ethnic group**

Please tick the appropriate box.

If you are descended from more than one ethnic or racial group, please tick the group to which you consider you belong, or tick the 'Any other ethnic group' box and describe your ancestry in the space provided.

White ☐ 0
Black-Caribbean ☐ 1
Black-African ☐ 2
Black-Other ☐
please describe

Indian ☐ 3
Pakistani ☐ 4
Bangladeshi ☐ 5
Chinese ☐ 6
Any other ethnic group ☐
please describe

12 **Long-term illness**

Do you have any long-term illness, health problem or handicap which limits your daily activities or the work you can do?

Include problems which are due to old age.

Yes, I have a health problem which limits activities ☐ 1
I have no such health problem ☐ 2

Answers to the remaining questions are not required for anyone under 16 years of age (born after 21st April 1975)

13 **Whether working, retired, looking after the home etc last week**

Which of these things were you doing **last week?**

Please read carefully right through the list and **tick all the descriptions that apply.**

* Casual or temporary work should be counted at boxes 1, 2, 3 or 4. Also tick boxes 1, 2, 3 or 4 if you had a job last week but were off sick, on holiday, temporarily laid off or on strike.

Boxes 1, 2, 3 and 4 refer to work for pay or profit but not to unpaid work except in a family business.

Working for an employer is **part time** (box 2) if the hours worked, excluding any overtime and mealbreaks, are usually 30 hours or less per week.

† Includes wanting a job but prevented from looking by holiday or temporary sickness.

$ Do not count training given or paid for by an employer.

- * Was working for an employer full time (more than 30 hours a week) ☐ 1
- * Was working for an employer part time (one hour or more a week) ☐ 2
- * Was self employed, employing other people ☐ 3
- * Was self employed, not employing other people ☐ 4
- Was on a government employment or training scheme ☐ 5
- Was waiting to start a job already accepted ☐ 6
- † Was unemployed and looking for a job ☐ 7
- $ Was at school or in other full time education ☐ 8
- Was unable to work because of long term sickness or disability ☐ 9
- Was retired from paid work ☐ 10
- Was looking after the home or family ☐ 11
- Other ☐ *please specify*

Please read A below, tick the box that applies and follow the instruction by the box ticked. This will tell you which questions to answer.

A Did you have a paid job last week (any of the boxes 1, 2, 3 or 4 ticked at question 13)?	Yes ☐ No ☐	If **yes** ticked, answer questions **14, 15, 16, 17** and **18** about the main job last week, then go on to question **19.** If **no** ticked, answer **B.**
B Have you had a paid job within the last 10 years?	Yes ☐ No ☐	If **yes** ticked, answer questions **14, 15** and **16** about the most recent job, then go on to question **19.** If **no** ticked, go on to question **19.**

14 **Hours worked per week**

How many hours per week do or did you usually work in your main job?

Do not count overtime or meal breaks.

Number of hours worked per week ☐

15 **Occupation**

Please give the full title of your present or last job and describe the main things you do or did in the job.

At a, give the full title by which the job is known, for example: 'packing machinist'; 'poultry processor'; 'jig and tool fitter'; 'supervisor of typists'; 'accounts clerk'; rather than general titles like 'machinist'; 'process worker'; 'supervisor' or 'clerk'. Give rank or grade if you have one.

At b, write down the main things you actually do or did in the job.

Armed Forces - enter 'commissioned officer' or 'other rank' as appropriate at **a** and leave **b** blank.

Civil Servants - give grade at **a** and discipline or specialism, for example: 'electrical engineer'; 'accountant'; 'chemist'; 'administrator' at **b.**

a Full job title

b Main things done in job

Please turn over ▶

16 **Name and business of employer (if self-employed give the name and nature of business)**

At a, please give the name of your employer. Give the trading name if one is used. Do not use abbreviations.

At b, describe clearly what your employer (or yourself if self-employed) makes or does (or did).

Armed Forces - write 'Armed Forces' at **a** and leave **b** blank. For a member of the Armed Forces of a country other than the UK - add the name of the country.

Civil Servants - give name of Department at **a** and write 'Government Department' at **b**.

Local Government Officers - give name of employing authority at **a** and department in which employed at **b**.

a Name of employer

b Description of employer's business

17 **Address of place of work**

Please give the full address of your place of work.

If employed on a site for a long period, give the address of the site.

If not working regularly at one place but reporting daily to a depot or other fixed address, give that address.

If not reporting daily to a fixed address, tick box 1.

If working mainly at home, tick box 2.

Armed Forces - leave blank.

Please write full address and postcode of workplace below in BLOCK CAPITALS

Postcode

No fixed place ☐ 1

Mainly at home ☐ 2

18 **Daily journey to work**

Please tick the appropriate box to show how the longest part, by distance, of your daily journey to work is normally made.

If using different means of transport on different days, show the means most often used.

Car or van includes three-wheeled cars and motor caravans.

British Rail train ☐ 1

Underground, tube, metro ☐ 2

Bus, minibus or coach (public or private) ☐ 3

Motor cycle, scooter, moped ☐ 4

Driving a car or van ☐ 5

Passenger in car or van ☐ 6

Pedal cycle ☐ 7

On foot ☐ 8

Other ☐ 9
please specify

Work mainly at home ☐ 0

19 **Degrees, professional and vocational qualifications**

Have you obtained any qualifications after reaching the age of 18 such as:

- degrees, diplomas, HNC, HND,
- nursing qualifications,
- teaching qualifications (see * below),
- graduate or corporate membership of professional institutions,
- other professional, educational or vocational qualifications?

Do not count qualifications normally obtained at school such as GCE, CSE, GCSE, SCE and school certificates.

If box 2 is ticked, write in all qualifications even if they are not relevant to your present job or if you are not working.

Please list the qualifications in the order in which they were obtained.

* If you have **school teaching qualifications,** give the full title of the qualification, such as 'Certificate of Education' and the subject(s) which you are qualified to teach. The subject 'education' should then only be shown if the course had no other subject specialisation.

NO - no such qualifications ☐ 1

YES - give details ☐ 2

1 Title	2 Title
Subject(s)	Subject(s)
Year	Year
Institution	Institution

3 Title	4 Title
Subject(s)	Subject(s)
Year	Year
Institution	Institution

Declaration

This form is correctly completed to the best of my knowledge and belief.

Signature	**Date** April 1991

1991 Census Wales

Iw form for making an individual return

Please complete this form and have it ready for collection on Monday 22nd April.

Completion of the form is compulsory under the Census Act 1920. If you refuse to complete it, or give false information, you may have to pay a fine of up to 400.

Your answers will be treated in strict confidence and used only to produce statistics. Names and addresses will not be put into the computer; only the postcode will be entered. The forms will be kept securely within my Office and treated as confidential for 100 years.

Anyone using or disclosing Census information improperly will be liable to prosecution.

After completing the form, please sign the declaration on the last page.

Thank you for your co-operation.

P J Wormald
Registrar General

Office of Population Censuses and Surveys
PO Box 100
Fareham PO16 0AL

Telephone 0329 844444

This form is available in English and Welsh. If you have not received the version you require, please telephone 0329 844444

Mae'r ffurflen hon ar gael yn Gymraeg ac yn Saesneg. Os na chawsoch y fersiwn y mae ei eisiau arnoch, ffoniwch 0329 844444

To be completed by the Enumerator

Census District

Enumeration District

Form Number

Serial Number

To be completed by the Manager, Commanding Officer, Chief Resident Officer, or other person in charge of the establishment or vessel.

Name of Establishment

Address

Postcode

To be completed by or for the Individual

Please answer question by ticking the appropriate box or boxes √ where they are provided.
Please use ink or ballpoint pen.

1 **Name**

Please write in your name and surname (BLOCK CAPITALS). For a baby who has not yet been given a name, write 'BABY' and the surname.

2 **Sex**

Please tick the appropriate box.

Male ☐ 1
Female ☐ 2

3 **Date of birth**

Please write in the day, month and year of birth.

Day Month Year

4 **Marital status**

On the 21st April what is your marital status?

If separated but not divorced, please tick 'Married (first marriage)' or 'Re-married' as appropriate.

Please tick one box.

Single (never married) ☐ 1
Married (first marriage) ☐ 2
Re-married ☐ 3
Divorced (decree absolute) ☐ 4
Widowed ☐ 5

5 **Position in establishment**

Please write in your position in this establishment.
For example, write 'Guest'; 'Patient'; 'Inmate'; 'Staff'; 'Student'; 'Boarder'.
If you are completing the form in a private household, your relationship to the person making the return for the rest of the household should be stated.

6 **Whereabouts on night of 21-22 April 1991**

Not applicable to this form

7 **Usual address**

If you usually live here, please tick 'This address'.
If not, tick 'Elsewhere' and write in your usual address.

If you are a student or a schoolchild away from home during term time, your home address should be taken as your usual address.

If you live away from home for part of the week, your home address should be taken as your usual address.

This address ☐ 1
Elsewhere ☐

If elsewhere, please write your usual address and postcode below in BLOCK CAPITALS

Post-code

Please turn over ▶

8 **Term time address of students and schoolchildren**

If not a student or schoolchild, please tick first box.

If you are a student or schoolchild and you live here during term time, tick 'This address'.

If you do not live here during term time, tick 'Elsewhere' and write in the current or most recent term time address.

Not a student or schoolchild ☐

This address ☐ 1

Elsewhere ☐

If elsewhere, please write your term time address and postcode below in BLOCK CAPITALS

Postcode

9 **Usual address one year ago**

If your usual address one year ago (on the 21st April 1990) was the same as your current usual address (given in answer to question 7), please tick 'Same'. If not, tick 'Different' and write in your usual address one year ago.

For a child born since the 21st April 1990, tick the 'Child under one' box.

Same as Question 7 ☐ 1

Different ☐

Child under one ☐ 3

If different, please write your address and postcode on the 21st April 1990 below in BLOCK CAPITALS

Postcode

10 **Country of birth**

Please tick the appropriate box.

If the 'Elsewhere' box is ticked, please write in the present name of the country in which your birthplace is now situated.

England ☐ 1

Scotland ☐ 2

Wales ☐ 3

Northern Ireland ☐ 4

Irish Republic ☐ 5

Elsewhere ☐

If elsewhere, please write in the present name of the country

11 **Ethnic group**

Please tick the appropriate box.

If you are descended from more than one ethnic or racial group, please tick the group to which you consider you belong, or tick the 'Any other ethnic group' box and describe your ancestry in the space provided.

White ☐ 0

Black-Caribbean ☐ 1

Black-African ☐ 2

Black-Other ☐
please describe

Indian ☐ 3

Pakistani ☐ 4

Bangladeshi ☐ 5

Chinese ☐ 6

Any other ethnic group ☐
please describe

12 **Long-term illness**

Do you have any long-term illness, health problem or handicap which limits your daily activities or the work you can do?

Include problems which are due to old age.

Yes, I have a health problem which limits activities ☐ 1

I have no such health problem ☐ 2

This question is for all persons aged 3 or over (born before 22 April 1988)

W **Welsh language**

Do you speak, read or write Welsh?

Please tick the appropriate box(es).

Speaks Welsh ☐ 1

Reads Welsh ☐ 2

Writes Welsh ☐ 4

Do not speak, read or write Welsh ☐ 0

Answers to the remaining questions are not required for a person under 16 years of age (born after 21st April 1975)

13 **Whether working, retired, looking after the home etc last week**

Which of these things were you doing **last week?**

Please read carefully right through the list and **tick all the descriptions that apply.**

* Casual or temporary work should be counted at boxes 1, 2, 3 or 4. Also tick boxes 1, 2, 3 or 4 if you had a job last week but were off sick, on holiday, temporarily laid off or on strike.

Boxes 1, 2, 3 and 4 refer to work for pay or profit but not to unpaid work except in a family business.

Working for an employer is **part time** (box 2) if the hours worked, excluding any overtime and mealbreaks, are usually 30 hours or less per week.

† Includes wanting a job but prevented from looking by holiday or temporary sickness.

$ Do not count training given or paid for by an employer.

- * Was working for an employer full time (more than 30 hours a week) ☐ 1
- * Was working for an employer part time (one hour or more a week) ☐ 2
- * Was self employed, employing other people ☐ 3
- * Was self employed, not employing other people ☐ 4
- Was on a government employment or training scheme ☐ 5
- Was waiting to start a job already accepted ☐ 6
- † Was unemployed and looking for a job ☐ 7
- $ Was at school or in other full time education ☐ 8
- Was unable to work because of long term sickness or disability ☐ 9
- Was retired from paid work ☐ 10
- Was looking after the home or family ☐ 11
- Other ☐ *please specify*

Please read A below, tick the box that applies and follow the instruction by the box ticked. This will tell you which questions to answer.

A Did you have a paid job last week (any of the boxes 1, 2, 3 or 4 ticked at question 13)? Yes ☐ No ☐

If **yes** ticked, answer questions **14, 15, 16, 17** and **18** about the main job last week, then go on to question **19.** If **no** ticked, answer **B.**

B Have you had a paid job within the last 10 years? Yes ☐ No ☐

If **yes** ticked, answer questions **14, 15** and **16** about the most recent job, then go on to question **19.** If **no** ticked, go on to question **19.**

14 **Hours worked per week**

How many hours per week do or did you usually work in your main job?

Do not count overtime or meal breaks.

Number of hours worked per week ☐

15 **Occupation**

Please give the full title of your present or last job and describe the main things you do or did in the job.

At a, give the full title by which the job is known, for example: 'packing machinist'; 'poultry processor'; 'jig and tool fitter'; 'supervisor of typists'; 'accounts clerk'; rather than general titles like 'machinist'; 'process worker'; 'supervisor' or 'clerk'. Give rank or grade if you have one.

At b, write down the main things you actually do or did in the job.

Armed Forces - enter 'commissioned officer', or 'other rank' as appropriate at **a** and leave **b** blank.

Civil Servants - give grade at **a** and disipline or specialism, for example; 'electrical engineer'; 'accountant'; 'chemist'; 'administrator' at **b.**

a Full job title

b Main things done in job

Please turn over ▶

16 **Name and business of employer (if self-employed give the name and nature of business)**

At a, please give the name of your employer. Give the trading name if one is used. Do not use abbreviations.

At b, describe clearly what your employer (or yourself if self-employed) makes or does (or did).

Armed Forces - write 'Armed Forces' at **a** and leave **b** blank. For a member of the Armed Forces of a country other than the UK - add the name of the country.

Civil Servants - give name of Department at **a** and write 'Government Department' at **b**.

Local Government Officers - give name of employing authority at **a** and department in which employed at **b**.

a Name of employer

b Description of employer's business

17 **Address of place of work**

Please give the full address of your place of work.

If employed on a site for a long period, give the address of the site.

If not working regularly at one place but reporting daily to a depot or other fixed address, give that address.

If not reporting daily to a fixed address, tick box 1.

If working mainly at home, tick box 2.

Armed Forces - leave blank.

Please write full address and postcode of workplace below in BLOCK CAPITALS

Postcode

No fixed place ☐ 1

Mainly at home ☐ 2

18 **Daily journey to work**

Please tick the appropriate box to show how the longest part, by distance, of your daily journey to work is normally made.

If using different means of transport on different days, show the means most often used.

Car or van includes three-wheeled cars and motor caravans.

British Rail train ☐ 1
Underground, tube, metro ☐ 2
Bus, minibus or coach (public or private) ☐ 3
Motor cycle, scooter, moped ☐ 4
Driving a car or van ☐ 5
Passenger in a car or van ☐ 6
Pedal cycle ☐ 7
On foot ☐ 8
Other ☐ 9
please specify

Work mainly at home ☐ 0

19 **Degrees, professional and vocational qualifications**

Have you obtained any qualifications after reaching the age of 18 such as:

- degrees, diplomas, HNC, HND,
- nursing qualifications,
- teaching qualifications (see * below),
- graduate or corporate membership of professional institutions,
- other professional, educational or vocational qualifications?

Do not count qualifications normally obtained at school such as GCE, CSE, GCSE, SCE and school certificates.

If box 2 is ticked, write in all qualifications even if they are not relevant to your present job or if you are not working.

Please list the qualifications in the order in which they were obtained.

* If you have **school teaching qualifications,** give the full title of the qualification, such as 'Certificate of Education' and the subject(s) which you are qualified to teach. The subject 'education' should then only be shown if the course had no other subject specialisation.

NO - no such qualifications ☐ 1

YES - give details ☐ 2

1 Title	2 Title
Subject(s)	Subject(s)
Year	Year
Institution	Institution

3 Title	4 Title
Subject(s)	Subject(s)
Year	Year
Institution	Institution

Declaration

This form is correctly completed to the best of my knowledge and belief.

Signature	**Date**

April 1991

1991 Census England/Wales

L Form for Communal Establishments, HM Ships or other vessels

To the Manager, Chief Resident Officer, Commanding Officer or other person in charge of a communal establishment:

To the Captain, Master, Commanding Officer or other person in charge of a vessel or HM Ship:

I am seeking your help in conducting the Census. Under the Census Act 1920 you have a legal obligation to list the names of the people in your establishment or on your vessel, to distribute forms to them and to collect the forms on completion. In a communal establishment you must also complete the 'type of establishment' panel. If you refuse to complete this form, or give false information, you may have to pay a fine of up to 40 0. The instructions opposite tell you what to do and should be followed carefully.

The Individual forms with which you have been supplied are for the returns to be made by or for each person who spends the night of **21-22 April** at this establishment or on board this vessel. To assist you in issuing and collecting the individual forms, spaces have been provided overleaf for listing those people.

The answers given will be treated in strict confidence and used only to produce statistics. Names and addresses will not be put in the computer; only the postcode will be entered. The forms will be kept securely within my Office and treated as confidential for 100 years.

Anyone using or disclosing census information improperly will be liable to prosecution. For example, it would be improper for you to pass on to someone else, information which you have been given in confidence on, or for completion of, an individual form.

Thank you for your co-operation.

P J Wormald
Registrar General

Office of Population Censuses and Surveys
PO Box 100 Fareham PO16 0AL

Telephone 0329 844444

To be completed by the Enumerator or Customs Officer

Name of Establishment/Vessel/HM Ship

For communal establishments: address of establishment

Postcode

For vessels other than HM Ships: port of registry

Place at which the form is delivered, that is: name of town or port and of harbour, dock, wharf, mooring etc.

Name of master or person in charge of vessel

For Enumerator/Census Office use

CD No.	ED No.	Form No.

Instructions

Listing of names

List the names of all people present, as instructed overleaf.

You may start drawing up the list in advance of Census day, but before collection or despatch you must bring it up to date.

Distribution

An Individual form (I form) must be completed for each person listed. Where a person is incapable of making a return, you must arrange for a form to be completed on his or her behalf.

Before you issue each form, enter the name of the establishment or vessel in the panel at top right hand corner on the front of the Individual form (a rubber stamp may be used).

Please issue an envelope to any person who wishes to make a return under sealed cover.

For communal establishments, please give the type of establishment below.

When you have completed this form please fill in and sign the declaration overleaf.

Collection of forms

Communal Establishments

Please have all the completed forms ready for collection by the Enumerator, who will call on Monday 22nd April or soon afterwards.

Vessels other than HM Ships

Please have all of the completed forms ready for collection by the Enumerator who will call on Monday 22 April, or return them to the Enumerator in accordance with the instructions issued at delivery.

HM Ships

Please despatch the completed forms as soon as possible after 21st April to:

Office of Population Censuses and Surveys,
PO Box 100 Fareham PO16 OAL

Communal establishments : type of establishment

Please give a **full description of the type of establishment** and if the establishment caters for a specific group or groups, please describe; *for example mentally ill or handicapped, physically disabled, elderly, children, students, nurses.*

Hospitals, homes and hostels only

- **Please specify type of management:** *private, voluntary (charitable), central government, local authority, housing association, health authority etc.*
- **Please indicate if the establishment is registered** with a local authority or health authority

Hotels or boarding houses only

Please enter the number of rooms in the establishment, including any annexes in which meals are not provided. Do not count kitchens, bathrooms, WCs, rooms used as offices or stores.

List the names of all people present, that is:
everyone who spends Census night **21-22 April 1991** in this establishment or on board this vessel; and everyone who arrives in this establishment or on board on **Monday 22 April** before the forms are collected by the Enumerator (or despatched in the case of HM Ships) and who was in Great Britain on Sunday but has not been included as present on another Census form.

In communal establishments do not list the names of any non-resident personnel who happen to be on duty on the premises on Census night.

Please put a tick in the appropriate column when you issue each form and when you collect it.

Name	**Individual** form		Name	**Individual** form	
	Issued	Collected		Issued	Collected
1			31		
2			32		
3			33		
4			34		
5			35		
6			36		
7			37		
8			38		
9			39		
10			40		
11			41		
12			42		
13			43		
14			44		
15			45		
16			46		
17			47		
18			48		
19			49		
20			50		
21			51		
22			52		
23			53		
24			54		
25			55		
26			56		
27			57		
28			58		
29			59		
30			60		

Enter the number of **Individual** forms collected on this L form. ☐

Declaration - If more than one 'L' form is used, only complete this panel on the first form

Enter the total number of **'L'** forms completed for this establishment/vessel. ☐

Enter the total number of **Individual** forms collected (sum of all L forms). ☐

Signature

Date April 1991

Appendix 2

Advice on Usual Residence and Whom to Include/Exclude in a Private Household

Everyone present on Census night must be included on the form which should be completed to show their usual residence at Question 7. For those 'usually resident' tick 'This address' in Question 7, and for 'Visitors' tick 'Elsewhere' and write in the address of usual residence. In addition to people present on Census night, the form-filler is asked to include 'any other people who are usually members of the household, but on Census night are absent on holiday, at school or college or for any other reason' (tick 'This address' at Question 7 for any such people).

You may be asked questions where the form-filler is in doubt about the appropriate usual residence for someone who is present or is not sure whether or not to include somebody who is not present. This may be particularly so in the case of names entered in Panel B of the H (W, C) form.

It will usually be obvious from a person's circumstances whether they are usually resident or not. In more difficult cases the following guidelines will help. If still in doubt accept the view of the person involved.

REMEMBER: EVERYONE PRESENT ON CENSUS NIGHT MUST BE INCLUDED ON THE FORM.

FOR PEOPLE NOT PRESENT ONLY THOSE USUALLY RESIDENT SHOULD BE INCLUDED.

GUIDELINES

	Present	**Not Present**
Au Pair - on long-term engagement of 6 months or more	Usual Resident	Usual Resident
Boarder - returns to another address at week-ends	Visitor	Exclude
Business Person, Coach Driver or HGV Driver - works away from home but usually lives here	Usual Resident	Usual Resident
Child (parent completing form) - at boarding school, university, college etc, if not married	Usual Resident	Usual Resident
- adopted or foster-child (however temporary)	Usual Resident	Usual Resident
- in the forces or working abroad	Visitor	Exclude
Family Member (but see spouse) - working and living away from home	Visitor	Exclude
Member of HM Forces - who normally lives here, unless a child of the family (see Child)	Usual Resident	Usual Resident

	Present	Not Present
Member of Religious Order - usually living in a monastery, convent etc	Visitor	Exclude
Merchant Navy Personnel - works away but usually lives here	Usual Resident	Usual Resident
Offshore Worker - works offshore but usually lives here	Usual Resident	Usual Resident
Nurse - usually living away at nurses' home, hostel etc	Visitor	Exclude
Person in Prison - prisoner on remand	-	Usual Resident
- prisoner convicted and having served at least 6 months of a sentence	-	Exclude
- prisoner convicted and having served less than 6 months of a sentence	-	Usual Resident
Person in other Institution - has been in institution for less than 6 months	-	Usual Resident
- has been in institution for 6 months or more	-	Exclude
This sort of case can cause distress, so only offer it as a guide. For example, 'We have a general rule that if he/she has been in hospital for 6 months of more he/she is regarded as living at the hospital, but it is really for you to decide. We will accept what you do'.		
Regular Visitor (eg elderly relative living here part of the year) - if living here most of the year (6 months or more)	Usual Resident	Usual Resident
- if less than 6 months, or less than 4 nights a week	Visitor	Exclude
Shift or Night Worker	Usual Resident	Usual Resident
Spouse - separated but occasionally visits	Visitor	Exclude
- separated but never visits	-	Exclude
- normally lives here but works away from home, abroad, in forces etc	Usual Resident	Usual Resident
Student - for form completed at home address	Usual Resident	Usual Resident
- for form completed at term-time address (away from home)	Visitor	Exclude

1991 Census England & Wales

Definition of usual address

UA

For use in Hospitals and certain other types of Communal Establishment

This leaflet gives advice on how the question about address (Q7) on the Individual Return (I form) should be answered. Please pass this advice on to the patients or residents concerned before they fill in the form. The definition of 'usual address' for patients in your establishment is given opposite.

Residents or Patients in:	Usual Address:
a Homes and Hospitals taking residents or patients mainly on a long stay basis: Homes for the elderly Homes for epileptics Homes for the terminally ill Homes for the blind Homes for the deaf and dumb Homes and hospitals for mentally handicapped Almshouses Eventide homes Nursing homes	**Answer:** **'This address'** Note: Some patients or residents may be staying on a short term* basis and these should give their home address * If in doubt, we have a general rule that if the person has been in the same home/hospital for 6 months or more, he/she is regarded as living there.
b Homes and Hospitals taking residents or patients on a short-term basis: Convalescent homes and hospitals General, maternity or special hospitals (not psychiatric) Homes for unmarried mothers Maternity homes Sanatoria	**Answer:** **Give the home address**
c Other Institutions taking residents or patients on either a long or short term basis: Chronic sick hospitals Psychiatric hospitals Geriatric hospitals Homes for drugs or alcohol abusers Homes for ex-offenders	**Answer:** If **6 months or more** in hospital -'This address' If **less than 6 months** - home address

INDEX

All references, with the exception of those to the Appendices and Annexes (given as App 1 or Annex A, etc), are to paragraphs.

ENQUIRY POINTS FOR FURTHER INFORMATION

Enquiries about Census definitions and classifications, or about further information generally on 1991 Census output, may be addressed, in England and Wales, to:

Census Customer Services
OPCS
Segensworth Road
Titchfield
Hampshire PO15 5RR

(tel: 0329 42511 ext 3800)

and, in Scotland, to:

Census Customer Services
GRO(S)
Ladywell House
Ladywell Road
Edinburgh EH12 7TF

(tel: 031-314 4254)

Printed in the United Kingdom for HMSO
Dd295044 5/92 C25 G3390 10170